PROBLEMS OF AMERICAN SOCIETY
Bernard Rosenberg, General Editor

| *Governing Nature* |

Governing Nature

EARL FINBAR MURPHY

Quadrangle Books | *Chicago*

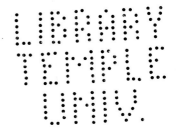

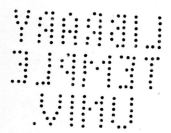

Pro omnibus propriis magistris

Acknowledgments

The writing of this book was made possible through a sabbatical leave for the academic year 1965–1966 by Temple University and through grants from the Temple University Law Foundation and from the University of Wisconsin Law School Research Funds.

I am deeply grateful to Professors Jacob H. Beuscher, Fred A. Clarenbach, Joseph J. Hickey, J. Willard Hurst, and Gerard A. Rohlich of the University of Wisconsin; to Thomas Calabresa, Wisconsin State Supervisor of Well Drilling; to Charles Montemayor, Planning Officer, Dane County, Wisconsin; and to Ray H. Kocher, Acting Chief, General Sanitation Section, Indiana State Board of Health.

Research for this book could not have been completed without the assistance of the general staffs and these persons particularly in the following libraries: Professor Erwin C. Surrency, Librarian, Temple University Law Library; Miss Eleanore Devlin, Chief Reference Librarian, Temple University; Maurice D. Leon, Associate Librarian, University of Wisconsin Law Library; and Mrs. Florence McMaster, Librarian, Indiana University Law Library, Indianapolis Division. I am, of course, solely responsible for the facts adduced and the opinions expressed in this book.

I am especially grateful to the Law Schools of the University of Wisconsin and Temple University, and to my mentors and colleagues in the field of property law, John S. Grimes, Myres Smith McDougal, J. H. Beuscher, and Willard Hurst.

My thanks also are due to Dean Ralph Norvell, to Dr. Benjamin F. Boyer, and to my other associates at Temple University, who have maintained such a pleasant atmosphere for the teaching of law; to my typist, Mrs. Marie Crockett, who was indispensable; and to my editor, Jack Thygerson.

E.F.M.

Philadelphia, 1967

Contents

Governing Nature

1

The origins of environmental control

THE CHALLENGE TO TRADITIONAL VIEWS
OF MAN'S RELATIONSHIP WITH NATURE

The ambition of man has always been to control completely not only his immediate environment but all of nature. In antiquity and during the early centuries of Christianity, magic, both white and black, was the traditional means of seeking that control. Then, toward the close of the Middle Ages, those ambiguous scholars, the alchemists, offered a different way for man to establish his dominion over nature. They started to talk of a great new beginning in human affairs, during which man would master the techniques of manipulating the whole universe. Woodcuts of a technocracy scarcely conceivable in any previous period began to appear in fifteenth-century Italy and Germany; from that time, there has been no turning back to any other ideal as a way of life.

The concepts of a technological culture emerged in a favorable milieu. If Western Europe had been a static social structure, such ideas would have meant very little more than the scientific discoveries that had previously appeared: concepts to be ignored or else incorporated with as little general change as possible. But for reasons not yet understood, fifteenth-century Western Europe stood at the edge of vast social changes. A wholly different view of nature and man's relationship to it was in process of formation. The wars of religion, the collapse of the feudal system, and the American, French, and Russian revolutions were to be mere parts in the changing formulations of that new view.

Previously, man had seen nature as the vast immutable, with himself as the most trifling part of its reaches. Religious literature might confer divine importance upon him, placing him only a little lower than the angels, but the fates of individual men were, in man's own eyes, scarcely more significant than the falling of sparrows. In all of ancient learning, nature was infinite and man was only one more finite, mortal creature of no consequence.

This had been accepted lore until the fifteenth century. Only then did humane knowledge begin to alter the classic base of expectations. It was inevitable that the Faust legend should have begun to burgeon from that time, when man began to realize that he might process nature in his own schemes. In short, from the fifteenth century onward, the idea has persisted more and more that nature is finite and that only the imagination of man has no boundaries in time or space. It has been the sedulous effort of modern science to alter everything that the ancient philosophers of Greece, India, and China believed about man's relationship to his environment.

At first, the challenges were either advanced very timidly as pronouncements or simply took the form of ways of living. The Church inquisitors knew that Copernicus and compound interest were equally destructive to certainty. It is no accident that the areas of the inquisitors' greatest influence—the Two Sicilies and the empires of Spain and Portugal—were almost devoid of the new view of nature, after there had been a brief, losing struggle by the rising intellectual and economic forces in those regions. A similar victory for conservatism occurred during the religious revival that swept Islam at about the same time. In these cultures, as well as in the scarcely stirring Orient, traditional society won only what has proven to be a delaying action rather than any final victory. Eventually, change penetrated, and men began to live the new ways of life.

History, after all, notices the abrupt discoveries, the shattering revolutions, or the *pronunciamento* more than it heeds the steady, gradual change which alters a subsistence to a market economy. It is very hard to say precisely when this alteration occurred in Europe. The perfect model of the feudal system never existed everywhere at all times in Europe any more than the ideal of the self-sustaining manor enjoyed a universal European existence. But, generally, the bulk of Europe's population lived either outside of or else very peripherally to whatever markets continued to function after the decay of the Roman Empire. The retying of those populations to a market economy came about very slowly.

Yet when the market economy had been re-established in Europe, it was more pervasive than any that had operated before, not excluding ancient Rome's. To it was joined a growing industry that, with the application of steam power, gave to market operations an impetus that had been lacking in prior times. The needs of this vigorous market pushed the Europeans out into the larger world and—this was at least as important as any voyage to the Indies—forced an expansion of sales possibilities through the expansion of credit.

By the time the English settlers had arrived in North America during the seventeenth century, these forces had created the mesh of a world-wide market of resource purchases and product sales, a credit mechanism, a flourishing industry in Europe requiring continuous expansion of both sales and sources of supply, and a European public with rising expectations of material comfort that saw nothing wrong either in these expectations or in the economic operations that made them possible. The English settlers in North America were extensions of that European public; from their arrival in the New World, they worked tirelessly to establish and to maintain the market connections.

THE CHALLENGE TO RENEWABLE RESOURCES

Although the English apparently worked their soil prudently, in the tradition of northwest Europe, English settlers in America frequently lacked such caution. They assumed an attitude toward nature which was very different from the one that had prevailed in the economically stable, socially static resource picture of the Old World.

From the beginning, human settlement in North America was highly mobile. This meant that relationships in local society partook of an instability inherent in the need of a moving population to mobilize quickly the capital potential of available resources.

In Europe, even the shift from the self-sufficient manorial economy to dependence upon the market could not produce results upon the resource base as extreme as those routinely caused in North America. There was little absolute loss in Europe's rural population, despite the shift to the cities that began in the early eighteenth century, and the local dynasties of gentry and petty nobility have held a firm grip upon rural resources in England and northwestern Europe right through to the present. Under these conditions, there was a possibility of planning for the distant future in resources. Such a situation was not present in North America until some of the larger, more fully capitalized corporations began to feel strong enough in the twentieth century to make such plans.

The southern plantation owner in North America might have seen himself as the last genteel remnant of the medieval knighthood, but this image could not have been more in error. His work force was unattached to the land, being the merest chattels, whether slaves or indentured servants. This kept him free of the kinds of limitations on economic activity that had bound the feudal lord. The planter's tie was primarily to the market, since only through the market could he get the wherewithal to maintain his social pretensions. Those pretensions were sustainable only through the development and extension of the fullest credit. Unlike the enfeoffed feudal lord, the plantation owner lacked loyalty to any locale; and frequent removals of the plantation to new lands were common. The great houses were jerry-built, and the planter society was a geographically mobile, socially unstable, and economically insecure order. The succession of exhausted soils that marked the passage of planter society from the Tidewater to Texas was simply the clinching proof that the planters were business people and not gentlemen.

The grain farmer of the American Midwest and the rancher of

the far West operated in like fashion, for the same reasons and almost to the same degree. Conservatism has never marked American economic practice where the organization of society and the exploitation of resources were concerned. The clearing off of the hardwood forests, the breaking of the plains, and the extermination of the perennial native grasses were results of the radical decisions that typified the way economic operations functioned on the North American continent from the time the first settlers reached Virginia.

Some authorities have attributed this to the enormous riches of the New World, which seemed unaffectable by anything the settlers might do. Others have said it was the spirit of adventure that caused Western man to extend himself against nature. Similar psycho-social explanations have been added to these. Whatever validity these theories may have, they lose some preordinate importance when the economic market drives that had begun before the North American settlement are considered.

English settlers brought to the frontier ideas which precluded the sort of accommodation with nature and the native peoples that marked Spanish settlements from Florida to California, or the sort of self-contained agrarian economy descriptive of most of the French settlements. To the English immigrants, all of North America was a vast preserve of resources waiting to be processed. What proved satisfactory to the conservative pioneers from Normandy who settled French America, or to the Spanish communities in the Southwest, was not suitable at all for persons having a more aggressive attitude as to what nature's proper role was. North America was to be an extension of the most market-conscious forces existing in Western Europe. This relationship has persisted from the Jamestown settlement until today.

What was true of the historic past for Western Europe and North America is true for their current conditions and for the situations that have come to exist for societies in many other parts of the world. The simple technical devices of the fifteenth century and the formative period of the market economy have been replaced by more sophisticated developments. These alterations have themselves produced profound changes, and as technology and the market have become more complex, they have enlarged the impact that man has been able to make upon his immediate environment and the total sweep of nature.

The demands which must be met by nature have grown in scope and depth, to the point where nature's finiteness clearly has been established. At the same time, the techniques for the manipulation of nature have been developing. Although man is still less sophisticated in his creative role than in his destructive function, he has arrived at the stage of technical development where, if he wishes to make the effort, he can keep his activities and those of nature in a reciprocally sustaining balance that will preserve the human environment's inherent viability.

MEANS OF CONTROLLING THE HUMAN ENVIRONMENT

Technical proficiency, however, is not enough. It is only the base for creating a livable balance between man and his environment, just as it was the means that made possible the enormous modern demands upon nature and the possibility of a human conduct that could make the environment unbearable for all forms of life. The opinions of scientists as to the possible perfection of the world through technique are therefore to be taken seriously, but not to the exclusion of other forces. The very scientist who insists on rigid proofs and controlled experiments within his own laboratory feels no shyness in issuing oracular prophecies about the salvation of the world through some set of scientific techniques. What made science applicable to mass conditions in the past were the operations of the economy, the social structure, and political institutions; it is through these that science will be made applicable in the future.

The social aspects are inescapable. Often, indeed, they have not only provided the means of making scientific knowledge widely available, but have generated the pressure that produced the curiosity from which scientific knowledge ultimately developed. The gasoline-combustion engine is a serious air polluter, but knowledge of its effects has been developed only recently. Such information has grown out of the air pollution control work in Los Angeles, which in turn was the result of widespread public apprehension over the progressively worsening smog conditions that had developed over the years. Much of the "common sense" about air pollution in the pre-1940 period has proved to be wrong. Out of subsequent work by air pollution–control personnel in Southern California has come much of the knowledge that identifies auto exhaust as a chief culprit and that has led to the enactment of the most comprehensive exhaust regulations in the world.

This control of combustion-engine exhausts serves as an example of the constant interaction between technique on one side and social forces on the other. Technically, such exhausts are not yet fully controllable. Socially, the available choices up to this point limit technology to the gasoline-combustion engine as an object of study without regard for mass rail transit, or electric engines, or alcohol fuels in lieu thereof. But it is plain that designating either technology or social forces as superior to the other is a jejune exercise.

Modern demands upon nature result from an intricate relationship between technical knowledge and some need for it in current economic, social, or political operations. These demands, once fulfilled, lead on to still increased needs, which only the natural resources in man's environment can supply. The fear that these demands would exhaust the supply did not appear until the nineteenth century.

Fr. M. C. Fourier (1772-1837) lamented at what he saw done to the woods, waters, and soil, but in this he was exceptional, both because he expressed fears at all and because of the precise fears he recorded. The popular view throughout the nineteenth century, as in earlier periods, was either that man could make little impact upon the vastness of nature or that nature would always heal itself. That Fourier believed neither premise was unusual but scarcely unique in an age when Malthusian economics had strong adherents. Where Fourier departed most sharply from his contemporaries was in concentrating his worry upon "life cycle" or "fluid" resources that possessed a capacity to renew themselves after use in the human economy. Other men in the minority of the concerned were more upset over the possible exhaustion of resources having physically fixed quantities not renewable through natural processes: coal, oil, ores, or gem stones, for example. Those elements which replaced themselves scarcely seemed subjects for alarm.

But technology and economic conditions have produced a reversal in fears. With the disappearance of the best forms of fixed or stock resources, it has been possible to utilize poorer and poorer levels of any given resource. Copper is now taken from material that nineteenth–century entrepreneurs barely would have called copperous earths. Once the last pool has been drained, oil can be extracted from shale. Extraction of these resources acquires new refinements that seem almost to rule out any chance of their exhaustion in the future. And to extraction are joined the advantages of substitution and the synthesizing of new elements containing only some part of the old, common, stock resources. The light metals have opened a new era in construction that has profoundly affected the amount of iron ore and limestone needed in building operations. Simply to consider the quantity of such materials that would have been needed in Manhattan's post-1945 office building boom without the light metals should be a sufficient reminder of what technical change can mean for the employment of the stock resources.

But if comfort can be taken in what progress has meant to the irreplaceable stock resources, no such sanguine view can be taken concerning the resources that, by their renewing abilities, seem to pose the lesser problem. When uses are light, of course, the renewable resources do cause little difficulty. Flowing water has a purifying function; moving air currents can displace emitted waste; the soil can receive and hide much solid junk; game, grass, trees, and fish will recover from a selective taking and perhaps be the better for it. Indeed, in all of these examples, the ability of the renewable resources to continue their renewing function is remarkable, considering the demands made upon them.

It is still possible to fish in many rivers, to walk in shady forests, and to take game near the heaviest industrial centers of the United States. Few people seem to have died from air pollution; burning dumps, gob piles, and culm heaps do not dominate the entire landscape; and all rivers are not dead. The fish caught may not be the most edible, though there are tasty ways to prepare carp. Game, except for the deer, is generally small. And the trees are second-growth or scrub of still later vintage. But even the most heavily populated, industrialized, and citified part of the United States is still a region of great natural beauty reminiscent of the scenes that inspired the Hudson Valley painters. A casual traveler who concentrated upon the beauties of the eastern United States might reasonably decide a workable balance had been struck between the modern economy and its natural environment.

Balance, of course, does not exist, although efforts made since the mid-1930's might have helped form the traveler's inaccurate opinion. Very often a balance means the measuring of equal parts of one static quantity against another fixed amount. If human activity and human environment could be balanced only under such static conditions, the situation would be hopeless. Nature itself is dynamic and ever-changing. Only by acquiring an economic apparatus more dynamic than nature itself has man been able to impose a finiteness upon nature in relation to his demands. Once man accepts any limitations upon his demands, he will lose his ascendancy and must slip back to a position of subordination under infinitely extending nature.

A balance with nature means equalizing dynamic forces upon both sides. It means not overall restraint but a modification of unnecessary aspects in the demands made. Such accommodation has existed in the American program of water improvement since 1940. Though the quality of water is still abysmally poor, enough has been learned to know that satisfactory stream conditions are possible without a return to sweet Auburn and Arcadian pastoral. Every American river cannot be made a trout stream, but its contents need not eat the metal off boat keels or dissolve the brass threads on the valves at water works either.

POSSIBLE HUMAN RELATIONSHIPS TO ENVIRONMENT

Man's relationship with the renewing elements in his natural environment is at an important stage in history. It appears that a total control of nature is possible in a not very distant future. Many ecologists deny this, claiming that nature is too complex to be reflected in the simulation of any computer technology. Such assertions indicate that we have not yet managed to describe nature completely. Until the subject has been fully described, it is not likely that the controller can freely manipulate it with a superiority to the natural processes.

But the means of acquiring that complete description are already well developed, as are the economic and social conditions that make a greater control of nature necessary. Furthermore, control can approach totality without having to be arbitrary. Once natural processes are understood and directable, a sufficient base for controlling the environment will exist, beyond which it is not necessary to push. Establishment of "total" human control over the environment does not mean that rubies must grow on rose bushes.

It might not even be necessary to go beyond an understanding of and accommodation with nature. This is probably the great hope and purpose of most ecologists and social biologists. By comprehending the functioning of what is ever renewed in nature, man can find his place therein and become a part thereof that will do minimal harm to the remainder. This goal does not require that man's aspirations be fixed, for most of them could be completely fulfilled once man has determined his place in the fully understood natural processes of the human environment.

Many authorities who view man as an organic part of nature, who believe he must be sick and marked for death when he is alienated from nature, take a very pessimistic view both of man's capacities and his capabilities of employing nature beneficially for himself and with minimal detriment to his environment. Too often, because of bias, the organicists laud the agricultural existence and allow man to have few aspirations beyond those of a well-behaved animal. Of course man is a part of nature, but he is apparently the only part that wants to transcend the whole. Those who insist upon man's merely comprehending nature and accommodating his activities to its processes too often overlook this human drive.

The static, limiting view, however, need not be an integral part of the opinion of those who want an accommodation with nature. Man's imagination and aspirations can both be free under such a comprehension and accommodation. But the possibility of total control rather than accommodation seems to hold far greater promise for human activity than accommodation ever could. Just as some of the theorists who call for an organic relationship between man and nature are advocates of stasis in human affairs, so many of those who speak of total control of man's environment are apologists for unconsidered change. In some respects, man seems to have *stumbled* upon his abilities to alter the environment profoundly. The biocides, for example, whose effects upon insect, plant, and animal life some observers fear so much, were developed after the late 1930's by people who had limited objects as their aim. Only after the effects upon the living community began to be perceived did talk begin about their utility in the enterprise of totally controlling nature.

Yet, whatever the modest basis upon which such talk began, the search for this goal of mastery is one now commonly discussed. Biocides are being used to make the outdoors more healthful, more amenable, and more economically profitable to human activity. To those chemicals are being added a wide range of growth inhibitors, plant regulators, fertilizers, and chemical aids to animal husbandry that are intended to govern the size, the texture, the harvest time and techniques, and the reproduction patterns of plants, insects, birds, and animals. Increased use of fertilizers could have cut American crop acreage by 30 percent in the years between 1960 and 1964, at the same time maintaining existing production. Depending upon how heavily fertilizers are used by 1980, there will have to be either an increase of nearly one-fifth in acreage or, under heavy fertilization, an acreage cut of over one-half.[1] The living community in nature is at the beginning of a course of treatment quite analogous to that laid out for the modern urban bourgeois, whose life is made more productive, more pleasant, and longer through the use of surgery, vitamins, drugs, and prosthesis.

Under such conditions, the life of man is highly artificial, but it flourishes materially. A similar artificiality, when it can be established, produces a like flourishing in nature. The benefits as well as the problems of this artificiality are already apparent.

Artificial regimes are being set up for river valleys so that silt carriage and deposit can be calculated and controlled. Ultimately, when such regimes are perfected, there will be neither a technical nor an institutional reason for the existence of the present huge loss of stream, lake, and reservoir space to sediment. Today, most of the major dams built since 1930 are being enclosed in envelopes of silt, and the beds of streams are aggrading at a rising rate. Under an artificial river regime that subjects the whole valley to total measurement and control, this deposit process can be materially slowed up. In its reduced form, the silt that remains in the streams can be treated as an important element in stream bed and bank maintenance.

For several decades, the artificial regime has been applied to the kind of forest that is intended to produce income directly. Much of the forest acreage in the United States is of course too low in quality ever to be used for lumber, and in many localities there is not enough wood to make up an economic supply for pulp paper. Such forests serve only to fasten soil against erosion, provide a refuge for game, and provide greenery for a budding recreational area. Some American native softwood forests, to be sure, have considerable powers of resilience in making a comeback after cutting, and lumbering still finds substantial virgin stands for felling in the Pacific Northwest. But the bulk of timber activities in the United States is already conducted in managed forests, and this quantity will increase. Although it may lack the manicured quality of a Rhenish wood, the American forest is under a silvicultural regime that is just as artificial as its German counterpart. The managed forest is sharply constrained as to the variety, size, spacing, and condition of trees, so that, however natural it may appear to be, its essential quality is its artificiality.

Such artificial regimes can be expected to proliferate in any environment which surrounds human activity. The cattle herds of the great late nineteenth-century drives were considered "domestic" animals in their own times, but the "wild animals" grazing on America's public preserves today are scarcely as untamed as the Longhorns were. If international agreements can ever be reached concerning marine resources, the way will be cleared for oceanographic studies that will make possible artificial regimes for the whale, anchovy, salmon, and other threatened species.

Of course, under ocean conditions, controls as close as those possible in forests and river valleys may not be possible.

Although regulatory measures may vary, they all contribute to the artificiality which characterizes the regimes for the control of land, water, and air resources which the next several decades will see developing. Given the size of the demands being made by modern technology and institutions, these same technical and institutional forces must intervene to create regimes that will make even greater demands upon man's natural environment routinely possible.

THREATS IN PRESENT USE OF THE ENVIRONMENT

In every artificial regime, instability is the inherent difficulty. This is especially true where the subject of the regime is some living community of fish, birds, trees, or insects. A monocultural forest containing only one kind of tree of one age is peculiarly subject to disease, pests, and fire. If one species in a living community is destroyed as a pest, the whole community is subject to invasion, displacement, or disruption. Even after human ingenuity is substituted for nature's own dynamic balances, it will still be necessary to rectify effects that stem from the original human intervention in any living community and to keep the artificial human constructs from slippage and decay.

The same problem of instability affects the regimenting of the non-living renewable resources. Balances in nature are never eternal, but they can have a permanency that comes close to being interminable. The wildest river in a state of nature has its pattern of conduct and limits of performance, at least until upset by some catastrophe like an earthquake or a basic climate change. But in its normal reach, the limits have been set in nature for this river.

When human economics, therefore, decides to tame such a river by dams, concrete banks, water withdrawals, effluent discharges, flumes, and canalization, something like a natural catastrophe external to the functioning of the stream has occurred. A new order for that stream has been created; and if any part of that new order is to operate for long, every aspect of the stream must be brought into a reciprocal relationship similar to the kind of interlocking functionings that had existed in the natural wild river. The refusal of authorities to recognize this duty has brought America's rivers to their present rather sad plight. Only very gradually has the need for this approach in various river basins caused the creation of institutions capable of organizing the required artificial regimes.

Since total arbitrary control of nature is not possible, there is often a great similarity in the actual work product of those who seek only an accommodation with nature and those who seek mastery over it. An accommodation capable of permitting vigorous economic and social growth to human institutions requires for its base a nearly complete ability to understand and manipulate natural process. Contrariwise, a control of nature demands that the putative controller understand the total effect upon nature of what he seeks to do and that he work with rather than against natural forces. Except for those men who want no change in natural conditions, or those who equate mastery of nature with the mere ability to knock out of the living community one or more species, both the accommodators and the controllers require a similar knowledge and share a similar purpose in continuing to further the use to which man can put his environment.

In traditional cultures, the risk is that man will not make enough use of his environment. Minimal use is not necessarily any more beneficial to nature than it is to human economic operations. In India, the demands made upon soil by agriculture are not great. But the very fact that they are so slight proves harmful to the soil, exposing it to leaching, exhaustion, desiccation, and erosion. India requires not less use of its soil but a degree of intensive soil development and employment for which there is little likelihood within Indian culture.

Yet, if the risk in traditional societies is that natural resources will not be sufficiently employed for either their own or for man's benefit, the danger in modern economics is the very opposite—overexploitation. This is not to say that the damage of underexploitation is a thing of the past even in the most modern economies. The auger method of coal mining, presently used in Appalachia, circles a mountain peak with drilled borings from which not over 20 percent of the emplaced coal can be pulled. In this pitted condition, the mountain is left to settle in upon itself. If the value of coal should so rise in the future that extracting the 80 percent remaining should seem profitable, then the tops may have to come off those mountains, because of the gutting damage done by the past augering of coal. Underexploitation still takes place, therefore, under sophisticated economic conditions.

However, it is not the failure to use resources enough that is the chief peril in urban, industrial society. The uses may be uneven in the demands they make, but their totality is both heavy and growing much heavier. Already, waters of considerable size in America are utterly dead, while others support only forms of life that do not require oxygen and exhale noisome gases. Even lakes, reservoirs, and streams having oxygen-breathing life in them are in a precarious condition. Enrichment from the nitrogen and phosphorus that are present in sewage effluent and run-off from fertilized land is causing explosive growths of plants and fish that ultimately will exhaust oxygen supplies. Furthermore, delicate plants and feeders in many American waters have been replaced by other species capable of sustaining themselves under coarser conditions. The use of American waters for removal of waste, for consumption in power and irrigation processes, and for cooling in industry has pushed to the very limits of the waters' present renewing capacities.

Soil and air seem to be plagued by the same excessive use. Americans are not the world's greatest consumers, but only because true consumption is scarcely possible in the totality of nature. This limitation, consequently, makes Americans the world's greatest producers of junk and waste. American cities, despite their skyscrapers and pleasant suburbs, are squatting in their own filth. Some claim that the disposal of solid waste will have become an impossible task by the year 2000; others say that by that time air pollution in some urban areas will have made human life impossible for anyone not wearing an oxygen mask.

Conditions of the renewable resources are not good in modern urban industrial society. Water, soil, air, wildlife, forests, and many other renewing or living things are in demonstrably poor and deteriorating conditions. It is easy to pass from this knowledge to despair for the future, and some sensitive students have made that short passage. Perhaps they are right to have done so, since society seems unconcerned with nature as long as human demands are being met. Business operations in the economy seem interested only in the size of the next quarter's dividend or the year's profit-

and-loss statement. Politics seems unable to transcend ideology and the personal ambitions of the politicians. If one assumes a fixed character to human response and shallow greed as the one dominant human characteristic, then the best that could be hoped for would be an ultimate thinning of population and demand such as occurs among overcrowded and overpampered zoo inmates. Under such an assumption in full operation, the bitterest contemporary Cassandra will come to look as sanguine as Voltaire's Dr. Pangloss.

INSTITUTIONAL DEVICES FOR RELATING MAN
TO HIS ENVIRONMENT

Fortunately, there is no need to make such a hopeless assumption. Nor must this refusal to be pessimistic about future possibilities require the adoption of a perfectionist philosophy. Altruism will have as little to do with future urban industrial processes as it has had in the past. What is beginning to show now is the very abuse of the renewable resources which has made so many commentators despair.

An economic reflection of this abuse is beginning to appear in the market. In addition, the economic processes of modern industry have given a greater leisure to greater numbers, so that the area of the renewable resources can turn amenity and aesthetics into direct profit through the recreation industry. This, combined with the reflected costs of correcting abuse of resources in regular industrial processes, produces a drive for change which makes it very hard to be sure the year 2000 will be any worse for nature, the human environment, and the renewable resources than most of the years since the fifteenth century.

While modern urban industrial methods certainly abuse nature on a scale unknown before, they simultaneously make possible protective measures which also were hitherto unheard of. In primitive societies or those of resource surplus, when soil or game or woodland are exhausted, the area is abandoned and the population moves on to an untouched region. This is true among the jungle peoples of the Amazon and among the lumbermen and coal miners of North America. But, modern urban industrial society has reached a stage from which a simple moving away is no longer possible.

It is now the whole of the atmosphere and the fresh waters that may be spoiled by society's acts and not a single forest, however vast, or some jungle patch which the tribe could ultimately abandon. The problem of the renewable resources cannot even be left for a future generation, though future generations will have to contend with it. Urban industrial society is being compelled by its own processes to take a stand at this time, without any chance of passing the task on to the future. The present has become the future on to which the past, ever since the fifteenth century, has been passing the problems that are created when human demands upon nature are so great that only total human comprehension of nature can make such demands sustainable.

At the present time, substantial investments are being made in space exploration. Quite apart from whether it diverts funds better invested on this planet, space investigation poses an added burden in that space expenditures appear to be made without regard to economic requirements. The supply of water to astronauts on long cosmic voyages, the provision of oxygen on the moon, and the synthesizing of food in astral space are all projects undertaken without regard to cost. If man is to put himself on barren planets, then in order to sustain his life there, cost-benefit ratios must take a leap upward nearly as astronomical as the voyage itself. This kind of shift in thinking has moved persons of a technocratic turn of mind to use projects in space as illustrations of what technology can do for, among other things, the renewable resources on this planet. If costs mean nothing in supplying air, water, and food to astronauts, why should they loom large in more earth-bound enterprises?

The analogy is tempting, but it overlooks the fact that even the expensive exploration of space is not free of economics, nor is technology in general ever likely to enjoy such freedom. Expenditures for space projects are made within the national and world economy. Investments are made in space at the expense of other tasks upon which they might be spent. The space studies represent a setting aside of some significant part of the national capital for reasons of national prestige and security in which thirst for knowledge and hope of financial returns from space play a small part.

Yet even here, the mesh of economics holds technology tight, for these space projects mean immediate profits to suppliers and wage earners, and also are a means of gaining knowledge that will prove valuable in other business ventures.[2] The task of fully describing the earth's atmosphere, which is but a trifling part of space exploration, will lead to a predicting, and perhaps control, ability on weather that will have a sweeping effect upon much of human economic activity. Not even the technology of the penetration of inner or outer space can be free of the operation of economic forces.

This relationship between technique and economics is an even more important factor in the mundane matter of protecting the renewable resources from insult and destruction. Man has often depicted nature as an inexhaustible cornucopia or as a treasure chest which he has inherited. Because it is self-renewing, nature is actually richer than any treasure chest. Similarly, it is more productive than the image of the cornucopia inasmuch as human activity can prime and enrich the flow of good things emanating from nature. But if man sees no responsibility to this supplier of his wealth, then he can look upon resources only as free goods to be engrossed for his personal profit or merely destroyed for his individual amusement. Normally, what is free holds little value to the recipient. This is true no matter how much morality, for example, attempts to assert such value by means of statutory prohibitions.

The statute books are crowded—for anyone with the patience to page through them—with bans upon conduct that would pollute water or air, overgraze a pasture, erode a field, strip a forest, fish out waters, maintain open dumps, or result in any of a wide number of other acts harmful to renewable resources, human environment, and nature. What is needed, instead of additional prohibitions, is a system of institutional restraints which would destroy the illusion that nature's goods are free. The law, despite its orders not to misuse resources, generally favors the destruction of resources. Progressively higher taxes on vacant land in highly populated areas force such land into development. Depletion allowances work most profitably at high rates of exploitation. There is the promise of low taxes once the resource region is exhausted. And the burden of resource maintenance is assumed by the general fund of tax revenue. It has seemed simpler to pass water purification costs on to the general taxpayer or to the water rate payer than to charge any part of such a burden to the pollutors causing corrupted water conditions.

The time has come to specify the character and the extent of the demands being made upon nature. When human employment of nature left little permanent impression upon the environment, the task of defining these uses would have been superfluous work. But when the demands require man to "vanquish open land and subdue nature," the specification of those demands is crucial. In addition, since the effect upon nature of human economic activity has become total, the old industrial threats of flight from regulation or withdrawal from the market lack the meaningfulness they could once have, because flight today would almost have to be from economic life itself once regulation had reached out to the full scope of specific resource use.

This specified use must be calculated in terms of its costs to the environment, which is the traditional—if false—area of free goods. Having been so calculated, these costs must then be internalized into the industrial processes themselves. The users of resources and the emitters of waste, on the one hand, and those who benefit from receiving the value of unabused and pure resources on the other, must both incorporate into their business processes part of the costs imposed by their demands upon nature. If renewable resources are to be best served, the legal institutions must aid in the complete specification and internalization of the costs inherent in resource use.

However appealing the radical sound of it may be to some minds, socialization of renewable resources is not a sufficient solution. Indeed, with an economy in which private capital plays basic roles, statutes declaring that certain resources (like water) are absolutely within the public domain simply encourage the illusion that resources are free goods open to anyone's engrossment. If the assertion of public ownership is to represent a meaningful control, such statutes must be accompanied by the means of making the publicly held resource available in economically viable units to private interests. Even in a communist state, where everything is publicly held, this lack of specificity can cause the production units of the communist economy, whether Stalinist trusts or Bakuninist communes, to view renewable resources as free supplies available for their advancement and the benefit of the economy.

Whether an enterprise is privately, publicly, or cooperatively capitalized, it is likely to find the sources of its work effort in substances that the general economy views as cheap or worthless, and to pass on as many of its production costs as possible to that same general economy. In its search for cheap coal to sustain cheap electric power, the Tennessee Valley Authority has been no more benign than privately capitalized coal operators to the coal-bearing Cumberlands. Nor has it been any more prudent in preventing erosion from its mining operations, even though the silt must collect in the TVA's own system of reservoirs. The lures of cheapness and the apparent passing on of costs have been too great. Similar kinds of economic thinking have produced water and air pollution in Poland, the Soviet Union, and other communist countries where these resources are in no better condition than those used for similar industrial purposes in the English Midlands or the northeastern United States. Not even national planners in communist or socialist economies, whose plans specifically prohibit abuse of natural resources, will succeed with general exhortations. For several centuries, statutory injunctions have failed all ideologies.

What is needed in any modern economy, whether it be purely communist or private-capitalist, is an institutional ability to specify the demands which the economy makes upon its environment and to internalize those costs into the productive processes of the economy. One means of accomplishing this end is the problem shed approach, which defines one resource in some particular area of use. Such definition is possible because water and air do not comprise an indivisible national entity so far as intensity of use and allocation are concerned. Streams are formed by the lay of the land in separate basin systems, and air moves in its own patterned fashion.

Demands also vary. On these bases of difference, administrative units can be set up to test the pertinent renewable resource in the unit's jurisdiction, to find the costs of its use, and to impose constraints within which those costs must be internalized by economic interests functioning inside the unit. The units necessarily differ in size, depending upon the resource, since an air shed is larger than many basin systems and basin systems themselves have widely varying sizes.

The concept is scarcely a new one, since the model for all resource shed approaches is the Ruhrverband, which has existed in one form or another in the Ruhr area of Germany from the end of the nineteenth century to the present. The Ruhrverband levies charges upon sources of pollution, calculating costs in terms of what must be done to dispose of waste. The monies collected are spent in the improvement of waters within the association's jurisdiction. The Ruhrverband plan is now being copied in England, Belgium, and other parts of Germany. Properly applied, it holds great promise for the future.

Such an arrangement is, of course, no cure-all. The Ruhrverband has been criticized by Ruhr industrialists, who have fought the jurisdiction's being extended to control of air pollution. Existing effluent charges to protect water already hurt the local coal industry enough, they argue, in its competition with rivals who are not subject to waste removal charges. Other Germans in the region claim that the improvement of the Ruhr has been bought only at the sacrifice of the Ems, the Lippe, and smaller streams. Besides, they say, the Ruhr is at the southern extremity of the region taking its name, so that the improvement of the Ruhr's waters has not been as great an accomplishment as it appears to foreigners.

Yet, even though the problem shed approach at its best still has critics, it offers opportunities for resource improvements if it is used to internalize costs and is backed up by national requirements. Merely to form problem shed administrations without powers to internalize resource use costs is to have created nothing more than a powerful pressure group which can assault the general treasury for subsidies. To fail to back problem shed administrations with national requirements for maintenance of renewable resources is to isolate such agencies and make them vulnerable to the blackmail of economic groups functioning within their jurisdictions. There must be a broad-based national policy both for renewable resource preservation and for specifying and internalizing the costs in renewable resource use, or else all attempts at coping with the problem will fail.

The problem shed approach, the idea of regional and industrial constraints, or the imposition of emitter or receptor charges requires other conditions to operate successfully. National tax policies, national criteria or standards for conduct, national surveys, nationally directed studies, and national coordination of federal, regional, problem shed, state, and local efforts are all required. Agencies below the federal level need not be replaced, but their efforts must be supplemented and all governmental programs brought into mutually sustaining relationships.

The size of the problem imposes this obligation, as just one example drawn from the American suburban residential building industry will show. The construction of one house selling for $20,000 in the mid-1960's real estate market requires of the finances of the local government $18,000 in capital service costs and $1,000 per year thereafter for the maintenance of those services.[3] Open space, which as a resource has been so attractive in expanding American cities, provides profit for the developer, some amenity for the home-buyer, and substantial hidden costs to be passed on to the local taxing authority. Some of it comes back from the taxes which the now-improved land pays, but increasingly such costs are being met out of various kinds of sales, income, and intangibles taxes, which prevent any internalization of the true costs of suburban building into the suburban building industry itself.

But the lack of cost specificity and internalization is so general, and the condition of the renewable resources of water, air, open space, forests, and wildlife is becoming so inadequate to the economic demands made upon them, that demands are rising to make up any needs out of investments from the general funds. Corporation executives, politicians, and conservationists commonly make these demands, sometimes because the necessity is unavoidable.

Despite the recent establishment of entry fees in national parks, the general federal treasury is still the chief source of support for these recreation areas. It is impossible to allocate specifically the costs or benefits of parks. The burden of maintaining them must therefore be put upon the generality of taxpayers in the knowledge that the parks offer enjoyment to the population at large and that every decade more persons utilize the parks' recreational facilities. The national parks, like historic shrines, can legitimately be kept up out of the general tax dollar without efforts to specify and internalize costs or to establish refined cost-benefit ratios.

The same is not true, however, for the bulk of renewable resources. Private fishing, lumbering, grazing, and recreation industries have no call upon the general treasury beyond some initial assistance. This may include the creation of self-sustaining resource protection programs and the provision of standards to be applied by resource problem shed administrations against those elements of industry which may be unwilling to help maintain the resource upon which the industry's future depends. The greatest value of governmental constraint is to take away from individual operators the chance for personal profit at the expense of the total resource. Performing that service, and assisting in initiating and coordinating resource preservation efforts, ought to represent the extent of governmental expense. Beyond that, the costs can well come from the direct beneficiaries of improved conditions in the renewable resources.

Once costs were specified, the anti-pollution levies imposed upon industrial users of renewable resources could justifiably be higher than appropriations which might formerly have been made from the general fund. Payment by beneficiaries of resource use could also encourage the establishment of specific legal interests in such hitherto publicly claimed resources as air, water, and ocean space. Despite inadequate legal protection and without much public notice, investments in the resources of ocean space have grown even more rapidly than those made in the exploration of outer space.[4] This kind of development would occur upon a still greater scale once legal and economic interests in the renewable resources became more specific and departed from the traditional pattern of merely engrossing free goods.

THREAT AND PROMISE IN THE RELATIONSHIP OF URBAN
INDUSTRIAL SOCIETY TO ITS ENVIRONMENT

The scope of economic demands upon the human environment
has reached the point where changes in property concepts, economic analyses, and institutional arrangements are imperatively
needed. Out of this need, changes have been slowly and partially
emerging, particularly in the decades since World War II. The full
impact of urban industrialization upon renewable resources and
nature seems finally to have come under close scrutiny in our time.

It is now apparent, too, that, just as economic demand, technology, and institutional adjustment have brought about this impact, these same forces can meliorate and alter the unfortunate
effects upon nature that they themselves created. A kind of balance,
it is believed, can be created between the human environment and
human demands upon nature. This balance can make possible a
healthful, prosperous, and continuous future despite population
growth, world urbanization and industrialization, and the apparent
limitlessness of human demands as expressed in economic, social,
and political terms.

Some observers may consider man's efforts at controlling human
environment a prime example of *hubris,* which can end only in
futility. They may be right. If so, *all* effort is vain, and the only
issue is the timing, scope, and permanence of the inevitable catastrophe. But it would be a pity if such a view should prevail by
default of enough effort to prevent the supposedly inevitable cata-
clysm. Since there can be no more certainty of catastrophe than
of security, and since it is evident that solutions to the problems of
urban industrialization do not come ready-packaged with the problems, man's hope would seem to lie in his exerting himself to establish a balance between human demand and the environment upon
which that demand is made.

A chronic state of despair has not been the human condition,
though man's efforts to overcome crisis have often failed. The
Roman Empire was not saved from its economic ennui, and the
irrigation economies of the Middle East were casualties in the total
destruction of the Mongol invasion. But all prophets of doom have

not been sustained by events, either. The effort to bring human demand to terms with the manner of operation, if not the finiteness, of the human environment must be made. Perhaps nature's abilities to meet human demand can be made as limitless as the demand itself. Perhaps new directions will have to be given to those human demands in order to preserve a bounded natural environment. But in any event, although man knows enough about resource problems not to feel euphoric, what he knows is still not sufficient reason to justify despair.

Even to reach a point of justified despondency requires an effort that has not yet been made. Once undertaken, that effort may make a viable solution possible. The task of coping with the environment under the growing demands upon it is a severe one. Urban industrial society, the wars, and the military expenditures of the twentieth century do not make matters easier. This task—this saving of nature from man for man's own sake in the future—has scarcely begun, however. Until it has been carried further, no one can fully predict its possibilities for futility, usefulness, or salvation.

2

Determining resource sufficiency

In 1865, the English economist W. Stanley Jevons published a startling little book called *The Coal Question*. The unpleasant message of it was that the substance upon which the growth of the Victorian economy was based, and upon which Victorian hopes of an ever-improving future were founded, would soon no longer be able to sustain a continued increase in economic activity. Needless to say, Professor Jevons—a scholar respected then and now—was pessimistic indeed as to what would then inevitably ensue. It is doubtful that he was much cheered by the optimistic predictions of the Royal Commission on Coal Supplies which his book prompted. In 1871, after a five-year study under its chairman, the Duke of Argyll, the commission indicated to Jevons that he had "notions utterly futile"—or so they wanted him to think.

Certainly he had his justifications for alarm. The development of coke from coal in the mid-eighteenth century had saved the rising steel industry at a crucial moment. With the disappearance of the last great stretches of English forest, the sources of charcoal, the traditional fuel, had been nearly exhausted. Without the providential discovery of the coking process, Jevons might well have thought, the industrial revolution would have been short-lived.

And where in the England of 1865 could an equivalent replacement for coal possibly be found?

David Ricardo had predicted early in the nineteenth century that as population grew, and as industrial demands increased, unit costs of all resources, including mined elements, would steadily rise. Back of Ricardo stood the grim figure of Malthus, with his prediction of a sustained population growth rate of 3 percent a year. It was a certainty that the quantity of material within the earth was fixed in geologic time, but that man was not. His expanding numbers and the rapid increase of his demands upon nature clearly foretold an early crisis. It seemed most evident that the crisis would come with an exhaustion of mineral wealth precipitated by the insatiable demands of modern industry.

The early American conservationists, led by WJ McGee and Gifford Pinchot, began to stress this theme in the 1890's. Perturbed by the quantities of coal and ores and oil that they saw consumed each year by the economy, they began to argue for a more measured use, a concern for posterity, and a demand that reserves be cut out of current production so that the future might be secured. In the absence of such action, they could envision only the disaster Jevons had foreseen. Nor were they comforted by the coal conference in 1913 which insisted, as the royal commission had insisted almost half a century before, that there was no chance of a world coal shortage for industrial use within the distant future.

Since 1913, there have been other authorities who have refused to be consoled, and who insist that the world verges upon some crisis in ores or energy sources. Either natural gas is about to be finally taken from the last dome, or oil from the last pool, or iron from the last range. Thereafter, they conclude, all industrial process must stop, for urban civilization in the twentieth century will have lost its essential fundament. They keep their mowers sharpened for the grass they expect to find growing in the streets.

In the past, it has been the stock resources—materials like oil, gas, ores, coal, stone, and commercial earths like sand and gravel that cannot be replaced except in terms of geologic or astronomic time—upon which the pessimists have concentrated their attention. If the Reverend Mr. Malthus had been correct in his population predictions, such observers would have been quite justified in their apprehensions: a mass of humanity, like maggots crawling on festering carrion, would at this moment cover the earth. All construction and mineral exploitation, like food production, would have been brought to a condition no better than one purely static and immutable in its character.

Yet, since the eighteenth century, there has been little of a static quality in industrial existence. Perhaps the development of the coking process to save the burgeoning English steel industry *was* providential. If so, it was about the last specific act of providence in the technical processes of the industrial revolution. In any event, the fact of socio-technical change has served as the motive force of Euro-American culture in the past three centuries, and has prevented the fulfillment of prophecies otherwise quite reasonable in their expectations.[1]

In the latter part of the twentieth century, world reserves of ores and fuel present no serious problems. With the aid of technology, ample quantities of both will be found in deposits of low content or in remote locations, and modern transport will move them cheaply from source to use. As early as the mid-1950's, American coal, extracted by almost completely automated methods, was selling at the pitheads of the Ruhr for less than the local coal; technology will make this sort of thing common in the future.

CHANGED ATTITUDES TOWARD SUFFICIENCY OF RESOURCES

Not long ago, Europeans were still talking about the "necessity" of empire to supply their industry with raw materials. The most reasonable-sounding remarks in Hitler's tabletalk were elaborations upon this idea. Now that the empires have reverted to native control, the Europeans have turned their attention again to their own continent. As Pierre Laffitte, a mining geologist, has said, "Small and overcrowded Europe, the cradle of industrial civilization, can develop her mineral resources to . . . face the increasing difficulties of supply." [2] What recently appeared to be the makings of a severe economic crisis which would require the most extreme political solutions is currently discussed as a technical problem.

The reason for this altered attitude lies in a different apprehension of nature. Karl Brandt, the agricultural economist, in a remark summarizing current economic thought, has called it a "hard fact that whether some feature of our environment is at a specific time potentially a resource or not, or one of high, medium, low or no value, depends on many changing social, economic, political, and national security factors." In this view, nature is passively waiting for human ingenuity to find within one of its elements an asset to man. The environment stands for "nothing more than opportunities for man to apply his ingenuity, inventiveness, and skills, as well as his manmade resources . . . [since environmental resources] contribute wealth in any degree only in response to this human action and in relation to the changing needs of society." In the ultimate analysis, the only vital resource is man: all else is cumbrous substance waiting for him to confer value upon it.[3]

In recent years, therefore, the expressed alarm at human misuse of stock resources has moderated. But previous misgivings concerning stock resources have been replaced with concern over another portion of the spectrum: resources which are renewable. The renewable resources, sometimes called life-cycle or fluid resources, are those which continuously replenish themselves in the course of nature. They include air, water, soil, and all living organisms such as trees, grass, and animals. Human activity can aid in the replenishing process, but sometimes no replenishment is possible: once connate waters, trapped during the geologic past, have been pumped out, the water layers surrounding them become impermeable. Changes in soil through erosion may make it impossible to reforest a lumbered-off area; breaking the prairie may destroy an irreplaceable grass cover; or climatic differences may extend the desert over previously fertile ground. The more normal course in nature, however, is for grass, trees, soil, water, air, and animals to replace themselves. Aware of this self-replenishment, man did not originally worry much about the "renewables" as opposed to the stock resources—coal, oil, or ores—which nature cannot replace within the limits of human time. Yet, it is upon these renewable resources that attention has been focused increasingly since 1950 and in relation to them that alarm currently is most often expressed.

The main reason for man's not worrying about renewable resources earlier is that he had not managed to make much of an impact upon them until this century. In the interval between World

Wars I and II, more soil was lost through careless farming than in all of man's previous history. It has been discovered since 1960 that the biological metabolism of Lake Erie has been so disrupted that a 2,600-square-mile patch in the center, about one-quarter the lake's area, contains no oxygen for ten feet up from the bottom. Accumulating medical evidence shows such a high correlation between the incidence of air pollution and lung and heart disease that, empirically, smog and other conditions in the air can be considered as possible causes of lung cancer, emphysema, and a variety of related lung or cardiac or circulatory disorders. What was a nuisance to the Victorians appears to be a menace today.

Traditionally, economics has treated resources as a single entity for analysis, as if ores, crops, and water were of the same aspect. The more recent trend, however, is to discern a difference in kind between resources that renew themselves and those which do not. The resource economist S. V. Ciriacy-Wantrup, who has emphasized this distinction, has also stressed the greater delicacy in the physical condition of the renewable as opposed to stock resources. It is an emphasis strikingly illustrated by his calling the renewable the "life-cycle" resources. They are interrelated in a manner that causes them to be considered as the single entity called the biocycle, or the "wheel of life." Water, air, and soil are each necessary to sustain some form of living organism. Indeed, much of what is considered as soil is itself composed of living subjects whose life and death processes go to make it up. Beyond this need for water, air, and soil, all living things depend upon other living organisms for sustenance, fertilization, or some similar life-sustaining function. Man, whose mind describes this process and whose demands upon it are so large, is as much a part of it as any insect, reptile, carnivorous plant, or sweet pea. Plainly, that which composes the biocycle, in which man is a unit, must be of great importance to mankind.

All living things draw their sustenance from air, water, and soil, in various combinations, and make their home within one or more of these aspects of the universe. They are the ambience of the living creatures within them. To them, living creatures make contributions that either renew (as with soil) or else modify for the benefit of other living organisms (as with water and, to a lesser degree, air). Any change which occurs in these elements works a massive effect upon any life within them, even to precipitating its occasional disappearance.

But in the life of creatures there are more subtle interrelations than their direct participation in whatever ambience each finds itself within. Ecosystems, or ways of organizing habitat and food supply in nature, are myriad. All living creatures do not have straight connections with each other. Rather, they are organized in pyramids within which one form draws upon another for existence. The pyramids are predatory systems within which X is fed on by Y, which is fed on by Z, upon which nothing in particular preys. This last creature constitutes the peak of the pyramid, the final predator in a particular ecosystem. What lies beneath it in the pyramid is kept in its place by the predatory powers of Z, while Z is constrained by what is available for food supply within the ecosystem.

The unconscious diplomacy of ecosystems is what has made the totality of life possible. Insects, plants, birds, and animals in this plan have a relationship that may be non-predatory or only partly related to the search for food. Insects cross-pollinate plants, birds and animals spread seed and fertilize plant roots, and the plants through their breathing assist in creating and maintaining the atmosphere necessary to some of these other creatures. In these particular processes no killing occurs, and the participants are not parts of each other's ecosystems. Yet it is impossible to deny the need which plants, insects, birds, and animals have for each other.

Man is the supreme predator for all the world's ecosystems—a kind of omnipotent Z. To make his life more convenient, to increase food and fiber production, or to protect his health, man takes out the peaks of the pyramids in the various ecosystems and reduces or increases numbers at other levels within those ecosystems. By his actions, man extinguishes certain species and regionally extirpates others, doing so by his mere existence as often as he does by intent. Man's extending his civilization into all parts of the earth and his enormous increase in numbers during the past three centuries have done about as much damage to other life forms as policies of deliberate control.

The growth of human population and the development of industrialized urban agglomerations are having a profound effect on such elements as air, soil, and water, as well as upon all forms of wild life. President Lyndon B. Johnson said in his 1966 Conservation Message to Congress that pollution of air, water, soils and living organisms "already adversely affects the quality of our lives. In the future, it may affect their duration." [4] Whether this should prove true or not, the end of the twentieth century is likely to see "man monopolizing the biological production of the earth's surface solely for his own benefit—such a monopoly being created at the expense of wild life. All wild life will . . . certainly be considered as competitive with man and therefore destined to extermination." [5] If such extinction does occur, man had better be prepared to substitute his own artificially created and sustainable biotic community.

PROBLEMS OF PREDICTION IN THE USE OF RESOURCES

The Greek city planner Constantinos Doxiadis believes that by the year 2065 the world population will "level off at around 25 to 30 billion people" and that there will have occurred by that date a 200 or 300 percent increase in autos and machines. By that date, he expects nature to be "suffering" in a manner and degree unlike any it has previously experienced from human activity—unless drastic action is taken to limit the effects upon the human environment of this expanding and intensifying human activity.[6]

Such projections into the future, of course, are extremely difficult to make. In 1908, Charles Richard Van Hise, a conservationist much impressed with the prospects of thermal pollution due to man's greater use of energy sources, praised the prospect of an artificially increased temperature for the earth. As he saw it, such a feat would increase precipitation and thereby reverse the trend toward aridity that conservationists then thought they saw, and extend the temperate zone to Greenland. Through these changes, scientists of the time thought, the American Southwest would blossom and Eurasia would be able to support much denser populations. On the basis of anticipated industrial activity and a condition which others would regard as an unfortunate side effect, he projected a future of great artificial improvement.[7]

Temperature changes such as those Van Hise advocated would,

of course, cause absolute catastrophe, with flooding that would drive man to subsist upon the poorest of the earth's soils, and, probably, with freezing temperatures at the equator. Neither the increased industrial burning of fuels, which Van Hise foresaw, nor the gasoline combustion engine, whose importance in air pollution he did not envision, has produced these thermal disturbances. Van Hise erred in attributing to man's actions a potential influence upon nature which they have not yet had. It is the sort of error which few predictors have made, and, aside from a blind optimism rather peculiar in a conservationist, not as harmful as the more typical, tradition-bound type of projection. .

The problems inherent in prediction can be seen in relation to the widely quoted statements on stream pollution control made in 1960 by the United States Senate Select Committee on National Water Resources. After stating that by 1980 the demand for water in the United States would exceed the country's surface stream flow, the committee stressed the importance of maintaining water quality. In such conditions, the re-use of water is the obvious means of preventing disaster. Given a relatively fixed quantity of water and ever heavier demands for greater quantities, repeated re-use would seem to be more likely than a continuation of such practices as those of New York City, which flushes pure mountain water into the ocean after the most trifling utilization.

The Senate committee, concentrating upon better water quality in the future, claimed that it would cost a minimum of $100 billion (at 1954 prices), expended between 1960 and 2000, to control water pollution. This estimate assumed that the relationship in 1960 between population and economic activity concerning waste would remain fixed, that four parts per million of dissolved oxygen should be maintained in all streams, and that "standard biological treatment and augmentation of low stream flows for waste dilution would be the only devices used to deal with pollution loadings." [8] Yet even now there are persons who claim that much of this work can be done at one-tenth the cost through mechanical re-aeration of rivers, and that joint river basin treatment projects would also reduce the need for gigantic dilution reservoirs.

Certain expenses may be reduced in ways of this sort, but the world will have to make an enormous investment to protect, salvage, or bring into market use the renewable resources. Michel Batisse, Chief of the International Hydrologic Decade, has said that the amount of money spent for water supply between 1964 and 1984 may reach one million million (a Franco-American billion) pounds or $2.8 billion. In the presence of prospective investments of this magnitude for water alone, immediate attention must be focused on the problem in all of its complexities. It is not sufficient to say that the task is difficult, or uncertain of success, or one to be left to pragmatic disposition when the proper time arrives. The problems of our times are numerous, complex, and very expensive. To consider how, and to what degree, capital shall be allocated is something that must be done at once.

Stanley Cain, a subcabinet officer for Presidents Kennedy and Johnson, dealt with the matter by quipping, ". . . complex natural-resource problems have no *single* solution. As the saying goes, 'All cats are gray at night,' but, as we shall see, under illumination some cats still are gray." [9] Insofar as major difficulties are concerned, the issues involved in the planning and management of renewable resources lie chiefly in economics, public finance, and legal and governmental arrangements. The technical problems requiring attention relate to the quantities and qualities of resources now and potentially available, the costs of these as registered in the market, and any external effects of a physical-biological character upon the natural environment. When data of this sort are available, the decision can be made as to whether the deserts shall be made to bloom.

DIFFICULTY OF SPECIFYING FUTURE RESOURCE USES

A certain careless rapture seems to mark the attitude of otherwise careful scientists when it comes to considering man's ability to "re-create" the natural world. God, at low noon before the first day of creation, may have felt more inadequate than the physicist Willard Libby, who has told his lecture audiences, ". . . man's place in the physical universe is to be its master, . . . and by controlling the natural forces with his intelligence, to put them to work to suit his purposes, and to build a future world in his own image." [10] In the presence of such supreme confidence, which is common among the physical if not among the biological scientists, the economists and political scientists seem like pale creatures of the dusk in the presence of harbingers of dawn.

The economists insist their discipline "is central to progress . . . for it is economics alone that can formulate those problems in the terms to which they must finally be reduced, namely, the balancing of our varied desires . . . against the costs of satisfying them in various degrees." [11] In political science, we are assured, the politics of ecology, or the science of environment, will provide a deliberate management of the physical environment greatly exceeding any previous governmental experience. This will place the managers of public policy at the head of a "strategy of organizational development for stability." In any case, each discipline—physics, economics, political science—sees itself as supremely important for the future disposition of environmental problems and the allocation of the use of renewable resources.[12]

This perspective does not suggest what other disciplines think of the social sciences, for example. Anne McLaren, a specialist in nerve viruses, charges economics and political science with having done "little hard thinking . . . on the basic question of how the world is likely to develop economically." So far as she is concerned, the social sciences are still caught within the confines of the moral theology from which they originated, maundering on about "feelings of decency and humanity and rationality" as being the determinants of the future.[13] The disciplines concerned with organizing the institutional aspects of human life have not engaged the sympathy of the scientific imagination. They are so alienated from science, in fact, that they are in danger of contamination from their enforced association with lawyers and politicians— notoriously untrustworthy, subjective, unscientific personalities. Yet whatever the prejudices of the scientists who work in media more capable of measurement, the "policy sciences," as H. D. Lasswell dubbed them over a generation ago, must continue in their course. Whether they will ever be capable of exact quantification or a role of omnipotence, the policy sciences have long since passed from moral theology.

Science and policy interrelate. Public policy, affecting the development, allocation, and quality of resources, refers to the action of governments at various levels and in the three branches of government, with the unifying principles being supplied by the viewpoints of the scientific observers and a governmental ideal which seeks to coordinate purposefully otherwise random actions. In part, this is revealed in the planning function of government where it is necessary to bring together the surveys of an area's physical and economic bases, the environmental moderations in local conditions, the inventory of "the backbone and vital organs" of the community, the forecasting of development, and public participation under orderly democratic procedure.[14] In such a situation, compromises are constantly being struck and both gains and losses tallied. In the process, the possibility of a proof of scientific certainty is likely to be lost.

But economics and poltical science are as much techniques of social psychology as they are of more mathematical studies. The technical economist Maynard Hufschmidt, whose work consists of the most arcane model-building, is nevertheless the man who said, ". . . the appearance of *belief* in some kind of environmental crisis changes the normal pattern of political decision and response. . . . 'Decision-making under uncertainty' . . . is probably the *only* condition under which political decisions are ever made." [15] This sort of process is clearly seen in the response of industry since 1960 to the growing public pressure against air and water pollution, "with little complaint and a good deal of action." It means heavy expenditures and continued public demand for still further effort. And the public demand is quite correct: as the President's Science Advisory Committee pointed out, everything currently planned in pollution control, if fully carried out, will enable Americans to stay about where they were in 1966 so far as harm to the human environment is concerned. It is through this sort of understanding, or perhaps even undue alarm, that the necessary change in belief has to occur. After that, the modifications in human activity necessary to preserve or restore the natural environment can be started.

DECISION-MAKING IN A CONDITION OF UNCERTAINTY
CONCERNING RESOURCES

It is to be expected that politicians will capitalize upon the use of technology for social and economic ends and that the values they bring with them will be severely attacked. Though there is doubt among scientists as to how much control man can expect to exercise over weather, Secretary of Commerce John Connor predicted, "If we . . . were to acquire the ability . . . to augment precipitation, to blunt the thrust of hurricanes, . . . to suppress hail in crop areas, to cope with lightning discharges in forest areas, and to dissipate all types of fog . . . we would be able to expand our national economy . . . to a degree now inconceivable." [16] These vast Promethean powers would be used primarily to increase the gross national product and lower insurance premiums—objectives widely concurred in as important enough to justify the effort.

John Kenneth Galbraith, however, has scathingly attacked this kind of thinking. He has indicted "the nation's planners for sacrificing urban survival to the growth of the gross national product. . . . Economists are 30 years behind the times in specifying 'it is the growth that counts.' " [17] At this time, such a charge can only puzzle and confuse political decision-makers. The public administrator, seeking a consensus on future actions, turns always to the areas of general agreement in social and economic values. He extrapolates them with the optimistic help of the growing technology—and he is assured by voices currently in a minority that he is planning society's disaster.

In such a predicament, the public man tends to take the middle view, to be eclectic, and to seek the areas of agreement. Normally, this is the intelligent political decision; it may also be the correct course of action in dealing with the life-cycle resources. Merely because demands are made in the political arena does not mean that all of them are equally valid or that any one must be met entirely.

But the crucial choices are present. Shall society seek a wildlife management program in which there is a balance between man and the biological processes, or should we scrap nature and aim for an artificial ideal of environmental conditions? Shall we control economic demands through standards, prohibitions, and strict planning, or should we split all resources into units bearing proportionate shares of total social cost and then allow the market its invisible play? Shall we determine a point of condition at which human activity should "level off," or should we accept as immutable the need for never-ending growth?

These are the basic issues in man's future use of the renewable resources. As issues, they may transcend this problem. There may be other, more difficult issues in the total social picture. But no issues present more difficulty in the making of decisions. Until now, decisions have been made both incidentally and fragmentarily. Subsequently, they may be made unconsciously or by default. But decisions will be made. Whether the answers must be framed in terms of an absolute "either . . . or" is the problem. The drive is for compromise, but compromise may be a conscious way of reaching decisions by default.

CHARACTER OF MAN'S RELATIONSHIP TO HIS
NATURAL ENVIRONMENT

The twentieth-century economy is both very far from and very close to the economic ideas of the ancient Greeks. Modern theory is at cross purposes with Aristotle, who viewed resources as static and looked upon nature, not man, as the source of wealth. According to Aristotle, man might organize and program nature, but this created no wealth. Like Xenophon before him, however, Aristotle argued that man must adjust to physical nature and must harmonize with rather than seek to dominate it.[18]

On this last point, the Greeks establish contact with the eighteenth-century Physiocrats, the nineteenth-century agrarian populists, and the twentieth-century welfare economists. It is a contact of varying intensity, to be sure; but in the latter part of our own century, the issue of man in harmony with nature is a critical one.

The problem of public attendance at the national parks is a good illustration. In 1917, the year the National Park Service began functioning, there were half a million visitors. In 1934, which was designated "National Parks Year," about four million people visited the parks. In 1940, which was designated by presidential proclamation as "Travel America Year," the number of visitors exceeded 16.5 million persons. Without any special effort on the government's part to encourage park visitors, 110 million persons attended National Park Service recreational areas, exclusive of the National Capitol Region, in 1965. This total represented a 77 percent increase over the period 1952–1960. The total acreage grew from ten million in 1941 to 25.7 million in 1960 to 26.2 million in 1965. As the National Park Service expressed it to President Johnson, "more intensive use has grown by leaps and bounds." And the increase within the next twenty years can be expected to be far greater than any in the past.

Such an increase in the use of renewable resources is not purely a matter of population increase or concentration. There has been a more subtle and hard to measure transformation that is best summed up as a "change in the quality of living." This new pattern offers both great risks and simultaneous promise of salvation.

For two centuries, men have been reminded that the industrial revolution worked a profound change on what had preceded it. Whether that previous society was organic and natural, or whether it is better described as having been static and subsistential, what came after 1750 in Western Europe was quite different from what prevailed in prior centuries. English writers, from Oliver Goldsmith to George Eliot and D. H. Lawrence, lamented what had been done to man and nature. With few exceptions, art has refused to treat sympathetically any of the positive effects of the change. Here and there, however, sometimes on its lesser levels, art did record some aspects of the change—in Frank Norris' *The Pit* and Upton Sinclair's *The Jungle,* for example. Such works considered the exaltation of the dynamics of the market, the super-importance of production, the significance of the margin in profit, and the stress upon whatever could be expressed in cash. These phenomena have come down to the present day as the vital subjects that dominate the life of Western man.

Yet something has been happening in the past generation that now appears to be a change as enormous as anything which occurred in the eighteenth century. Whether it will bring as much suffering as the industrial revolution did is still to be determined. But that it involves pronounced social changes cannot be denied.

It is called the automation revolution. It promises to render 80 percent of the population "economically useless," so that 20 percent of the population will be able to feed, clothe, and service the remainder. It bids fair to be an unusual situation in which "the intellectual and professional elite shall reduce at an ever-increasing rate the need of the non-professional and less intelligent."

Whether or not Clyde Kluckhohn was right in calling economics "applied anthropology," the automation revolution is as full of problems as anything produced as a social by-product of the steam engine or the spinning jenny. The production-orientation for Western man seems about to be changed to a recreation-orientation for masses of humanity; and this is bound to alter the relationship human activity bears to its natural environment.

The prophets of this new condition see the elite as happily continuing under the old work ethic that Max Weber and R. H. Tawney found at the base of capitalism, throbbing in theological and business documents alike after the fourteenth century. The rest of mankind, having been deprived of a production function, will provide only what Malthus would have called "effective demand," thereby giving a purpose to the labors of the elite. The masses will labor no longer but divert themselves in lives of never-ending extension courses, arts and crafts, science-hobbying, outdoor recreation, and activity justified only by the activity itself. Maintenance will come from the elite who will be the only ones still concerned with working for cash income, although for them, too, wages will be highly attenuated.[19] All this is said to constitute the near future —assuming that the elite do not administratively liquidate the masses as drones, or that the masses do not purge the elite as insufferable queens.

Whether or not some deficiency in knowledge of human psychology is present in this view, the economics of North America and Western Europe are already beginning to show the influence of the automation revolution. The trend is very much apparent when the United States government means "to unite beautification and anti-poverty programs," when the Rural Community Development Service of the Department of Agriculture will "coordinate natural beauty activities," when the Recreation Advisory Council of the Department of the Interior will "make natural beauty a council concern and create a coordinating center," and when, for the first time in history the President of the United States finally chose to write directly to county executives, his elected topic was natural beauty. To "natural beauty" has been attached an importance in social, economic, and political affairs that could have developed only after World War II.

Uncle Joe Cannon fought every conservation measure of Theodore Roosevelt and William Howard Taft with the then popular phrase, "Not one cent for scenery." President Johnson declared it his intention to repeal "Cannon's law," because "if future generations are to remember us more with gratitude than with sorrow, we must achieve more than just the miracles of technology [because] clear water [and] warm sandy beaches are a nation's real treasure." The biblical diction is nothing new in presidential utterances, but the images it evolves are specifically set in the context of a drone society. If the future is one of almost universal human leisure, "clear water" and "warm sandy beaches" will be the truest measures of the nation's economic worth.[20]

Germany's Ludwig Erhard addressed himself to the same problem in his *Formierte Gesellschaft*. He claimed that the social order has already moved beyond the "social market economy" into a "society of achievement." He would create a "communal fund" with 1 percent of the annual gross national product for, among other things, "scientific research, studies of air and water pollution, creation of parks, and planning for backward economic areas"— an effort to deal now with what others are still calling the future. Erhard's *Formierte Gesellschaft* could plainly be the mainstay of the at-leisure masses in 2000.[21]

There are other signs in the wind, besides the current concern of political figures. By nearly every standard, except gross national product, there was a serious deterioration in the quality of the environment in North America in the century between 1840 and 1940. Since 1940, however, there has been a marked reversal, and, despite some rather emotional accounts to the contrary, the grosser forms of pollution have been reduced in scope. Abel Wolman, a sanitation engineer relying upon sixty years' experience in studying environmental pollution, said that every year since 1956 has seen an annual improvement in correction, if measured in dollars, greater than the amelioration of the previous half-century. The reason for this change was the creation of the pressure group that grew out of the five-day work week. The five-day week made it possible for people to become recreation conscious. Large numbers of people, in other words, became more aware of the quality of a stream as it affected trout rather than as it had to do with driving power shafts or receiving waste.[22] It is, therefore, no coincidence that the United Auto Workers Union, pushing strongly for the shorter work week, also pushes hard for the improvement of water, air, and forests. The traditional indifference of the old AFL to the conservation of renewable resources is by necessity over because the link between job and further resource destruction is being broken.[23]

THE VALUE OF LAND AND THE MEANING OF ITS ALTERATION

Steadily, the average American seems to regard the land less as an economic object than an essentially aesthetic one. Between 1945 and 1965, the farm population of the United States sank from 20 to 6.8 percent of the population. In 1965, one man did the farm work four men had done in 1939. Yet of the nearly three million farms in existence in 1965, over half—or 1.5 million—were subsistence farms, producing only about 5 percent of the gross farm income of $43 billion. These low producers have never been eligible for the agricultural subsidy program and are destined for elimination from the agrarian economy, departing in 1965 at the rate of 356 farms daily. In the past generation, crop land acreage has been cut 11.5 percent, despite enormous increases in agricultural output, and the Agricultural Act of 1965 foresees retirement of another 13 percent by 1975. Ultimately farm population will be well below 3 percent of the total population if present trends continue for another generation.

Yet does this mean that land has truly lost its economic value except as it is part of urban sprawl? The answer is unequivocally "No." The American farm in 1965 was worth 50 percent more than in 1958. The humorist who said he looked forward to the day when the last four farmers split the federal subsidy check among them referred to a trend. It is a trend that will have cut out the bottom 90 percent of the farm population between 1945 and 1985, but which, up to the mid-1960's, has produced more food than any other agricultural system in the world and cut the food share of the consumer dollar in 1965 to 18½ cents, the lowest in history. Agriculture has joined the ranks of industry in rapid technological change.

Apart from this, however, land is increasing its value for recreational purposes. There existed in 1965 over one-half million farm ponds, most of them for purposes very indirectly concerned with farming. As subsistence agricultural areas have been abandoned for farming, efforts at reforestation and wildlife restoration have been undertaken in the hope of converting these lands into money-earning, recreational areas. Even on farmed lands, land management programs with non-farm purposes have been adopted: contour plowing to keep streams clear by stopping erosion; hedge maintenance that avoids the "clean" fence row so deadly to wildlife; cropping to prevent the dust storms that empurpled urban sunsets in the 1930's. Non-urban land values, which had declined steadily before 1953, have dramatically taken an upturn that future social needs are likely to push higher.[24]

Economically and socially—and hence politically—there is every reason for a heightened apprehension of the value of the life-cycle resources: air, water, soil, wildlife, and forest and grass cover. Dangers to them no longer stem from man's indifference. Instead, they involve: a) processes used in the economy that have an increasingly subtle effect upon the environment; b) the difficulty of devising systematic ways of evaluating the external effects of many activities, so that enlightened decisions are possible; c) too rapid increases in the demands for what may be inevitably decreasing supplies; and d) the doubt that our present social, economic, legal, or political institutions can cope with anything so complex. It is this last difficulty, among others, that led the planner Melville Branch to say in 1965, "The next ten years are pivotal. Unless you grab it now, it's gone forever."

They probably will be, since every decade in this century has been "pivotal" in one way or another. Other observers are probably also right in saying that the continuation of man's present practices means the doom of the life-cycle resources—and, presumably, the doom of some considerable part of humanity, since mankind is very much a part of the life-cycle, however aloof humanity may feel. In the mid-1960's, Americans continue annually to cut more trees than are grown as replacements, to make barely noticeable progress in water pollution control, to increase generally the degree of air pollution, and to disturb the biotic community continuously with processes which are technically more "economic." Despite the factors for optimism, a sharp cry of doom, uttered in the style of Jeremiah, would seem suitable to the occasion.

RISKS IN PREDICTING RESOURCE SUFFICIENCY

Yet the example of Stanley Jevons on the Coal Question remains as a warning to any potential Jeremiahs. Given consistency and persistency in conduct, disaster may seem easy enough to prophesy. Observing the insatiable demand that society in the 1860's was showing for paper, and knowing how straitened the supply of rag-stock paper must ever be, Professor Jevons was convinced that the world must soon suffer a severe paper crisis as well as his predicted shortage of coal. Acting on his convictions, he reduced himself to using odd scraps which might better have been thrown away. Meanwhile, he accumulated large stores of paper against the coming shortage. Technical changes after 1880 rendered his sacrifices and precautions alike useless. His family had failed to exhaust his stored supply even sixty years later, and society might have faced a similar surplus problem if Jevons' opinion had carried the day on the issue of a coal shortage—this despite the fact that his logic had persuaded John Stuart Mill himself.[25]

Lord Keynes has rather coolly dismissed Jevons' projection, attributing it to "a psychological trait, . . . a certain hoarding instinct, a readiness to be alarmed and excited by the idea of the exhaustion of resources." Still, Jevons was the first who tried to use statistical accumulations, traced back into preceding centuries, for evidence of fluctuations that might make the future more amenable to predictions. If a man who "had genius and divine intuition and a burning sense of vocation" at the time he wrote

The Coal Question could make such a mistake, persons of lesser talent may have an equal fallibility. Since 1865, mathematical economics has improved astronomically; but any examination of the processes reveals the amount of estimation, informed intuition, and arbitrary fiat which underlies calculations that are, presumably, valid on their own terms. This should not impugn the utility or integrity of the methods or of those using them. It merely raises the possibility in the minds of resource economists that man has not "learned how to avoid something comparable to diminishing returns in the quality of life." [26]

Whether society is to prepare its doom through misuse of the life-cycle resources, or to receive salvation as a peripheral benefit of market operations, or to cope with increasing complexities through carefully articulated planning, no one can be certain. These represent alternatives yet to be settled upon as the century proceeds. The one certainty is that a serious problem exists and that the possible developments fit into one of these three categories —or perhaps cut across all three, with a modicum of doom, accidental salvation, and planning mixed together.

Any of these alternatives must be worked out through institutions not primarily associated with either the exploitation or preservation of resources. It is doubtful that a "constituency" can be developed to support any institutions that might be created primarily for managing life-cycle resources. There has existed, instead, an amorphous enthusiasm that enabled the Cabinet Committee on Natural Beauty to report: "The Vice-President . . . never fails to get a warm response when he suggests that [the police] might give out as many tickets for dirty alleys as for illegal parking. People seem to be sold on natural beauty; they want to be told what to do to achieve it." [27] Since the "telling" will be expensive, since it will interfere greatly with many established patterns, and since the ticket-writing policeman is not likely to play a large role, it is doubtful how happily the majority will respond to the orders—if, at the present state of knowledge, there was agreement on how the orders should be cut.

The problem of man's effect on his environment and of how much of a place he can carve for himself within the life-cycle is very amorphous in scope. The course of any solution might be so ambiguous that no one could be sure whether the solution had proven beneficial or harmful. The choices comprising any solution might have to be absolute, or perhaps their differences could be glided over. Everything is very vague, and there is the chance that this present generation may be as wrong about the renewable resources as Jevons was in 1865 and as the American conservationists were any time before 1920 about the stock resources. In any event, stock resources are not the problem. Renewable resources, on the other hand, are a matter of pressing concern for the present generation. The problem may be induced to go away, or it may be something for planning to eliminate. But it *is* here. This is not another Coal Question, nor will any royal commissions exorcise it as a myth. Man in relation to his environment may be the only reality by 2000.

3

The costs of working against
nature

USE OF RESOURCES AND THE NATURE OF ECONOMIC DECISIONS

The North American continent (with inconsequential exceptions)
was not settled or developed by people interested in founding an
isolated, autarchic, subsistential society. Beginning in the seventeenth century, North America has been tied into world markets.
As the newly created society grew and prospered, it became steadily more production conscious and aware of the importance of
profit margins. Under these conditions, the location of human
activity had to be determined by economic demands, and the use
of land, soil, and water had to be controlled by the profits returned
through the prevailing economics.

The presence of swamps, the existence of deserts, the recurrence
of floods in particular plains—none of these has been recognized
as a barrier. If nearness to market, if the need for a transport
junction, or if being within the environs of a city or recreation
area has meant the return of a profit, North Americans have
changed even the most hostile landscapes in order to make them
serve current economic demands. Natural conditions which in
feudal Europe had seemed insurmountable obstacles were merely

delaying nuisances in North America. Jesus of Nazareth preached in parables against building on foundations of sand, but his advice has been wasted on modern economic man. The filled land of the Florida coast, the sandy seashore colonies of New Jersey, and the desert cities of California are thriving examples of man's defiance of that parable. ("Ignorance" would be a better word, so far as most investors have been concerned.) In North America, economic onslaughts upon nature have been supported by an amalgam of shrewdness, defiance, and ignorance. The dominant motivations have been the economic and social drives based on utility, amenity, and cash return.

It has been the American pattern—the pattern of urban industrial civilization and, therefore, increasingly, the pattern for the world—to develop against and in spite of nature. Half a century ago, Gene Stratton Porter's novel, *Girl of the Limberlost,* depicted a swamp culture in northeastern Indiana. The oozy gloom evoked and preserved in that book has been replaced in present-day reality by the clear open fields of truck farms, and what was once wilderness traversed by pirogues is now the "Muck Country." Any heroine of that region today would have to be shown picking tomatoes, not poling her boat. Nor is this an isolated kind of transformation; progress in the eastern United States has largely been identified with drying up wet land.

In his quest for change, man completely transforms the face of nature. An example, one of many, can be observed in eastern Dane County, Wisconsin, which was a maze of marshlands in 1900. The marshes were universally regarded as economic and social nuisances. They could not be farmed or used for industrial sites. Indeed, one could not even live near them comfortably, because of mosquitoes and other insects. Owning them as swamps was unprofitable to any man. Marshlands were simply not moneymakers.

A seemingly paradoxical condition of Wisconsin and other stretches of the United States' northeast quadrant is that, in areas of relatively low rainfall, marshlands play crucial roles in water storage. But no one in Dane County was interested in the retention of waste and silt by the marshes, although the area is one of shallow lakes with already high natural rates of growth for water plants. Nor was there any regard for the marshes' action of holding back the flushing of waste until periods of high rainfall, when the basin's streams would have their fullest and swiftest flow. In lieu of such concern, there was local, state, and federal assistance for draining the marshes and converting them to farms. As a program, drainage was well under way by World War I and almost completed by the mid-1960's.

Most of the eastern Dane County marshes now are gone, their trees cut down, their soils put to the plow, their waters dissipated, their functions unperformed.

The lakes in the region show the consequences. Of one lake, Kegonsa, the center of a new suburban development built precisely to take advantage of a view of the lake, the water experts say: "Don't worry about Kegonsa! In forty years we'll have a cheap housing development in its bed. We'll be worrying then about keeping the streets clean rather than a lake." It is not a statement that makes the investors in lakeside real estate happy. At this point, some "forward-looking" people have begun to wonder if the marshlands truly lacked monetary value. Talk has started in Dane County about the public acquisition and preservation of remaining marshes as valuable "moist lands" instead of noisome swamps destined for drainage. But a month's deluge can alter such attitudes, because the neatness of a dry field has both greater human appeal and more variety of economic utility. Even if the drained field was originally a bog and returns to a boggy state during heavy rains, even if the original bog was part of a recharge system for a region's water resources, the economy will always exert strong pressure to subsidize drainage or to maintain a bog's dried-out status.

To the American pioneer, this change in nature would have seemed to be all to the good. Often racked by fevers, always short of capital, and constantly driven onward by ambitions that required an alteration in nature and his relationship to it, the American developer, from the seventeenth through the nineteenth centuries, was impatient for the power to drain the swamps, build in the deserts, and so bank the rivers as to let cities spread over the flood plain. Americans refused to stay off the prairies merely because of devastating tornados, or to be blocked from low-lying coasts because of hurricanes, or to be barred from building the

American skyscraper in California simply because one of the world's worst ground faults runs along that Pacific shore. It has been the American way. It is becoming the way of the world. Hence, can there possibly be anything wrong with it?

The answer is "No," if several facts are accepted. The first is that these changes do not represent any permanent "conquest" of nature. Instead, changes of this sort are characterized by a transformation to an unstable condition that will have to be maintained through great, concentrated effort. This means that if the effort should falter, or if a temporary combination of natural forces, greater than the human effort, should exert pressure, a prompt, if doubtless transient, return to the preceding natural condition will ensue. It also means that when this sort of reversal occurs, the losses and suffering on a human scale will be just as heavy as the weight of the force required to overcome the human changes.

In a sense, the last is a poetic sort of justice, because the harm worked upon natural conditions is massive. Nature represents a balance, worked out over time, that has numerous ramifications throughout the related biotic or living community. No balance in nature, of course, represents stasis. Even the most stable balance has within it dynamic factors that keep up the tension of competing and complementing forces which are necessary to its maintenance. Even in nature, changes occur that overturn existing balances and compel the biotic community concerned to work out a new balance of greater or lesser stability.

But catastrophes such as these are more commonly the result of human intervention. The presence of human activity introduces a new biotic element to which nature will adjust at some level in the life cycle. The adjustment may take place outside that cycle altogether, as at the point where the Buffalo River empties into Lake Erie. Slime samples, pulled up from the river's bottom, have been lifeless.

Sometimes it is vital for man to take action to keep the life cycle functioning in any degree. In the future, certainly, human action will be necessary to counteract itself in order to hold the life cycle at maintainably high levels. Whether man's pride is hurt or not, he must recognize he is biologically part of the life cycle. As John Kenneth Galbraith phrased it to the Joint Committee on the Economic Report, "I am not quite sure what the advantage is in having a few more dollars to spend if the air is too dirty to breathe [or] the water too polluted to drink." [1]

ECONOMICS IN EMPLOYING FLOOD PLAINS AS SETTLED AREAS

In the matter of the flood plain, the American economy has set itself firmly against the forces of nature. Since the adoption of the Flood Control Act of 1936, losses from floods have grown every year despite enormous expenditures to prevent them. That act marked the beginning of a steady, concerted federal policy to encourage settlement and building on flood plains. To make this possible, a non-reimbursable program of levee and reservoir construction was launched, financing to be obtained exclusively out of the general funds of the treasury. In the eastern United States, expenditure for flood control and waste dilution reservoirs had reached $1 billion annually by 1965, and the United States Army Corps of Engineers predicts that by 1980 the allocation will have to be $2.5 billion in that region alone. Since 1936, there have been no local contributions to flood control; the costs of flood plain settlement have been passed on to the general public. This flood control expenditure has been an equivalent water investment for the eastern United States to match the water investments made in the West since the Reclamation Act of 1902. It has resulted only in the steady growth of potential loss to flooding.

This freely subsidized activity has been carried on over the vigorous protests of economic geographers, who have argued that flood control means merely exchanging a series of small floods for an occasional disastrous one. "After all," runs their argument, "that is why the flood plain is there!" It is the refusal to accept this statement as a fact that marks most thinking on the use of flood plains.

Invasion of the flood plain by settlement causes any subsequent flood to cover greater areas of land than were encompassed in the original flood plain. Also, building on that original plain is automatically a hostage to natural catastrophe. The effect has been to tie up large quantities of equity capital in flood plain construction and to bring about a rise in local tax assessments and revenues.

This benefits local banks, local businesses, and local governments at the cost of the general federal taxpayer. For the federal government will have provided all of the money for the levee and the dam, and much of the money for the guaranty of mortgages, for the construction of bridges and highways, and for putting up public structures like hospitals and schools. Local investment is relatively small, but it does involve risk, in the committal of too great a part of local wealth, enterprise, and population to a perilous location. When the catastrophe, the reversion to nature, occurs, there is then a rush of supplicants to the federal government for restoration of the artificial situation at as near complete federal expense as possible. The number of "disaster" counties grows to monotonous lengths each year during the vernal and autumnal equinoctial storms.

Various suggestions have been made as to how to avoid or minimize losses from the use of flood plains. These have ranged from putting buildings on stilts, so that the space beneath could be used for highways or parking and the flood waters could swirl about the plain when in spate, to a program of flood plain zoning. The latter would zone flood plains for low-intensity use and would educate appraisers and mortgage-lenders to place low estimates on such locations. Both approaches have been used, but with little popularity.

Nor will such measures ever be popular as long as flood plain users can pass on to the federal treasury all, or nearly all, costs of that use. Under economic conditions current since the Flood Control Act of 1936, owners and users of the flood plains have been beneficiaries of free largesse in the amount of billions of dollars. In place of this gift, a compulsory insurance program has been suggested, with premiums paid by occupants of the flood plain to cover losses to them and the general public and with the premium costs figured in terms of risks. Such a scheme would promptly apprise potential settlers on the flood plain of the risk and cost of living there. In each year, the amortized private and social costs would be imposed upon the occupants, who presumably would not move in unless they had calculated that there would be an excess above the cost of the premium. The cost of supporting flood plain settlement would be thrust upon the individual occupant, and only the expense of the flood control works' initial construction might still be carried exclusively by the federal government.[2]

But why should any of these proposals be appealing? The 1936 and subsequent flood control legislation has brought such quantities of population and private investment onto the flood plains that the very success of the public policy of flood plain settlement renders a more rational sharing of costs politically difficult to accomplish. It is a little late to regress on even a mistaken policy that has been pursued for thirty years with such enthusiasm and quantitative results—whatever the potential risk of loss. Having encouraged settlement in areas not well suited for it, the federal government and the general fund now have to resign themselves to bearing the costs. The only issue still to be contested is how far such subsidies will extend.

DEMAND FOR SUBSIDIZATION OF OTHERWISE UNINHABITABLE LAND

California's Coachella Valley is significant in the continuing debate over subsidization of potentially "uninhabitable" land. The problems inherent in the use of this valley do not seem very much like those of flood plain invasion or settlement upon the sand bars along America's Atlantic coastline, but the difference is only illusive.

The destructive element in the Coachella Valley is not water. In this desert area, gusting winds commonly blow between forty and eighty miles per hour. When the first settlers arrived, they built along the sheltered base of nearby mountains to avoid the wind and dust storms. But the pressure of settlement kept growing, and the amount of sheltered land was limited. By 1950, new developments were spreading onto the desert plain. These new communities found the commonest indigenous plant, the squat creosote bush, unsightly and ripped it out methodically. To serve the new residents' needs, highways were cut through the mountains. Winds which had previously been excluded now came blowing into the valley along man-made routes. The natural tendency of the valley floor to keep in motion was highly accelerated by the heightened human activity. Without anchorage, and disturbed by the now concentrated winds, the valley soil seems destined to blow away entirely, taking with it the investments of banks and insurance companies.

Needless to say, desert specialists have reacted with a shrug: what is happening is what they predicted. But investment and population have reached the point where withdrawal is not to be thought of—at least by local residents. A "Blow-Sands Committee" has been formed with the support of insurance companies, local government, and the state to get the federal government to *"do* something." The enthusiasm shown for federal action is hardly unexpected since other agencies have failed completely in their efforts to cope with the blowing sand. Whatever their own failures, however, they expect the United States Soil Conservation Service to launch a project in soil stabilization over the entire area, either by developing a heat-resisting grass cover or planting sand barriers of tamarisk trees. Efforts to develop the former have not succeeded, and the tamarisk project presents special problems. Sand barriers of tamarisk, to be effective, would require one tree for every linear foot of barrier and an irrigation system to keep the trees alive. Neither of these conditions could be achieved without considerable expense.

The irony lies in past efforts of settlers and government agencies alike, from the local to the federal level, to destroy the tamarisk (known as the salt cedar) as a species in the American Southwest. The tree is a phreatophyte (i.e., a deep-rooted plant draining directly from ground water levels), and many experts feel that it creates an unwarranted burden upon the water in an arid region. Having dedicated themselves to complete destruction of the tamarisk, these men are understandably dismayed to hear of new proposals to propagate and to nurture the salt cedar, at great expense.

Even if the soil stabilizing efforts should succeed, the result will be converting desert into low-quality reclaimed land. The economic attraction of the Coachella Valley has been its desert character; when that has been "improved" away, the mainstay of the area's economy, the tourist and recreation business, will be withdrawn.[3]

Meanwhile, if sand anchorage should prove possible to some degree, there will be pressure upon the federal government to assume the financial burden—whatever the cost—of such a project. Washington can expect petitions of this kind from all quarters. The 1962 hurricanes along the New Jersey coast, for instance, prompted suggestions for an anchoring and seawall program that could match in cost any scheme for securing blowing desert sands or controlling floods in the Mississippi Valley.

Settlement and resource use traditionally make their demands upon natural environment to the point where continued use means either diminution of profit or dead loss to resource users. Throughout recorded history, this usually has meant an abandonment of the resource and even of the region in which it was located. The practice has served many groups, from primitive, "slash-and-burn," semi-nomadic agriculturalists to nineteenth-century timber barons. In the United States, one region, just below the Canadian border from Maine to eastern Washington, is a particularly good example of resource abandonment. As timber, ores, and thin-soiled farming lands have been exploited to near exhaustion, man has left them behind in his restless progress across the face of nature.

PRACTICES FOR AND AGAINST SUBSIDIES IN RESOURCE USE

The orthodox conduct for market-oriented entrepreneurs has been to equalize their marginal costs and revenues. If this mode of economic behavior had been continuous, the private participant in the market, who lacked monopoly, would have had to act automatically. Under such conditions, ultimately he might be saved by the very intensity of the shortage which behavior such as his had created, if it could be coupled with applicable socio-technical improvements. Certainly there are examples of this, as in the reworking of the Mesabi range waste for taconite now that the rich ores are exhausted. The severity of the shortage also simply could compel a reduction in the output, with a consequent sharp rise in prices. This has happened with the Nova Scotia salmon; but what is tolerable for lox in a delicatessen would be intolerable in an economy so dependent on capital-goods expansion as that of late twentieth-century urban industrial society. Another possibility would have the private user acting to save the resource when changes in the legal constraints on the market forced him to discount not his revenues and expenses but, instead, his actual rate of output. A system of charges presently imposed might thereby induce him into a degree of conservation by giving future social costs a current private significance.[4]

All of these ideas, however, are presently out of fashion. Amercans have been for some time in a neo-Keynesian economic universe in which it is the function of government to prevent the traditional cruelty of abandoning the lands and populations of exhausted regions. Nassau Senior, the man who made economics the "Dismal Science," would not only have urged government to permit such relics to die; he would have fretted because death did not come swiftly or severely enough. His muttering over the Irish bills of mortality during the starvation and pestilence of the Great Famine was memorable: "Too low, too low." There had to be more deaths to save that wretched country; and Nassau Senior would write out the same prescription today for Appalachia and what Michael Harrington has called the "New Poor" of the American metropolis: those masses unsuited for any function except consumption in an automated urban industrial culture. Nassau Senior's approach is not suitable for contemporary economic planners in an age when it is the function of government to so spend money that the private economy is stimulated to ever-increasing efforts at production. In this context, it is only natural for the private sector to expect government to absorb the expense of what have been called infrastructure or social costs.[5] Even anti-Keynesians in the American political scene see nothing wrong in expenditures like these.

EXAMPLES OF SILTATION AT PUBLIC EXPENSE

The problem of river siltation and how to cope with it illustrates the neo-Keynesian atmosphere which prevails today in economics. Although Plato was concerned over soil erosion in Attica and Pliny the Younger over sedimentation in the Tiber, American hydrologic experts prior to 1940 paid little attention to siltation. Silt might be a soil expert's worry, or a troublesome source of expense when it ruined hydropower equipment, but costs of this sort were hard to calculate and seemingly too peripheral to be of consequence to dam builders. Before 1940, silty streams were regarded as mere aesthetic nuisances, despite the existence of considerable data indicating that silt was a more serious matter.

It was known, for instance, that silt altered the quality of aquatic life by changing conditions to suit those species which required less oxygen and were therefore well adapted to thriving in situations when much oxygen was taken from the water. Silted streams, it had been observed, had difficulty in purging themselves by natural aeration processes. The swirling flow of sediment caught and held pollutants; the water became turbid and, with conditions favorable for anaerobic bacteria, gave off exhalations of sulphates and methane. Muddy bottoms rose because of silt deposits and because of the accumulation of rotting algae whose growth had been stimulated by plant nutrients contained in what originally had been soil meant to sustain the growth of land vegetation. Slowed by having to carry a burden of silt, the water flow was heavier at freshet time. This same heavy silt content gradually made water sports, such as fishing and swimming, impossible in many streams.

Perhaps if the high-speed modern sports of motor-boating and water-skiing had been popular before 1940, it would have been noticed that certain waters contained gritty loam which could abrade boat bottoms at an alarming rate. Skiers would not have been happy with the film of lighter wastes that floated near the surface. (These wastes cannot sink because of the silt beneath them and because both the surface and the depth of streams are invaded by run-off from the land.) But water sports as a form of mass recreation did not get well started until after the Korean War, so that pressure from this potential lobby was late in developing.

Before World War II, builders of dams and reservoirs and rectifiers of channels gave little thought to silt. True, it did hold bacteria in the water, but these could be killed by chlorination. Silt was also destructive to machinery coming in contact with raw water, but filtration could sieve the sediment out. And, of course, silt did destroy the navigability of certain streams, but there were faster alternative modes of transport. Silt raised the stream beds, but the same silt built out the deltas at the river mouths. The solutions above might involve high costs, but such costs did not concern river engineers very much. Occasionally, engineers might bother to dredge out some stretches of water, but the re-deposit of silt, the formation of islands, the slowing of water flow, and the rising of beds continued. Men who concerned themselves with silt at all could take comfort in the fact that, in reports to travelers about certain streams, the Indians had complained about the same old silt problems.

What caused the ultimate change in viewpoint proved to be the river engineers' very ignorance. Dams and reservoirs built without regard for silt carriage factors soon began to suffer acutely from the condition of the water. Although some silt studies had been conducted before 1940, the first disastrous reports came out of Ethiopia. Brief as the Italian Empire there was, Italian engineers, between their arrival in 1935 and their expulsion in 1941, managed to build a reservoir that had silted up completely by about the time they departed. In lieu of the original valley, or the artificial lake that had replaced it, there was a boggy plain. At great effort and expense a field of quicksand had been created. It was a horrible example; combined with other situations, reports of which had begun to gather, it caused the construction experts to re-examine their premise that the significance of silt was basically and only aesthetic.

THE COLORADO AS AN ILLUSTRATION OF ARTIFICIAL REGIMES FOR RIVERS

As Mussolini's engineers discovered, every reservoir loses capacity to silting, and this loss is both rapid and of major proportions. In the United States, the Colorado River presents the problem on a grand, though not a unique, scale. The alluvial valleys draining into the Lower Colorado had a naturally aggrading, silt-building effect on the reaches of the great river. Spring freshets from the snowmelt provided by the Rockies had moved tremendous amounts of sediment down into the river. Because the river was unconfined, the waters flooded out and deposited much of the silt on the flood plain. Yet, difficult as the river was to control, it was too important economically to the region where it ran to be left in any natural state.

Improvements on the river have made important changes at great expense to the public treasury. With the closing of Hoover Dam in 1935, Parker and Imperial Dams in 1938, and Davis Dam in 1950, a controlled artificial type of regime was forced upon the river, tightly confining it so that the plain would no longer be flooded and the water would be channeled effectively for irrigation and hydropower. Under this regime, sediment had to be deposited in the reservoirs, and the clear water releases from the sluices below each dam degraded the banks of the river, sweeping further sediment into the thread of the stream. A condition of aggradation above and degradation below came to characterize every dam on the river, so that the water surface rose and fell erratically. Irrigation projects complicated the artificial regime further by excluding normal tributary stream flows.

It is the way in nature for new constraints to give rise to new regimes which acquire characteristics as natural as any preceding them. River cycles of degradation and aggradation eventually establish stability through shifting smaller particles downstream and leaving behind coarser particles to armor and stabilize the bed. Unfortunately, so far as the human economy and natural stability are concerned, the period of time required to set up new regimes is too long to fit within the confines that human demands impose upon the Colorado. To correct this, the river engineers must undertake to channelize the river. Starting with the unstabilized conditions created by the man-made structures, the river is channelized; this process compels a readjustment to the rectified conditions. Eventually, the theory is, a stable regime will function in the river, so that siltation will not disastrously affect the reservoir system.

Unfortunately, it is very hard to prevent silt's causing disaster to reservoirs. When sediment enters a reservoir, the silt loads far out to form deltas which have an astonishing effect in diminishing the contour area of the reservoir. As the deposit of sediment increases, the successive layers encroach upon the deepest part, which is immediately behind the dam. The reservoir acts like a stilling basin in a water treatment plant, settling out the sediment loads that enter it. The capacity for both water and silt depends upon the area and depth of the reservoir. Once the silt reaches the sill of the conduit outlet (or the power inlet if the dam is hydroelectric), the sediment-laden water wears down any pipes or blades it contacts and builds up the beds below the dam.

At first this outflow of silt-laden water tends merely to reverse the degradation process which the clear water had previously carried out. But as it continues, the lower channel is built up, with deltas spreading out along the banks and eddies of the stream. The early deposits lapping over the dam will be carried farthest because of the clarity of the receiving water and the degraded conditions of the channel. But as stable silt slopes are built up, the deposits right at the dam become heavier. Ultimately, this means that a dam built at great cost of concrete is enclosed in a silt envelope.[6]

DIFFERING PROBLEMS IN WESTERN AND EASTERN AMERICAN WATERS

This is what has been happening to the Colorado River under the widely hailed improvement program that was begun forty years ago. The same pattern has been applied to many other western rivers under the impetus of the image of economic productivity that high-dam construction promises. As the high dams have been built and their reservoirs formed on other western streams, the expensive silt problems of the Colorado have appeared; and it has been necessary to construct for those streams similar artificial regimes to which the streams must adapt.

The creation of these artificial regimes is neither a cheap nor an easy process for engineers working on the rivers in the American West. First the total sediment load must be calculated. The data required for this includes such information as the channel width, area and average depth, the water temperature and discharge during sampling, and the concentration and distribution by size of suspended sediments. Western streams carry primarily a sand-element load; but since they do not carry it in a uniform fashion, data must be gathered in differing hydraulic conditions and the samples must be discretely analyzed to make up a total view.

In all of this, many steps are essential to compute the total sediment load. The erratic behavior of any stream requires the engineers to remain poised to modify their computed values at any time the data changes during their gathering of the bits and pieces of information supplied by their sampling. Needless to say, since total knowledge is not possible even for a stream carrying only one sediment element, assumptions have to be hit upon in the calculations that have a trial-and-error aspect. Knowledge gathered from observing many streams which have a single-element sediment load serves as the basis for these assumptions; and, for western American streams, the engineers can at least predict what will happen under the imposed artificial regimes. Often, when action means something on a smaller scale than dredging out Lake Mead in back of Hoover Dam, this information serves as a guide for correction of deterioration in the operation of the artificial regime.[7]

Even when used on the single-element sediment load in the western American streams, this method cannot be very exact. It is adequate for planning control of a system like the Colorado, but it is not suited for the more complex problems of eastern American waters. The rivers in that part of the United States are laden with multiple sediments and, because of long persisting misuse, have deep layers of pollution on their bottoms.

But even these eastern river problems seem simple when compared with the difficulties of coping with polluted sediment loads in estuarine waters along the ocean shore. There are no data on the patterns of sorting in tidal waters, nor is there a rigorous method for learning the effect of ebb flow on the normal shoreline process of sorting and grading deposited particles. The measuring of waves, currents, and other shore processes presents an awesome number of variables to the engineer who proposes to regulate them in some artificial regime. His task is complicated by the fact that the best sorting takes place where the ocean's actions make the water most turbulent and therefore casts the sediment in crescent-shaped fans over the floor of the sea. The heavier the sediment load, however, the more poorly this sorting process functions, and the nearer to shore the wastes are dropped. It is a design like the sediment-deposit being let down in reservoirs and natural lakes fed by tributaries, only upon the grander scale of the ocean and the ocean's shore.

To move from west to east in the United States is to move steadily from less to more complex difficulties in setting up artificial regimes to regulate water. This is largely due to the greater population, industrial and agricultural activity, and extent and depth of resource use in the eastern states. Actually, because of their greater natural clarity, eastern rivers started with a decisive original advantage. If their current condition is worse, it is the result of uses greater and longer in time than have yet been made in the West. And where estuarine waters are concerned, the greatest adverse natural conditions exist in the East conjointly with the heaviest resource demand upon waters as receivers of a sediment that is composed of eroded soil, sewage, and industrial waste.

EFFECT OF WASTE AND SEDIMENT LOADS ON TIDAL AND OTHER STREAMS

Yet the presently critical condition of waters in heavily populated and industrialized regions does not deter man from making ever greater demands upon the ability of streams, lakes, and inlets to receive waste. The current situation is the best argument for a close look at refuse disposal schemes like those of Otto Thope which are attracting favorable world-wide attention.

As director of public works for the city of Hanover, Germany, Thope has pushed a plan to dispose of solid dry refuse through a vast nationwide pipeline system. Its blueprints call for a plant at Hanover to crush and grind waste, with pipelines connecting the plant to other north German cities such as Hamburg, Bremen, Kiel, Emden, and Wilhelmshaven. It would do for dry refuse what sewers do for wet wastes, with pumping stations every forty miles on the flat north German plain until the pipes reached their outlets in the Baltic and North Seas. "Remnants of junked automobiles, castoff furniture, tires, bottles—even the slag and waste of steel mills—would pass through crushing and grinding machines in each city and then be flushed into the pipeline. Refuse, once sorted, crushed, and ground up, would be diluted in sewage or other waste water in sufficient quantities to make it fluid." In this condition of sludge, the waste would be flushed into the shallow, narrow, stormy waters of seas which, unfortunately, already carry a heavy pollutant load.

The Thope plan has seemed very appealing to many American municipal planners. True, it might be disastrous to dump wastes treated in this manner into waters like those of Chesapeake Bay or the Great Lakes. But the rising cost of urban land, the surfeiting of existing dumps and landfills, and the discarding of an average of four pounds of junk every day by every American makes such disposal ideas very appealing. Considering present conditions along the seashores and in the estuaries of urban industrial countries, however, the Thope plan is not a "solution" to be accepted without considerable thought.[8]

Studies of the Potomac before it empties its wastes into the estuarine waters of Chesapeake Bay suggest why the Thope plan might not work there. During his administrations, Theodore Roosevelt, like John Quincy Adams three generations before him, swam daily in the river. If any President in recent years had possessed the stamina or the curiosity to leave the heated, disinfected, filtered, enclosed White House pool, he would have found that a river impossible for swimming had been developed since 1909. And supporting the industrial and municipal waste and sewage poured into the water has been an increasing silt load brought about by the changing character of the valley. The minerals entering the Potomac from mine wastes and industry act to hold back the settling of the clay and silt washed into the river. By 1961, nearly three million tons of sediment entered the Potomac annually—probably about fifty times more sediment entering the river than the total amount prior to settlement of the valley.

The significance of sediment loads in the Potomac is determined by the uses existing in the valley, as is true of any river. Therefore, to treat sediment load as an isolated problem makes it impossible to grasp the magnitude of the damage being done. Yet this is the approach that has been taken. Beginning in 1880, sediment has been dredged from the river and estuarine waters near Washington at a rate of 1.5 million cubic yards annually. The ultimate futility of this as the sole approach was obscured by the utility of the dredged matter as fill. Now that the more available disposal areas have been used and it is necessary to move the sludge further at higher cost, the inherent difficulties of dredging have made themselves more apparent.

Natural contributions of silt do not constitute the major part of the Potomac's problem. Normally, larger sediment particles drop before the smaller ones. In fact, clay has a tendency to settle more rapidly in raw Potomac water than in distilled water. But chemical wastes in the Potomac interrupt the normal settling proclivities of sediment. These chemicals cause the particles to adhere together in adhesive masses which, depending upon the composition of the substance, will settle quickly or float further down river. Or, the chemical wastes may prevent suspended matter from settling at all. As can be seen, chemical waste converts soil sediments into material similar to non-degradable industrial waste. In the Potomac, this material damages the water far in excess of the valley's industrial potential. In regions that are more industrialized, such damage can kill all life in a river's waters.

The significance of chemical pollution depends upon what the river is to be used for. Tolerance in industrial processes ranges from ten to several hundred parts per million (ppm) of different kinds of minerals. And chemical pollution cannot be regarded as having a uniform effect. Silica, which is not significant to humans, livestock, fish, or plants, has an upper limit for most boilers of 1 ppm; and a limiting concentration of 0.1 ppm in the steam has been recommended, the same suggestion being made for water injected into aircraft engines. Sodium, which is harmless to the average person, is deleterious to soil structure if combined with calcium and magnesium, since it causes soil to lose its permeability. If the water should acquire alkalinity, it cannot be used for irrigation since it would destroy plant life, although most industrial processes would be unaffected. Certainly the examples of possible harm to soil cultivation, metal maintenance, and plant, animal, and human health by chemical invasion of water are numerous; but when the waters already carry a heavy load of sediment prior to chemical invasion, the two separate conditions create an intolerable situation.

Of course sediment discharges occur in uninhabited areas, but the differing kinds of human use determine how much soil will be washed down into the waters of a river. Forest lands produce the lowest sediment discharge, which ranges under one hundred tons per square mile. Croplands produce sediment flows of from 100 to 350 tons per square mile. The urbanized land of the modern metropolis causes sediment flow to increase enormously so that, in areas undergoing development, discharge rates of sediment can run as much as fifty times greater than those in the average rural area. One fifty-eight-acre tract being developed near Washington, D.C., in the mid-1960's had an annual average sediment discharge of eleven thousand tons per square mile, and many gauging stations in the Washington urban district register almost two thousand tons of sediment per square mile.[9]

It seems needless to emphasize the effect this is having on the confined waters of Chesapeake Bay. Reservoirs and estuaries located in forest districts will not be lost to siltation, while those deriving water from urban or urbanizing areas are in for serious trouble. And, if the basic soil being broken up is high in chemical hardness and harm to human activity, then nature has merely added her fillip to man's actions. It is no accident that floods in heavily urbanized valleys have been growing in severity. Aside from the new construction in the flood plain and the more rapid run-off of rainwater from pavements and roofs of city areas, the waste and sediment from urban centers is choking river outlets, building up stream beds, and silting up lakes, reservoirs, and estuaries that otherwise would receive flood waters and perhaps do so more rapidly.

But schemes like the Thope plan to flush all solid urban waste into the rivers, lakes, and bays continue to be brought forward. The more popular they prove to be, the more contributive to chronic flooding urban industrial activity will become.[10]

COSTS OF ARTIFICIAL RIVER REGIMES

The scope of the problem of waste and sediment load on public waters having been suggested, is there no solution? Has there been contentment with rising river beds, accelerating siltation of reservoirs, and the steady erosion of soil? For many years in the history of the United States, an indifference about equal to contentment indicated that the answer to this question was "Yes." The frontier seemed to have been settled only by soil miners. The rapid push west had helped give mobility to the population and an instability to the social structure that made land acquisition a mere speculation. Such social and economic practices combined to wear down soil and run it off into the streams.

Economically, techniques that mined the soil may not have been waste. Land, and the resources upon land, were the American capital that had to be drawn upon quickly and heavily to build a new nation. The affluent America of the late twentieth century should not despise the ancestors who created the basis for the present capital through an expenditure of life and energy as extravagant as any drafts they made upon the land. Still, physically there was damage, even if economic values were simultaneously extracted. This fact was recognized early. In 1879, the Mississippi Valley Commission was established with the United States Army Corps of Engineers as its operating arm. This, supported by the Rivers and Harbors Act of 1888, began the enormous program of dredging, channelization, stream rectification, bank control, and levee building which has been pursued ever since. To this has been added since 1945 the erection of trap and impoundment reservoirs at great cost to overcome siltation effects, particularly in the construction of artificial regimes for rivers.

But the nineteenth-century innovators of these river programs could have had no notion of the size of the undertakings they had begun. Taken in combination with the traditional methods of stream rectification, the post-1945 program of trap dams and reservoirs widely scattered through a valley to support the function of major dams on the main streams was meant to create, ideally, perfect artificial regimes for every river basin. The initial costs for such artificial regimes were certain to be great. About $100 billion is the allotment for the Potomac River alone before the year 2000. Maintenance charges also tend to be high. Unfortunately, the artificial regime can be highly unstable if struck by unusual conditions of weather or ground stability. Such programs are simply added to the costs of existing flood control projects. If such costs are incurred, it is true that large tracts of low ground could be kept open for settlement for every period of time except a time of catastrophe. Under such control, huge reservoirs could be kept indefinitely functioning. Indeed, these artificial regimes would be sustainable on any river if costs were put to one side as an irrelevant factor.

But artificial regimes embrace more than construction in concrete and call for public expenditures to other purposes. Beginning in 1933, the United States Department of Agriculture started a program of land management that was designed to cut erosion, soil depletion, and sediment run-off. Secretary Henry A. Wallace brought to this program an evangelic zeal somewhat similar to what Gifford Pinchot had done for conservation as Chief Forester. Subsequent Secretaries of Agriculture have kept up this program or even intensified it. Land from which soil leaches rapidly and which loses its ability to maintain crops is land which ought never have been opened to cultivation. Its quick retirement is desirable; and since 1933 millions of acres—much of it this kind of land—have been put into grass and timber. Contour plowing, terracing, and windbelts of trees have tied soil to the land so that neither wind nor water can move it in great amounts. Anyone flying over the country in 1932, and then again in 1967, would see a land whose agricultural management has been almost completely altered. As a prolonged policy, it has cut back sediment run-off from rural areas and helped materially in the overall management of artificial regimes in river basins.

This soil program has scarcely been carried through at the expense of the rural farmer—except that, insofar as it has excluded the subsistence farmer from subsidies, guided its assistance programs exclusively for the benefit of the market-oriented farmer, and precipitated subsistence farms into land retirement programs, we can thank this program for having assisted the overwhelming majority of those on the land in 1932 to be off of it by 1967. At this point in American history, the shift from rural to urban living having been no cause for either economic or social regret, it has been regarded as a beneficial program.

Yet, whatever the effect on society, population movements, or land improvements, this soil conservation, it cannot be forgotten, has been paid for from the general funds of the federal government and made as a free gift to all beneficiaries. Educational programs, subsidies, crop controls, soil banks, and other programs were all necessary for such a transformation of the land. This has always been the intention, from the time of the early Grange to the Wild Jackasses of the West. The reduction in sediment run-off from rural land has been achieved almost entirely at general public expense. Putting aside the ignorance and carelessness of American farmers, any profit derived from soil mining and erosion went to private persons. The costs of correcting the physical damage have been borne by the public treasury; and direct benefit once more flows into private hands. Any social benefits have been in the indirect form of capital formation and current employment.

ECONOMIC INTERRELATIONSHIP OF SUBSIDIZED WATER PROJECTS

That benefits have taken this form should come as no surprise. As part of general practice, flood plain protection, sediment discharge control, and erosion prevention have all been subsidized. Free gifts from the public treasury have been the rule. Of the total rainfall in the United States, about 7 percent is managed; over half of this managed portion is a part of the great irrigation schemes in the western United States, which have been provided by the federal taxpayer. Yet little of this "managed" water is beneficially used in agriculture. In Arizona, 75 percent of all precipitation is lost, mostly to evaporation. Only about 1 percent of the precipitation is left to replenish ground water supplies. Water is lost through the very constructions built for irrigation. In the hot climate of the Southwest, water is more rapidly evaporated from reservoirs and canals and swiftly absorbed into the porous banks of the ditches. It may be that "every time a drop of water falls in Arizona, state and federal agencies examine it, name it, claim it, dam it, or fight over it," but up to this point, private irrigation farmers, who use more water on one acre of cropland than urban dwellers use on one acre of residential area, have had little occasion to save the water supplied them at government initiative and substantially at government expense.[11]

It is this factor which makes it so hard to talk about a western water shortage and which explains why planners in the American Southwest are hoping population growth may solve their water problems for them. Not only do urban populations use far less water per acre than irrigation farmers; but urban sprawl, lamented elsewhere, is rather welcomed through its conversion of land from heavy to light water use. Furthermore, urban populations normally pay rates much nearer the cost of water supply than have ever been paid by the politically favored, subsidized irrigation farmers. But most people do not want to hear about the possible demerits of subsidized water programs, especially westerners defending the irrigation service. A Wyoming native, working in the United States Bureau of Land Managament, was just that blunt when he said, "I don't want to hear about the faults of subsidizing western irrigation at the expense of eastern taxpayers. It opened the Southwest, in particular, to heavy settlement; and it's keeping the flow coming. It seems to me that the public has gotten its money's worth."

Whether this is or has been so, one result of the program is that an irrigation farmer pays only about one-third of the cost of the water supplied to him. Because of this, it is hard to get the irrigation farmers to take measures for water conservation. Federal subsidy of irrigation becomes even more ironic when one considers that cotton is the crop often grown on the irrigated acres. Cotton *also* has to have its price sustained by government support. In a study conducted in New Mexico by Nathaniel Wolman in 1964, it was calculated that an acre-foot of water created about $3,000 in values from industrial activity and only $40 to $50 in agricultural crops. Irrigation is one of the highest consumptive uses of water known. It is clear that UNESCO was right in predicting a cutback before 1985 in the use of water in the United States for irrigation.[12] This will certainly be true generally, and truest of all in the arid, population-burgeoning, rapidly urbanizing American Southwest.

But irrigation is only part of the whole problem of subsidized programs for conservation of resources. People prefer non-reimbursable systems of environmental control, whether those systems concern water supply, siltation prevention, building within flood plains, land management, irrigation, or air and water pollution control. Indeed, the evidence indicates people prefer help that is non-reimbursable, even if they get less value than the cost of the project and less utility than would be derived from alternatives for which all or part of the cost would have to be borne by the beneficiaries. Government subsidies in land management have been of more use than all the exhortations for farmers to be good husbandmen. The farmer was quite willing to forgo the chance of future rewards from good husbandry until the federal government launched plans that showed an immediate return in federal payments if certain specific steps were taken. The same course can be paralleled in every one of the renewable, life-cycle resources. The only surprise is that there should be any surprise at all.

FUNCTION OF GOVERNMENT IN ENVIRONMENTAL CONTROL

This is not to deny that "government has a basic responsibility . . . [in] the wise management of forests, wildlife, farm crops, grazing, and the land and water themselves." [13] Nor is it to claim that pressure groups should not be organized to prod, persuade, guide, and extract from government what each needs. Such "cooperative hunting expeditions" are, as one conservation lobbyist expressed it, "a matter of necessity." In this way the keen competition among the various pressure groups that affect government planning and investment can be adjusted in a democratic society in a way other than through benevolent federal orders issued to an indifferent and apathetic public. So long as government stands at the point of control, for so long will those private pressures be exerted—or until politics succeeds in producing the monolithic state. Government assistance—in setting standards, financing basic infrastructure that private persons cannot provide, educating the public and in particular the youth, and granting subsidies to stimulate action— is indeed a necessity in the late twentieth century. The only issue that remains is the wise and economic management of this government assistance throughout the future.

Anthony Scott, a Canadian economist, has said that "a low-interest, high-construction economy uses up stock mineral resources, and that a high-interest, high-consumption economy depends mostly upon renewable biological resources." [14] The former condition perhaps characterized the American economy from the Civil War to World War II; the fact that it did would help explain the facts which so alarmed the early American conservationists at the turn of the present century about the possible loss of stock resources. As a theory, it would also explain why there is less and less alarm in the 1960's about the possible exhaustion of the stock resources and why perturbation has steadily grown over the effect of urban industrial society upon renewable resources.

Of course, no statement implying the limitations of a static law should be accepted: the dynamics of change, which have occurred and which seem about to occur, make all limiting statements suspect. Yet in this remark of Professor Scott's there does seem to be a considerable concentration of truth.

Currently, the economy of North America and Western Europe is one of high interest rates and high consumption. It may be that this high consumption is dependent upon military expenditures only and would collapse without them. It may also be most unfortunate that there exists such an emphasis upon the growth of the gross national product, and it may be that this emphasis degrades the human purpose to a purely consuming function. It also may be true that the persistent rise in the interest rate is an inflationary threat to the strength of this consumer economy.

However, it *cannot* be denied that high interest rates and high levels of resource consumption do characterize our present economy. Naturally, efforts had to be made to pass along these high costs. This might have been done through more intense exploitation of the renewable resources, since, in our legal system, these are so often held by no one in specific title. Because of this common ownership, life-cycle resources are often treated as if owned by no one—as if they were free goods to be reduced to private owner-ship by whoever chose to possess them. In this way, someone ex-ploiting earth for taconite might divert streams and cast off soils without regard for the effect on the waters of the region. From the exploited earths, he would make profit in the form of income; from the polluted water would come profit in the form of savings. With-out doubt, such has been the traditional method of operation; and it is still the common course of action.

But recently there have been steps taken to interfere with this traditional and common recourse. Administrators now exist to gauge the effects upon environment of industrial processes. Min-imal quality requirements in environmental matters are set by ad-ministrative agencies which investigate conditions to see if these rules are maintained. The state and federal governments have as-sumed directly many of the costs of preserving renewable re-sources, and private persons receive governmental assistance in this task of resource preservation.

Traditional public indifference to the private engrossment of renewable resources has been increasingly replaced, as these re-sources have been exhausted or damaged, by the government's as-suming the burden both of maintaining renewable resources and of increasing their availability. In Texas, San Antonio artificially re-charges the water levels for the municipal wells at city expense. The underground water supply has been drawn down by pumping for irrigation to the point where the recharge is needed. This same pumping, of course, prevents the recharging from reaching maximum effectiveness. The irrigation farmers make no payment to San An-tonio for water supplied by the tax and rate payers of that city. Instead, farmers continue to pump the water as if it were a free gift of nature. On November 2, 1965, the people of New York State voted to assume a debt burden of $1 billion in order to im-prove water resources within the state. Since 1956, when the fed-eral Water Pollution Control Act was passed, federal monies have filled out state and local expenditures which would have been far less without these federal grants. Public opinion has been ever more insistently demanding a higher level of regulation of renewable resources; and government at every level has been responding with investments and expenditures to try to meet that demand. The statutes enacted and the monies expended have been spiraling, unevenly, since the mid-1950's at every level of government and throughout the United States.[15]

ECONOMICS BEHIND CHANGED ATTITUDES
ON RESOURCE MAINTENANCE

Popular opinion and governmental activity cannot have been merely responding to the educational, alarmist propaganda efforts of the early conservationists and the neo-Malthusians. Many of these persons have been in a state of chronic panic concerning the overwhelming of all resources by a population explosion that began its greatest expansion after 1930. Probably the public has been aroused to some degree of interest by the work of the conservationists in education and propaganda. And, certainly, the public's concern has been stimulated by the post-1945 leisure and affluence in the United States. These have made great numbers of people more thoughtful about recreation. They have been moved to worry over the loss of resources whose existence might make their new recreation time meaningful.

But though these are indubitable facts, they are not the entire explanation behind changed attitudes. The modern urban industrial economy exerts an enormous demand upon renewable resources. This demand has been growing and will increase progressively before the end of the twentieth century. So great is this prospective demand that some observers wonder if nature can accommodate it. Perhaps nature can, or perhaps man will have to replace nature with artificial regimes. At present, it is difficult to know which. Popular opinion and government do agree, however, in the certainty that human activity in modern urban industrial society has reached a point where its effects cannot be repaired by nature without human assistance. The managers of the economy themselves recognize this, and the issue that remains is: Who is to pay the cost and how is payment to be made?

Modern economy makes drafts upon the environment that require repayment; there should be no denial either of the drafts or of the debts their drawing has created. It is probably this realization that has created public consciousness of a renewable resource problem. In an age when any quantity of wilderness land within twenty miles of a large American city is a "remarkable anachronism," [16] there can be no avoidance of man's debt.

The landscape and the living environment have been transformed by urban industrial society since 1800, a transformation often at the expense of the public treasury and always as a charge upon social values. The economic and social rewards from this process have been great, but so have been the costs. And the time has long since passed when the costs could be dismissed as invisible and painless charges upon the total economy and the physical environment. For some time, these costs have been cause for substantial outlays of funds; the effect upon the physical environment is even more consequential. Economic decisions concerning use of resources may have been expensive in the past; but the size of future costs promises to dwarf everything that has gone before this final third of the twentieth century. In economic terms, these are costs payment of which has yet to be calculated and the burdens of which have still to be allocated.

Practices of the past have permitted single economic units to seize resources from the living environment in order to obtain individual profit, and pressure groups have been encouraged to protect themselves against this by procuring public subsidies to finance their own activities. It did not seem wrong for some developers to run off topsoil into a choked stream during a soil-skinning real estate project; or to pay for the dredging of that same stream out of the public treasury; or for the federal government to underwrite the costs of new erosion and soil-fixing control. The same sense of "nothing wrong" inured men to the effect upon the physical environment of resource exploitation, as it made them feel unconcerned with the dollar costs of sustaining, or correcting, such employments of the living landscape. Until demand grew to late twentieth-century proportions, this ambiguity or neutrality of man's attitude toward resources and their treatment, economically and physically, could be accepted. But what was formerly the nuisance of confusion had become, by the mid-twentieth century, an enormous burden in economic cost and physical damage. The decisions must be made to resolve this confusion very soon. Even if economic cost were to mean nothing in the future, the damage to the physical world would hardly be bearable by even minimum standards. It is this physical burden that threatens to be the heaviest and, eventually, the most costly by any standard of measurement.

4

Urban industrial culture and its living environment

It has been a commonplace that when urban industrial civilization develops, a profound change occurs in the world of insects, birds, plants, and animals. Game of all kinds tends to find its numbers reduced or its habits much altered, while even man himself is brought to a readjustment of his ways of life.

In the past, the effects of such changes have seemed to consist mainly of aesthetic losses or deprivations of small significance to the general economy. The cutting down of hardwood forests, the extinction of certain species and the regional extirpation of others, and the pollution of the overall environment were simply accepted as the price to be paid for what has been since the eighteenth century an ever-expanding economy in Western Europe and North America.

Certainly the old problems inherent in the competition between urban industrial human economy and other forms of life remain as acute as ever. Game still is threatened, forests cut off, and soils exhausted. However, since the late 1930's, the increasing employment of chemicals of all kinds has introduced an element of larger hazard into the situation: risks to the living environment are reaching still higher levels. There seems to be no limit to the rising demands made on the living resources of nature.

From very early times, fears have been expressed concerning the harm that chemical compositions could do to human constitutions. In the thirteenth century, coal smoke was regarded as far more deleterious than the products of burning wood or charcoal. Only the stripping away of trees near London compelled the use of the cheaper and more effective sea-coal from Newcastle. In the eighteenth century, the physician-novelist Tobias Smollett raged continuously against the foul pollutions of the English air and water by commerce and the growing cities.

In subsequent centuries, there has been no shortage of writers to be perturbed over some chemical newly introduced in industrial or agricultural processes. As the United States Agricultural Extension Service has observed, "In cycles of approximately 25 years, hundred of alarming stories have appeared in newspapers and magazines, some written by leading personalities of their day. These warned the public that 'agricultural poisons will be the death of us all.' Such charges have been proven unfounded—not once, but many times. One of the earliest . . . farmers' bulletins, No. 7, issued in 1892, dealt specifically with this subject." [1] Despite the reassurance in this statement, fears persist. Indeed, there is considerable evidence that—whether or not they will be "the death of us all"— the chemical biocides have been a considerable peril to many forms of life.

USE OF BIOCIDES

"Biocide"—the killing of life—is the inclusive term for any chemical which destroys a particular form of life; herbicide, rodenticide, nematocide, fungicide, insecticide, and pesticide simply specify the victims. Commonly, it is the word "pesticide" that generically covers all of them, because whatever is to be killed is regarded specifically as a pest. Biologically and legally, the definition of "pest" is a difficult matter. Congress has declared that a weed is "any plant which grows where not wanted," and the administrators of the federal legislation consider any form of "plant and animal

life and viruses . . . to be a pest . . . when [it] exist[s] under circumstances that make it injurious to plants, man, domestic animals,
other useful vertebrates, useful invertebrates, or other articles or
substances." [2] A pest, therefore, is something that is economically
costly, dangerous to human health, or inconvenient to the ameni-
ties of human life. It can be anything from a starling or lamprey eel
to a wild carnivore or mosquito. In any campaign of destruction,
it should be remembered that a pest is an abstract idea derived
from the operation of economics and the concepts of public health.
In nature, a pest is merely one more species existing in competition
with or complementary to another species which it inhibits or upon
which it is dependent. It may even simultaneously be performing
some service for the species it frustrates. Pests are not merely noisome excrescences provided by a malevolent deity, nor can they be
heedlessly expunged from the natural landscape.

But what is particularly worrisome to most persons is not this
broader ecological aspect. Any kind of pest control program, whatever the basis for its procedures, must mean the removal or reduction of the population that has been designated as pestilent. Man
assumes this as a matter of course. His main concern is with the
effect of the chemical biocides—used more and more widely since
the late 1930's—rather than with any ecological query as to
whether any species is truly a pest.

Certainly, most people believe they know what a pest is, in economic terms. As the United States Department of Agriculture said
in a public statement issued in response to senatorial questions,
"Chemical pesticides have helped and will continue to help make
possible the better living conditions this nation enjoys. The burst of
productivity . . . on U.S. farms parallels the increasing use of
chemical pesticides. . . . Without pesticides, many of the foods we
take for granted would be luxury items available to only a few." [3]
Farmers who have used the biocides have been generous in their
applications. Economics encourages them to be so. A single large
planting of lettuce, for instance, as of eleven days before harvest
had received applications of eight biocides: Chlordane, endrin,
dieldrin, DDT, toxaphene, malathion, cryolite, and rotenone.
Even for a commercial farmer, such volume and variety would not
be considered bad practice.

Yet, what constitutes a practical application is hard to determine. Biocides differ from the old inorganic pesticides—like arsenic, lead, or fluorine—in that in these new organic compounds minor molecular changes alter effects most profoundly. Sunlight, oxidation, combination with the remains of other biocides that have been used, and reactions within plants that have absorbed them can produce compound rearrangements that are vastly more active than the expected effects of the originals themselves. This potentiation or synergism can produce an admixture far greater in toxicity than individual members in the mix; and no one is able to say with confidence that all effects can be predicted or tolerances set in advance. Any claims made as to the safety with which biocides can be used must be accepted as subject to re-evaluation, so that sensible commercial use is hard to calculate.[4]

Concern over the effect of the new organic biocides was first expressed at the federal level in the late 1940's. An Interdepartmental Committee on Pesticides was created in 1945; the National Institutes of Health made their first grants on pesticidal research in 1946; and the Toxicology Section of the United States Communicable Disease Center was established in 1949 to "investigate the health hazards of pesticides and related materials." [5] Yet these, and the bulk of legislation and administrative regulations then current, were more concerned with the lethal efficiency of biocides, with problems in handling or applying them, and with antidotes for the poisoning of agricultural workers than they were with possible side effects on the living landscape. A reading of the Insecticide, Fungicide, and Rodenticide Act of 1947 and the administrative regulations issued under it indicates that concern was greatest in guaranteeing honest claims of lethal efficiency from manufacturers and in protecting handlers of the substances from direct toxic effects.[6]

However, in the 1950's, anxiety over consequences of using the new synthetic organic biocides took on a larger scope. In 1954, the Secretary of Health, Education and Welfare was required to set tolerances for pesticidal chemicals in raw agricultural commodities. He has been told by the courts that in doing this he need not consider "hair-splitting speculation as to whether the amount of poison used might possibly have been so nicely calculated as not to kill

or be of immediate serious injury." [7] In 1952, the United States
Department of Agriculture, which as early as 1910 had begun to
study toxic substances in soil and water, extended its research to
the persistence, accumulation, and effect of organic pesticides on
soil and water conditions. In 1956, the National Institutes of
Health, which for the previous decade had made no grants for
pesticidal research, assigned 0.4 percent of their budget to it. Thereafter, until the Toxicology Study Section was created in 1959, personnel of the institutes and others met frequently to discuss the
effects of pesticides. These meetings were significant in producing
a pesticide research act in 1958.[8] Motivation for the act was the
belief that a new research situation would have to be created, its
sole goal being the study of health problems that man's newly
created chemical environment presented.

In the summer of 1961, a Federal Pest Control Review Board
was set up, using as its operative arm the old Interdepartmental
Committee on Pesticides, and serving as the coordinator for federal pesticide programs.[9] The board's first chairman thought that
its establishment had been predicated upon the idea that the large-
area, rapid-coverage type of biocidal program—so typical of governmental activity—was the prime source of peril to wildlife values.
The result was that the board never reviewed more than 5 percent
of the biocides used in the United States and had no control over
the much larger problem of the biocides used by private agencies
—farmers, ranchers, and those householders who employed in their
homes 25 percent of all biocides made.[10] Dissatisfaction with the
work of the board was intense. The wildlife lobby, regarding it as
a way to head off legislative action, considered its work of little
value. By administrative agreement, it was given broader consulta-
tive powers on April 27, 1964. It was replaced July 27, 1964, by
the Federal Committee on Pest Control.[11]

But the latter body, too, does nothing but make recommendations; it deals only with federal programs or those in which there
is federal participation; and, through its chairman, it simply
"exercises leadership in seeking timely resolution of interagency
differences." These are important goals, but they have not gone
far toward solving the problem of biocidal effect upon the living
environment. As Stanley Cain, Assistant Secretary of the Interior

for Fish and Wildlife, told Congress in 1965, "Research to date has demonstrated some really disturbing facts about minute quantities of pesticide chemicals. . . . We have found them in penguins and seals in Antarctica as well as in animals in the far north, far removed from any local spray programs. . . . Residues accumulated in fish and wildlife as they consume other animals are greatly magnified to the point where acute poisoning and tissue damage ultimately result. We know almost nothing about the biological and toxicological significance of continued exposure to small quantities [or mixtures of small quantities] of these chemicals in animals or in man . . . over long periods of time." [12] Man has only started to learn what needs to be known about the biocides that have appeared since 1940.

RISKS IN CHEMICAL BIOCIDES

As early as 1962, the United States Department of Agriculture had concluded these new biocides raised or posed fourteen problems:

1. Persistence of residual action.
2. Destruction of natural enemies of a native pest previously held in check by them.
3. Adverse effects on pollinating insects, with loss of honey and services of these insects in pollinating some fifty agricultural crops.
4. Reduction of wildlife.
5. Resistance to pesticides.
6. Overdoses of toxic chemicals during emergency health or pest infestation crises.
7. Present inadequacy of biological control methods.
8. Inadequacy of surveys for detection of outbreaks of insect infestation.
9. An insufficiently informed public.
10. Misuse.
11. Ecological shifts in weed population.
12. Drift of pesticide onto crops adjacent to the target.
13. Accumulation of pesticidal chemicals in the soil.
14. Contamination of the water.

Farm groups have always pressed for greater biocidal lethality in lesser bulk. A general reduction of 1 percent in the required rate of application means an annual saving to them of about \$5 million every year for pesticides alone, to say nothing of such other chemical agricultural assistants as growth regulators, defoliants, and desiccants.[13] Farmers are concerned here, of course, with efficient application rather than with the effects of biocides on objects which are not intended as targets. Considering, however, that as little as two-tenths of a part of endrin to one billion parts of water can be lethal to certain fish; that the directions for the use of aldrin and dieldrin carry the same warnings for the lightest as for the heavier concentrations used commercially; that some biocides, like aldrin and dieldrin, are included as a matter of course in fertilizer formulations; and that biocide labels say, "Do not use where runoff will contaminate streams, lakes, or ponds," even man's discovery that smaller applications will suffice may not be very encouraging in cutting down on extraneous effects.[14]

It is unfortunate that of the two commonest types of biocides which have come into use since 1940—organophosphates and chlorinated hydrocarbons—it is the former type that has created the greatest fear. The first research on organophosphates was undertaken for the development of a powerful nerve gas. The popular novelist, Len Deighton, has made the enormous potency of these biocides a factor in a best-selling book, *Funeral in Berlin*. In an appendix, Deighton lists the dread stories: the crop sprayer who died when he retrieved a nozzle from the barrel; the horticultural workers who acquired transient schizophrenia, depression, amnesia, and aphasia while working with organophosphates; the potentiating of one relatively harmless compound into quite a deadly one. Indeed, there are organophosphates far more dangerous than those dwelt on with horror by Mr. Deighton, including one that is promptly fatal to humans if a spot the size of a nickel touches the skin. Still, these are not meaningful terror tales, for the organophosphates, in actual use, are not the group to fear. In fact, because organophosphates break down within a few days after use, ecologists often regard them benignly and recommend that greater reliance be put upon them.

The chlorinated hydrocarbons, on the other hand, such as DDT, have a persistent and accumulative effect; they are recognized as the true villains. Currently, no one understands precisely how the chlorinated hydrocarbon insecticides work. Their effects diverge so greatly that differing modes of action must be considered. In some animal species, death is caused by a chronic biocidal ingestion which results in such histological changes as fatty infiltration of the liver and heart. These stored residues are released slowly when application of the biocide ceases, or rapidly if the fat is drawn on for energy. Death for other entities like aquatic organisms comes from suffocation, or, if the residue is smaller, through toxic effects on the central nervous system.

With organophosphates, since they break down so quickly, it is the direct and highly toxic effect in their short active span that causes death. Even this effect is erratic, however, in that aquatic organisms are little harmed by doses fatal to terrestrial forms. The histological operation of organophosphates is quite complex. Yet, though they induce death in a complex way, they work fairly quickly. Death serves as chief criterion. In biocidal research, the number of deaths in the test population from a given dose is the standard by which a chemical's effectiveness is tested. The commonest basis for comparison is the lethal dose for 50 percent of the test population, the oft referred to LD50. The other useful percentage figure is LD100, the minimum dose capable of killing all the organisms tested.

Production of the new chemical biocides began in the mid-1930's. In 1925, an agricultural experiment station in one year might have worked with not over four chemicals; forty years later a total of eighty would be nothing unusual. Even at the very early date of 1938, A. J. Nicholson warned the Seventh International Entomologists' Congress in Berlin against reliance upon the new chemicals because they were likely to create biotic complications even more serious than the problems they were intended to solve. But the warning was put aside in the glow of the great promise the new chemicals showed.

For the first time in history, the new chemical biocides gave man the promise of eliminating forever all agricultural pests. Biocides have been so widely used since 1938 that it is almost impossible to gather uncontaminated soil samples. For comparative testing purposes, it is now necessary to use soil samples gathered in the mid-1930's. Despite their side effects, biocides have been very satisfactory as producers of a huge increase in agricultural yields and as the openers of regions which, because of pests, were previously uninhabitable. The claim is made, for example, that for every dollar invested in the new biocides, five dollars have been made. Given the accuracy of those figures, the popularity of the new biocides is not hard to explain.

But, apart from such commercial considerations, there has long existed a division of opinion between the disciplines of ecology and entomology as to the harm done to nature by the spillover effect of biocides. Some ecologists regard any chemical attacks on pests as potential producers of catastrophic side effects. Their objections fall into the three categories: deploring the change in the organic environment that accompanies any chemical use; believing that judgment values have gone so awry that it is no longer possible to weigh gains against losses; or concluding that the chemical biocides are self-defeated by the biological complications which their use causes. These ecologists often talk about switching from chemical to purely biological controls. Unfortunately, too little is known about how biological controls would work, and many of them are not effective enough in eliminating harmful pests. Chemical biocides have proven their lethal effectiveness—at least in the short run of annual crop production and income—and industrial research has been largely apathetic about other possibilities.

This indifference has not extended, however, to other kinds of research centers. In 1962, the United States Department of Agriculture devoted two-thirds of its research on insects to biological controls, to the use of chemicals as specifics for particular insects or as attractants, and to basic studies of insect physiology and pathology. Despite this, however, the Entomological Society of America charged that "support level in terms of dollar value and personnel" for this kind of work was smaller in 1962 than it had been in 1932. Since that charge, much more has been done. Secretary of the Interior Stewart Udall, for example, in September 1964, ordered that first priority be given by his department to nonchemical methods of pest control. But by late 1965, the promise claimed for bioenvironmental manipulation had not been realized. The biological controls which were known, claimed the President's Environmental Pollution Panel, were not being widely used; both farmers and extension and research workers relied almost completely upon chemical pesticides. Much education was needed to win public acceptance of bioenvironmental control, and a far greater research program than any previous one had yet to be inaugurated in order to make possible manipulation of the environment through biological control.[15] In the mid-1960's, chemical controls remained the major tools in the regulation of the environment.

POSSIBLE EFFECT OF CHEMICAL BIOCIDES ON
LIVING ORGANISMS

The prominence of biocides has caused many persons to scrutinize chemical pesticides for possible ill effects upon human health. But even the most perturbed critics of these chemicals have had to conclude that, so far, no greater susceptibility of man to disease, or increased sensitivities, or harmful consequences among the general population can be traced to the new biocides. In fact, the President's Environmental Pollution panel could only deprecate any claims that biocides had hurt human health in any way. After all, as they put it, "Lack of evidence to substantiate health claims weakens the case for control." [16]

It is possible, of course, that ill effects have yet to appear, that the chemicals have not accumulated to the level at which they can be harmful. Only experience with biocides on a general level in the economy can provide evidence one way or another.

Since 1945, there has been a great deal of concern over the effect of radiation as a serious cause of carcinogenic and mutagenic change. The two are very similar since it is action on the chromosomes which causes both changes and since cancers are likely to be caused by gene mutations that remove checks on overmultiplication. Indeed, it may be that the mutation causes an innocuous virus to alter its behavior so that host cells are induced to multiply without limit. Certainly, however the process operates, it is this which has perturbed the popular mind and fueled the production of much science fiction predicated on bizarre changes. The Late, Late Show on television after midnight seems to subsist on these possibilities.

But this emphasis upon the dangers from radiation may distract attention from other sources that cause similar harm to plants, animals, and other living organisms. As early as 1941, the Russian geneticist J. A. Rapoport theorized that radiation caused gene changes as a secondary result through first producing peroxides of which ozone is an example. According to his theory, the main force of change would be the oxidative effect brought about through such oxidants as the peroxides and epoxides, by alkylating agents, and by various other substances like caffeine. Subsequent research has sustained Rapoport's theory, and changes that previously had been ascribed to radiation have been found to have a wide range of precipitators. The cells most likely to be affected are those that must freely divide in order to replenish the body's supply, and the ones most unlikely to be affected are those that do not undergo division, the so-called "noble cells." Among the former are the skin, the intestinal and some blood vessel linings, bone marrow, lymph glands, and male reproductive tissue. Brain tissue is the most important of the latter group. It is the freely dividing cells in the skin, marrow, glands, and so forth that are most susceptible to chemical insults through gene damage.

Results vary widely. Poisons that kill most developing individuals in a tested species have been found to have no effect on mutation frequency in the survivors. Also, enzymes may break up airborne mutagenic agents like the peroxides as they enter the body and before they can reach susceptible parts. When this occurs, however, the cells in the ports of entry may be subjected to more than they can handle, so that they are killed off with an ensuing emphysema or lung cancer. In the case of mutagens ingested orally, such concentrations in the protecting port-of-entry cells, being in the digestive or excretory organs, may cause similar damage there. How such events take place is little known. To test just one agent as it affects gene mutations in mammalian germ cells demands a project costing over $100,000. Cheaper, cruder tests have been used; but even these underscore the complexities of what happens within cells as the result of chemical invasion. Though it is probable that advantageous mutations in higher organisms are far less frequent than those which are weakly detrimental, there are inquiry obstacles that will prevent a clear view of cause-and-effect for years to come.

What is presently certain is that changes once attributed exclusively to radiation damage are now known to be brought on by chemicals as well. Among these chemicals, though in quantity probably not as great as industry's contribution to air pollution of their related compounds, have been the biocides and fertilizers in ever more popular use over the past generation. What significance this may have for carcinogenic and mutagenic conditions simply cannot be determined. It may yet be shown that certain diseases and ill effects among humans are the consequence of discharges from industry and agriculture into the air, soil, and water.[17]

People have a way of becoming alarmed only when they themselves are threatened, or when they see a decline in productivity or observe the diminishing of some favored species. Before conditions like these are reached, there is a general lack of curiosity. The effect of DDT on fish and bird populations is an example. Anyone who recalls DDT's being sifted directly on the bodies of verminous beggars in Naples in 1943 can have little idea of how it has been spread broadcast in the subsequent years. The widespread application of DDT has made parts of Sardinia inhabitable for the first time since the Roman Empire, radically reduced the malarial death rate in Ceylon, opened parts of Central Africa to settlement, and made outdoor recreation more pleasant for millions of Americans. But, while it has proven fatal to mosquitoes, flies, and gnats, it has shown itself equally lethal to other species.

The establishment of cause-and-effect relationships is almost impossible; even statistical correlations are unsatisfactory in attempts to determine whether or not biocides have diminished this species or that. Following a program of biocidal treatment for Dutch elm disease in southeast Wisconsin, a survey revealed that 86 to 90 percent of the robins in one municipality had died.

Beginning in 1960, huge fishkills appeared in the lower Mississippi; in the fall and winter of 1963, the total passed five million. Government investigators, thinking that the chlorinated hydrocarbon endrin might be the prime cause, investigated the sewage outlets of the one manufacturer of endrin on the Mississippi. One sewer there was found to be holding thousands of pounds of sludge heavily loaded with endrin and dieldrin. The sewer was sealed, and the manufacturer built new waste-control facilities. To hope that this removed the major source of difficulty is probably not justified, considering the woeful general water conditions in the lower Mississippi. Other examples of possible biocidal harm to wildlife could be found. The serious wildlife losses resulting from a fire ant control program in the South in 1957, for example, first alerted many persons to possible risks in the use of the chemical biocides.[18]

Recently, the finger of accusation has been pointed most often at the chlorinated hydrocarbons rather than at the organophosphates, because the former are so persistent and accumulate in the tissues of plants and animals over the generations. Settling as they seem to do in fat, egg yolks, and reproductive organs of animals, their chances of working harm are high. Chlorinated hydrocarbons constitute the same risk for plant life. Having killed aquatic plants, the chlorinated hydrocarbons remain in the decadent matter that subsequent plant life uses for nutrients. On land, these chemicals accumulate in the top foot of soil, especially within the upper four to six inches. From this humus both plants and animals absorb further residues into their tissues. Run-off leaches quantities into nearby streams. Little hope can be drawn from the fact that some chlorinated hydrocarbons seem to break down. Frequently, the breakdown simply results in more toxic and long-lasting substances. Because of this, the tolerance level for residues of one chlorinated hydrocarbon, heptachlor, has been set at zero in the United States. In 1961, Great Britain's Nature Conservancy, by agreement with industry, procured a three-year ban on aldrin, dieldrin, and heptachlor as seed dressings. And, in 1965, the United States Department of the Interior "announced a more stringent 'when in doubt do not use' policy on pesticides." [19]

EXPECTED INCREASE IN USE OF FARM AND HOME CHEMICALS

But the use of chemicals as biocides—not to mention their other roles in agriculture and around the home—is only beginning. Any contraindications are minor indeed. In 1961, it was estimated that in the United States the new chemical pesticides had been applied to 4.62 percent of the total acreage. So far as particular land uses were concerned, this broke down into chemical pesticidal applications to: 15 percent of cropland and cropland pasture; 28.3 percent of urban and other built-up areas; 3.24 percent of deserts, sand dunes, wildlands, open salt and fresh water swamps; .25 percent of grassland pasture; and .28 percent of forest lands. By late 1965, so far as total acreage was concerned, the figures had not changed. Confronted by this apparently static condition, the National Agricultural Library launched a program to consolidate all information on pest control and make it available to cities, real estate developers, and the general public to help them protect their natural greenery.

Present research will probably soon produce chemicals able to increase tolerance of plants to low temperatures, to decrease plants' water needs, to regulate crop size in order to ease mechanical harvesting, to fix the size of ornamental trees and shrubs which otherwise might have to be sacrificed to our highway safety programs, to extend the harvesting time for ripe crops, and to defoliate as economically necessary. In addition, the use of gamma rays to control insects by making them sterile and the employment of high-frequency radiation, cathode rays, and other kinds of radiant energy against such pests may not be far off. At present, some of these methods require dosage levels that can damage the product they are meant to protect. Similarly, some currently used herbicides reduce the nutritive value of certain protected crops, affecting mineral elements, vitamins, proteins, and carbohydrates. Whatever harm the chemical biocides or other farm and home chemicals may have done in the past, the mid-1960's saw them only in their infancy. If use up to that time had produced harm, the future would almost certainly offer greater peril.[20]

RELATED PROBLEM OF DETERGENTS

Similar to the problem brought on by organophosphate biocides and by nutrient pollution of the triplesuperphosphate fertilizers used after 1945 are those created by the simple household detergent. After World War II, housewives turned from soluble soap to insoluble detergents that were displaced in water but could never be dissolved. Presented with a problem that covered rivers as large as the Ohio with layers of foam several inches thick, that suffocated fish, defied sewage treatment and water purification, and had even begun to bubble back out of water taps, technology was compelled to develop biodegradable detergents that could lose their foaming properties. Aesthetically the problem has been solved; physically it remains.

Detergents continue to be about 70 percent phosphates, one pound of which can trigger a growth of as much as seven hundred pounds of algae. Detergent residue is added to the heavy run-off of phosphates, nitrates, and biocides from highly fertilized and sprayed land. Both these sources merely add to an already burdensome demand made by industrial waste and municipal sewage upon the oxygen supply of waters. Pollution of underground water supplies by detergents, as in confined aquifers like Long Island's, is not ameliorated by use of biodegradable types. Aerobic action, which the biodegradables require, takes place only in the top few inches of soil. Furthermore, the average claim on septic tanks is a day's holding, which is not long enough to permit detergent degradation. This matters little, however, since that average claim is rarely met. Some biodegradable detergents, like the hard detergents which preceded them, may be filtered out by the ground, but the ground becomes saturated with these phosphates fairly quickly. For underground discharges of degradable detergents, only anaerobic action, which has no need for oxygen, can take effect. This treatment is not yet possible. The aquifer may be purged by draw-down and recharge; but the persistent, accumulative pollution of underground water supplies by detergents can be expected to continue indefinitely, with whatever ill-effects they may produce.

Here is a purely man-made, relatively limited problem which has shown itself not very amenable to solution. One water pollution expert in the mid-Atlantic states commented, "I hate to see the hard detergents go. Their foam made people see the problem every time they looked in a creek. But what happens when the stuff is invisible and still nearly as deadly?" He may have been too pessimistic, because the biodegradable detergents do represent an improvement; but they are an improvement only and not the final solution some observers have considered them to be.

PROBLEM OF DOMINATING NATURE AS A GOAL

With the biocides, whose spillover effects have been greater than those of the hard detergents, their very invisibility has been part of the problem. The only things visible have been the positive economic and social consequences of the use of the new chemicals, whether as detergents, biocides, fertilizers, or one of a wide range of other agents. The biocides have resulted in a decided growth in agricultural production, the numbers of livestock brought to market, and the feet of timber raised in sprayed forests. Food, fibers, flesh, and woods economically valuable to man have received protection from their natural pests; and man has been rewarded with stunning surges in production of these economically utile terms. If in the process the herring gull, bald eagle, peregrine falcon, muskie, or lake trout should be brought to regional extirpation, is this important? The larger carnivorous predators in the eastern United States are now extinct, and the loss to nature has been bearable. If this were to happen on a far larger scale, would it be a misfortune to man?

"No!" say men who believe it possible to control single pests through use of chemical biocides, and who believe it possible for man to build through chemistry an artificial environmental regime. They maintain that there is no bigger problem here than the one posed by spraying apple orchards with Paris green in 1900: it is simply a matter of eliminating pests, one by one in place by place, as the pests pose a threat to any part of man's economy. These are the people who want to simplify nature for the efficiency of maintenance, the ease of harvesting, and the managing of agricultural land. They deny that what they do has much detractive spillover effect on the physical or biological universe. A second group believes that in the artificialized universe of the future, little heed need be given to nature except as islets have been preserved for scenic viewing. If the former are right, what is substantially the present course should be continued; if the latter, then an enormous course of inquiry to prepare for the future should be undertaken right away.

This inquiry should be promptly pushed forward because, as John Lear has said, ". . . the pursuit of the 'we are conquering nature' philosophy . . . [is] the saddest of all the cruel deceptions man has practiced upon himself." The vision of a Nature tamed was an Eden bruited about at the court of Lorenzo the Magnificent in the fifteenth century, claimed among the Encyclopedists surrounding La Pompadour in the eighteenth century, and rather confidently assumed by H. G. Wells as the twentieth century dawned. In the sense that the natural universe can be radically altered as a by-product of human activity, there is now justification for these claims. But that the universe may be controlled to human purpose is yet undemonstrable. It is improbable that man can produce more rain than would have been released *somewhere* by the clouds themselves, and the theory by means of which man hoped to prevent hurricanes may have been scrapped by further study. The intensity of ignorance may be lessened, but absolute knowledge has not replaced it. Man persists, however, in his dream of controlling nature. Hence *Time* magazine can suggest casually that hurricanes may be prevented by covering the ocean with a thin film of fatty alcohol. A recent RAND study was interpreted by the *Chicago Sun-Times* to mean that China could ruin both the United States and the USSR through climatic devices which would bring back the Ice Age. Yet manipulation of the climate as an economic proposition is not something that will soon occur.[21]

There are those who insist that man will never control nature if he must *dominate* the physical world. Even the physicist Willard Libby, who believes men should "recognize their true happiness to lie in their control over their environment," talks at the same time about having them "come to live in complete harmony with their environment." The difficulty is that in nature, as we have already noted, there is no such thing as a "pest": there are only biotic communities in which one creature or plant is dependent upon another or upon the same environment. Men, on the other hand, who manage crops, livestock, timber, and wildlife, are solely intent upon converting all of that energy into economically useful products. Anything which in nature interferes with this goal is regarded as an impediment and, if it is a living entity, a pest.

But living things are not randomly associated; the existence of any population species is related to another through the provision by one species of food and shelter for another. This is what the ecologists mean when they speak of a biotic community or chain. As the United States Department of the Interior said in its 1965 Yearbook, "The integrity of this chain . . . of life to the lords of creation . . . is becoming increasingly apparent. Our exalted position atop the pyramid of life is secure only if the base is allowed to remain broad and varied."

In every biotic community, the form and function are predictable among its plant and animal components because the possible range of interaction as established by competition is a narrow one. If the community should be destroyed, the natural limitations are such that, as soon as the destroying pressures are removed, the biotic community will begin to reassemble itself in regular sequences until the original community is restored. The total of these successional stages of sequences is called the *sere,* with earlier changes being designated "pioneer communities" and the full restoration of the original community the "sere climax." Once the community is "crisped and sere," it will begin its push back to the original condition as if in the sere there were thoughts and memories of what had existed before. The sere is not merely the end: it is the point of beginning in a sort of eternal return.

But mythic terminology aside, it is obvious that any disturbance of biotic community must produce an unstable condition. This is not merely a matter of the use of chemical biocides; it is the effect of land conversion as instituted for almost any human purpose. Both agriculture and industry have imposed a permanent seral subclimax which the chemical biocides and other extant factors tend to simplify further in the creation of pioneer communities. As Erich Zimmermann said a generation ago, "Nature strives toward ecological equilibrium . . . Man crashed into the finely balanced nature structure like a bull in a china shop." [22] This equilibrium is not static but a dynamic, if slight, fluctuation in species content, so that any major change comes gradually. Human activity tends to reduce the number of species, to favor the multiplication of a few, and to sponsor rapid biotic changes. Human activity tends to be "single-minded," with a narrow specialization designed to remove one species, to produce one crop, to convert natural energy into cash and a richer human life. In short, man's actions ultimately impose the responsibility of sustaining the productive sources on which man's well-being depends and of simultaneously preserving those "objects of beauty, curiosity, or sport" which our "ecological conscience," as Aldo Leopold called it, should move us to guard. Having upset the equilibria in nature, man must maintain the resulting seral subclimaxes and pioneer communities.

Economic efficiency moves man to monoculture and to increasing production through elimination of forms of life that would divert energy. Fence rows and field roadways are kept clean, and herbaceous verges are mowed down. Any life they would have maintained therefore never comes to exist. The world-wide trend is toward a biota scarcely more complicated than the arctic tundra. Economic efficiency pushes so for simplicity that even the managed forests, for which other patterns have been strongly recommended by conservationists and economists, are monocultural. As such, they are not as stable as the virgin stands, because the simplicity of their biota makes them susceptible to diseases and exploitation by other life forms. As their creator, man must maintain them in their economically fruitful, ecologically unstable simplicity through frequent spraying, clearing, and nurture. The same is true for much of the agricultural land. This fact, as much as the need to raise production directly through pest elimination, makes the chemical biocides necessary. Monoculture and "clean" farming set up an artificial regime which the biocides thereafter have to help maintain, even as they intensify the artificiality of the regime and make the environment more unstable.

Unfortunately, the task of maintaining this artificial regime is complicated by the fact that there is considerable resistance in nature to the effectiveness of biocides, if they are used long enough. This is something quite different from "tolerance," with which resistance is often confused in the popular mind. Tolerance, which refers to an organism's ability to withstand exposure to increasing amounts of chemicals during its lifetime, varies from individual to individual because of differing body chemistries and physiological conditions. The new biocides, insofar as the species populations at which they are aimed are concerned, will not go on the market if their lethal dosage is below 50; very often they have an LD of 100 or close to it. Only in species at which it is not directed might tolerance be built up, and with them it is more often a case of cumulative poisoning than of developing tolerances.

But resistance is commonly developed in the surviving remnant of insect populations. The only requirement is that the LD be somewhere below, no matter how close to, 100. The very instability of gene structure in these lower organisms may come to their assistance. Once a resistant strain has evolved, metabolites can develop to counteract mutagenesis and to act as anti-mutagens.[23]

In the ephemeral generations of the insect world, changes can occur that in man's chronology would have required a period from the fifth-century fall of Rome to the present. Mutagenesis may not even be necessary to change, for insecticides often merely eliminate the most vulnerable individuals in the species and encourage the flourishing of resistant types. Continuing change does not require mutations where insecticides are acting as universal agents that select certain characteristics which permit insect survival under the new, man-made conditions. That is why previously effective biocides lose their power, so that it is necessary to switch from one to another.[24]

This is quite different from a related problem in the instability of the biotic community. Elimination of one species may cause a forward surge in the numbers of another species, either because its rival for the joint food supply has been taken away or because a predator has been liquidated. Heavy DDT spraying programs to remove mosquitoes in lake areas have been followed by gnat and mite infestations that render boating, fishing, and swimming more unpleasant than they were before. Or, the withdrawal of a species may destroy another's food supply; since low order forms of life are rigid in food habits, the removal of the one species may coincidentally remove the other. Mosquito control often results in a decrease in local bird and fish populations, so that the sportsman who complains of insect discomfort may later find himself hunting or fishing in greater comfort but to no purpose. Nature lovers have had a great deal of contempt for the city dweller who goes to an air-conditioned hotel in the mountains, confines his exercise to an elevator ride from bed to dining room, and plays bridge with his back to the window. Perhaps such behavior is contemptible. But far more dangerous to the living community in nature is the sportsman who wants his way to be easy and pleasant while he is in the woods and waters.

DIFFICULT MAINTENANCE OF NATURE
UNDER COMMERCIAL DEMANDS

Commercial interests can be more deadly still to nature. Fishers for the anchovy in the plankton meadows of the Humboldt Current, furious at a decline in the catch for 1965, began a program to kill the guano birds, each of which eats its weight in anchovies every twenty-four hours. By the spring of 1966, over fifteen million guano birds had been killed and the Peruvian guano production cut by five-sixths. Since guano has been about the only fertilizer cheap enough for Latin American farmers, the effect upon their agriculture may ultimately be very severe. In addition, fish experts predict that the guano birds will have died for nought. Pursued as they are by electronic sonar equipment and spotter planes, anchovy schools will continue to prove ever harder to find.[25] It is doubtful that sporting interests are ever this ruthless.

To a considerable degree, American conservation programs have been geared to the needs or aspirations of the sportsman. There is, after all, no reason why this substantial section of economic demand should not receive satisfaction. With the decline of commercial hunting after the 1880's, most nimrods left in the woods were there for sport. Commercial hunting declined because it had eliminated the reason for its existence. After 1885, there were no longer buffalo sufficient to supply eastern markets with robes, hides, and horn, and only in the late 1950's did herd management bring buffalo meat back to the butcher shops. Demands for buckskins and venison reduced the deer by 1899 to a point where its fate almost appeared to be the same as the buffalo's.[26]

The exorbitant demands of commercial hunting in North America by the white man were actually mere extensions of the practices of the indigenous population. Considering that the average Indian brave expected to consume about ten pounds of buffalo meat daily, and that consumption of twenty pounds at a single serving was not uncommon, the demand of the Plains Indians in the heyday of their culture, between the introduction of the horse in the late sixteenth century and their overthrow by white settlement in the mid-nineteenth century, was substantial. Only the simplicity of weaponry and the small numbers of these nomadic peoples preserved the buffalo from meeting its fate two centuries sooner.[27] In the eighteenth century, the aboriginal populations of Alaska took, on a conservative estimate, about 33.5 million pounds of salmon per year, while in 1959, after years of declining yields, the catch was 47 million pounds. Only the reduction of the native peoples by Russian and American administrations gave the salmon a biological rest prior to the start of commercial fishing in 1878 and made the fabulous early commercial catches possible. Even so, the naturalist Tarleton Bean warned in 1889 that it was folly to treat salmon as an inexhaustible, undiminishable resource. But in the presence of native example, market demand, and apparent plenitude in the species, such warnings were shunted aside in the nineteenth century.[28]

The counterforce to this disregard for wildlife came as much from sportsmen as it did from more altruistic conservationists. The first sportsmen's clubs (as something other in form than social gatherings) made their appearance after the Civil War. In the 1870's, the state fisheries, forerunners of the later conservation commissions, were founded. Pressure grew for the setting up of closed seasons, the encouragement through tax relief of game preserves, the setting of bag limits, the appointment of wardens, the posting of premises against hunters without the owner's permission, the requirement of hunting licenses, and absolute prohibitions such as those against shooting does and fawns. It was to take from after the Civil War to almost World War II before these provisions were widely enacted, enforced, and accepted in the United States. But by 1939 game populations had increased substantially.

There were, of course, exceptions. Between 1815 and 1965, the

United States lost forty species of birds and mammals, half of them after 1900. And in 1965, nearly eighty kinds of birds, mammals, reptiles, fishes, and amphibians were threatened with extinction. In some areas the situation was quite acute: half of the local bird species in Hawaii, for instance, were on the endangered list. To counteract such developments, the federal government has a program to "raise rare specimens, train the young to contend with conditions of the wild, and release them to the world for hoped-for survival and propagation." [29]

Since fish releases were first made in the 1870's, this has been the hope: to replace through man's care species which man's actions have reduced. Occasionally this effort has been rewarded. In 1907, Pennsylvania, reacting to a kill of only two hundred bucks, imported a thousand deer to see if the species could make a comeback. By 1963, after substantial annual kills going back to the 1920's, the kill was 48,000 bucks and 36,000 does and fawns. The restocking of deer has been aided by the breakup of the prairie (which permitted the invasion of scrub growth) and by the lumbering off of heavy forests (which were replaced with similar scrub). This kind of vegetation is very favorable to deer, and the restocking came at just the right ecological moment. But in most situations, restocking has not worked out. Many naturalists regard it as a waste of money, about on a par with setting out either exotic trees or plantations of white pine, which nature meant for a transitional phase in most areas. Such efforts, if they do not fail, can be maintained only at the greatest expense.

After decades of field experience, ecologists believe that there is only a minimum which man need or can do to maintain game populations. Beyond this minimum, they maintain, all extra effort is to little purpose. Natural forces must carry most of the burden of maintenance; if they are inadequate, it is unlikely man can supply the slack. Artificial protection can be harmful if it is enforced without due regard for natural conditions. There is a limit to the numbers of any species which a tract of country can support. Once that maximum has been determined, programs to ban hunting of the species, or to limit sharply the bag to be taken, or to liquidate the predators of the species become harmful to the game which is being protected. Its general health will deteriorate; it will contract specific diseases; its predators will increase; its food supply will prove inadequate; and its death rate will rise sharply. At this point, human food supply programs will prove to be not even palliative, and the species will fall below its maximum sustainable in that region. Records kept over generations in North America show increases and decreases in predator and prey species that fully support this cyclic view.

Man's best contribution is to do as little as he possibly can to upset the process and not to undertake to redress the balance of nature. Deer increased in the eastern United States on lands where lumbering had most butchered the landscape, leaving a burned and slashed area in which scrub was allowed to grow up as best it could. In this neglected secondary growth, deer flourished far better than in managed forests. Deer protection programs had very little to do with increases in the herds. As these areas continue their seral recovery, the beginning of which goes back as far as the 1890's, a level will be reached unencouraging to deer. Heavy foraging can delay the change, but ultimately the scrub forests that have been such favored haunts for deer will be replaced by a thicker growth in which fewer deer can live. There are probably more deer in the United States in the 1960's than there were before the arrival of white settlers. But it should be no cause for astonishment if deer populations go into decline again in the future. When this occurs, there will be very little that can be done about it, since it is unlikely if even deer enthusiasts can encourage another assault on the forests in order to give back to the deer the environment in which the species flourishes.

Of course where game like deer, moose, elk, buffalo, and other wild herbivorous species are sharing grazing land with domestic cattle and sheep, it is possible to permit larger or smaller wild numbers by controlling the quantity of domestic animals turned out to grass. In 1964, almost three million big game animals on United States public lands consumed one-fourth of all the forage growing there. Overgrazing is such a serious problem outside the United States that in all but a few regions the question is not of protecting wild grazing animals but of preserving vegetation and soil matrix. The shores of the Mediterranean are monuments to man and his urge to exploit. First, their not very heavy forests were cut off; then their not very deep soils were subjected to protracted grain farming; and finally, herds of cattle, sheep, and goats have been put to grazing there for the past thousand years. It is rather doubtful if much could be salvaged at this point from the soil resources of the area's past. What renders the doubt almost a certainty is that in a choice between the goat and any other resource such as forest or grass or soil, no one can fail to guess the preference of the Arab, Andalusian, Sicilian, or Levantine peasant.

The most pessimistic critic could not say that conditions in the United States had come anywhere near this point, though the Mediterranean coast is a horrible example of what can occur if Americans fail to act. In 1854, mesquite and cactus were confined to small areas of Texas. By 1887, after a generation of commercial cattle raising on the native grasses of the prairie, the Texas countryside west of San Antonio had been invaded by mesquite and many other worthless flora commonly found in desert conditions. The native grasses and their prairie had perished, and the run-off this permitted precluded the retention of moisture necessary for the land to make a comeback. By 1937, the grazing capacity of those ranges had declined up to 25 percent below the level they had reached half a century earlier.[30]

From Wisconsin to California, the native grasses have perished. The Indians periodically set raging fires to burn off the prairies, probably to make hunting easier. It was a careless disregard of resources, perhaps, but it preserved the eastern reaches of the prairie from forest encroachment. White settlement stopped the fires, and the forests swept into areas capable of sustaining them. Plowing, grazing, the introduction of new seeds either deliberately or through land procedures encouraging to invaders—all combined to eliminate the rich variety of native flora and reduce it to today's relative sparseness. The most complete elimination of native flora occurred in California where, at this date, it is simply not possible to reconstruct, by elaborate detective work, all of the original stock of grasses. In the nineteenth century, the native grasses, which had been perennials, were replaced by invaders, which were annuals and better able to resist change. Maximum stocking for an immediate profit without concern for maintenance of future grazing conditions seems to have typified herders and ranchers from the Mediterranean to the Pacific slopes of California.

The reason for this rapacity does not lie in the herdsmen's greater stupidity or greed. Nor is it to be explained by the herds' need to compete with wildlife or to graze within too narrow physical limits. Rather has it been due to the difficulty of extracting enough profit from the business at any point in history to create the surplus necessary for acting prudently in relation to the wildlife, forest, grass cover, run-off, or soil matrix resources necessary to sustain the raising of any sort of cattle. Public lands in the United States have been viewed by ranching interests as the prairie was before them: a great free good supplied by nature for the benefit of their industry.[31]

Perhaps it was a mistake, as cattlemen have long argued, to permit "nesters" to break the plains with the plow. But the virgin wealth was stripped off the prairie by cattlemen before farming settlements were founded. It was mostly overgrazing that broke the California cattle industry in the 1860's, and the pitiable range conditions reported in west central Texas in the mid-1880's could not have been created by farming. Under the Taylor Grazing Act, which was passed in 1934 to try to bring some measure of control over the use of public lands for private herd benefit, the Grazing Service and its successor, the Bureau of Land Management, have been pressed hard to permit as much grass use as any particular local herding interests desire. Indeed, there has been an unremitting effort to convert the grazing licenses into permanent, alienable property interests and for the herders to speak of the public lands as peculiarly their own. That such is not the case is being stressed more and more with each decade.[32]

At one time, aside from graziers, lumbermen, miners, and other consumptive users, most Americans took only a rather abstract interest in the federal lands. Generating public interest was an uphill battle, and the conservationists had to garner their victories slowly. Although John Quincy Adams set aside a live-oaks preserve in 1828, and Wisconsin created the first state forest in 1878, it was not until the 1890's that the movement began to gather any momentum. From these earliest days, the sportsmen's clubs were often the conservationists' allies—though perhaps it was a union somewhat like that existing between the Temperance-men and the Bone-drys in the Prohibitionist movement. Ultimately the sportsmen did have designs on nature; out of those designs the recreation interest has grown.

Many sportsmen are as sincere as conservationists in lamenting the development of recreation as an industry. Others in the sporting community see no cause for grief. They envision, instead, a powerful, new, prospering economic bloc of hostelries, restaurants, equipment manufacturers, and other enterprises reaching right into the heart of the private sector of the American economy—the auto industry. This bloc will support sport and conservation, in the name of recreation, against the old consuming interests. So far as the public lands are concerned, the timber men and miners are no longer righteously indignant at not being able to engross them; and the graziers will have to come to the same modest estimate. At one time, the prospect of cutting the number of grazing cattle and sheep from the public lands so that the game might better be provided for would have provoked nothing but cries of derision. Today, this is specifically a program of the Bureau of Land Management. Some observers say that game is not given enough consideration. That it is considered at all shows how far removed public opinion and government policy are from attitudes current even into the 1950's.

ALLOCATING THE LIVING ENVIRONMENT
AMONG ECONOMIC DEMANDS

Resources, which at one time were used as a capital freely supplied by nature for Americans to convert to cash as individual profit, have become in recent years something which is potentially exhaustible in very short order. Of the 3,700 miles of shoreline on the Atlantic and Gulf Coasts, only 105 miles, or less than 3 percent, were available in 1965 for public use. Whenever land is declared surplus by the Defense Department, there is an executive order that first choice be given to the federal conservation and park agencies in order, as President Johnson put it, "to see if somehow, somewhere, the little people of America might not be able to enjoy this in the few hours of relaxation that is theirs on a weekend." [33] The reason for this shortage is that "the great natural resources of a virgin territory, many of which had to be sacrificed for the social goals of the moment, . . . helped to create a spendthrift attitude subsequently institutionalized in a social and economic pattern of production for maximum consumption." This aspect of American history is the basis of the problem. Though disregard of the harm man can do nature is no longer an immutable fact in American culture, the priority given productive forces remains; what these do incidentally to nature is crucial.[34]

What, precisely, constitutes pollution of the environment is not yet known. Nature can never be restored to pristine conditions, despite President Johnson's insistence that there must be a new conservation which "must be not just the classic conservation of protection and development, but a creative conservation of restoration and innovation." [35] Still, whatever good intentions there may be, the almost primordial fact of American culture remains its emphasis upon production. Whatever is done for the renewable resources and the human environment will have to be done within that constraint.

Until time histories of concentrative levels have been kept, man cannot know at what point the accumulation of pollutants will reach the critical stage. With past experience as a guide, man tends to ignore all pollutants until concentrations begin to cause some kind of noticeable detriment. Despite contemporary aesthetic demands for a "clean" environment, man will probably be well occupied in working out a "threshold" environment: how much spillover from production, man must ask, can the air, water, and soil absorb before living organisms are affected to the point of being nuisances or menaces to human society and health? With new chemical combinations coming on the market by the hundreds every year, this "threshold" represents the best goal toward which human effort should be directed. There may be a better ideal, but at the present time the very least that must be done is to seek the natural tolerance levels for spillover from the various production processes and to set guidelines for the modern economy.

Pressure for an even greater gross national product, including the tacit assumption that this means a higher material standard of living, continues to build. Man must set in counterbalance to this a concern for such factors as health, the aesthetics of a clean environment, and the benefits of a flourishing renewable resource complex. The total environment must be examined in terms of each economic, social, and political interest whose demands require reconcilement. This process may have to take place at the federal level; but it is not a procedure which can be successful exclusively because of government action. The economic community must be drawn in, and there has to be support in the national culture more generally.

Whether this is called "education" or something else, governmental effort will fail without it. Jacob M. Arvey of the Chicago Park Commission has said, "I would rather see one swimming pool than 200 trees, or one tennis court than 100 trees." When both recreation and production are at cross purposes with nature, the situation has reached critical proportions. However radical the idea may seem, the time has come to take "the position that all native animals—even starlings and coyotes—are resources of inherent interest and value to the people of the United States. Basic government policy . . . should be one of husbanding all forms of wildlife." [36]

Aside from the huge demands made upon natural environment by the mere existence of urban, industrial, production-centered civilization, an ever-increasing spillover or spatter effect is taking place because of the use of biocides, fertilizers, detergents, and similar materials on farms and in homes. Pollution by these substances involves ever more complex problems which lie behind the ones to be solved first. Invisible, odorless, and insubstantial elements may be more harmful than the piles of rotting carcasses and vegetable matter which slaughterers and canners used to dump into streams. To deodorize and polish away is not enough, as the public health reformers learned in the nineteenth century. At that time, invisible bacteria and viruses were the troublemakers. The twentieth century will have to cope with the more subtle, obdurate chemical effluents.

The gross problems of renewable resources must be solved—whether they produce utterly dead rivers like the Buffalo or soils like those in Texas gullied to a depth of two hundred feet—but beyond them are still more complicated, almost incomprehensible difficulties whose very scope has yet to be defined. To warn of cancer that comes out of corrupted air, or soil, or water may not be scientific. Even so, such parts of the modern economy as the biocides have been profoundly disturbing in their effects upon bird, fish, and small animal life.

Some fright may prove unjustified. Synthetic organic components designed to regulate plant growth as crypto-fertilizers could scarcely be a menace since they rarely accumulate; they degrade into harmless particles, and they resemble natural plant constituents. Even radioactive elements may be held so tightly in the soil that the peril is minimized.[37] Yet it is all a question of minimal peril, whether the cause is radioactivity or a persistent, non-degradable biocide.

Long-term, peripheral, and sub-lethal harms have rarely been examined in past generations. Only recently has ecological understanding developed in connection with the fluctuation in game numbers, the reasons for increases or decreases in different kinds of wildlife, and the relation which modern civilization can have with wildlife. The difficulties encountered in acquiring this knowledge may seem to have been trivial compared with the problems posed by the impact of chemicals. The chemical revolution, which has poured so much into the environment, has proved since 1940 to be a continuing, almost fulminating, process, the side-effects of which must now be scrutinized carefully.

In 1965 over four hundred new chemicals went into industrial production. This number will increase.[38] It scarcely seems quixotic to study these substances before observable losses begin to occur. This economic demand—like the demands urban industrial culture makes generally upon the living environment—has yet to be allocated prudently. The time to do so is now and not later. The promise of such biological controls as synthetic juvenile hormones that would retard insects in a pre-adult phase is not far off; despite the danger to bees and other pollinating insects, its developers insist "the substance could be used to advantage now." [39] The real problem is not chemical or biological biocides, or anything else so limited. It is, instead, the possibility that our urban industrial culture may consume its living environment. That possibility exists, and all subsidiary problems sink to insignificance.

5

The risks of pollution

The Indiana State Air Pollution Control Board, as a New Year's gift for 1966, consoled citizens with the news that there were very few cities in the United States meeting "the level desirable" for clean air. This announcement is typical of those made by public agencies in charge of protecting the air, or water, or soil. They defend themselves either by saying that practically nobody meets the minimum standards, or that conditions would be much worse if it had not been for the existing regulation of resource use, or that conditions are better than they appear if they are not examined in absolute terms. Or they offer some other extenuating excuse.

The excuses are not entirely rationalizations. Deterioration of American waters has been slowed since 1940, and in the past generation American soil conditions have been shown a heretofore unknown consideration. Nevertheless, absolutely dead streams exist in western New York, northern New Jersey, and elsewhere. Lake Erie may become the largest cesspool in the world. New industry continues to destroy major rivers in Georgia and the Southeast. New fertilizers and plant growth regulators make possible a growing economic indifference to soil depth. And there is the still-ascending spiral of increasing air pollution. Whenever man feels the urge to congratulate himself on what has been done, he should remind himself of problems that still exist. Clearly, the twentieth century is like no other. Human enterprise has so managed affairs that there is simply no place to turn. If man does not make his present enviroment livable, he faces a morbid future.

Nature has been invaded and profoundly "insulted"—as biologists would say. Man begins as a sort of swimmer in an "ocean of neutral stuff." Immediately around him is the "fringe" of matter that he can convert to his resources. Beyond that is the vast sea of what he cannot control, or of which he is unaware, and which does not affect him one way or another. But every portion of this hitherto "neutral ocean" which he converts to a resource gives rise to a matching resistance. Between man's "fringe" of resources and the "neutral" waters of the world ocean is a "range" of resistance that has been provoked by man's employment of the elements. A resource therefore is a human contrivance, shaped from nature, which creates an effect in nature that will resist and be hostile to what man devises.

Man's relationship to air illustrates the process. Initially, man has only a mythic awareness of air and atmosphere. Then he begins to employ air as a free good in a more positive, economic sense, to receive the waste emitted from his production processes. Gradually, the emissions increase. In certain districts the air cannot cope with what it must take. Businesses previously accustomed to draw on pure air begin to suffer. Smog thickens. Eyes smart. Respiratory death rates soar. And dark mutterings of cancer in the air are heard. In brief, the "range of resistance" has materialized. That resistance promises to be of massive depth by the end of the century.

AIR POLLUTION CONDITIONS IN AMERICA

The use of air as a resource is obviously on the rise, and the probable future holds little cheer. It appears that, without control devices better than those which existed in 1966, carbon monoxide discharge will go from the 1960 volume of 90 million tons annually to around 370 million tons in the year 2000. Hydrocarbons will rise from 8.6 million tons in 1960 to around 37 million tons in 2000. And oxides of nitrogen, for which no control devices of any sort exist in the mid-1960's, will increase from 2.8 million tons in 1960 to around 12 million tons in 2000.

A "poor" day for air pollution is determined by multiplying the air contents of a "good" day by three. (Even on a "good" day in an urban area of the United States the air may be three times as polluted as that in a rural area.) Motor vehicles, the generation of electricity, industry, space heating, and refuse disposal—in that order—are the sources of air pollution. It is calculated that in 1965 the vegetation in half the states showed damage from photochemical smog, ozone, sulphur dioxide, fluorides, and ethylene. Deposits of these substances are not the only sources of harm. What the plant breathes and what may cut it off from needed light are far more pernicious.

As the kinds of damage done by discharged elements in the air are discovered, measurement of the existence and harm of air pollution is growing ever more complex. The typical black or rusty pall of a nineteenth-century city is increasingly being dissipated. Emissions are becoming smokeless. Yet the problem is greater than it was: in the future, it will not be deposited grit but what is carried in suspension that will serve as the measure of air pollution.

The monitoring of air quality started on a small scale nationally in 1953. By 1965, the United States Public Health Service, cooperating with states and localities, had set up a meshed national network for measuring suspended particulate matter, sulphur dioxide, and oxides of nitrogen over a twenty-four-hour period. A few cities measured for carbon monoxide, oxidant, ozone, carbon dioxide, hydrocarbons, and salinity over a shorter period, but such measurements were very scant.

Although measurement of air is necessary, it may be a potentially unfortunate borrowing from the regulation of water pollution. Many water specialists assume that the corruption of water is inevitable. They concentrate on treating the water in order to make it once more potable or useful to industry. By analogy, authorities on air pollution have come to regard waste treatment as "still the old standby." But to accept a degree of air pollution comparable to what has been tolerated in water would be suicide, at least in some regions.

In any combustion, of course, there is a gas-phase reaction, so that many contaminants must remain. To this extent, air and water are similar in having to receive apparently unavoidable wastes. But no number of high stacks and no amount of research on the movement of pollutants in the air will ever permit man to rely on "air sewers" to carry off wastes as water does. Ultimately, auto exhaust and the sulphur in fossil fuels will have to be almost completely eliminated and other outpourings of wastes sharply cut. So long as man remembers that air cannot be treated like water, he can measure air pollution without apprehension. Otherwise, such measurement is like that of the libertine who keeps a precise medical check on his health as he breaks it down.[1]

There is still some tendency to accept air pollution as fixed constraint, and man has adjusted his life with that constraint in mind. Building materials have been developed that will weather under the impact of suspended matter in city air. For existing structures, there is an epoxy resurfacing mastic that becomes self-cleaning two years after application. It chalks mildly—about one five-thousandth of an inch each year—and the soot and dirt particles flake off with the chalking.[2] If carbon dioxide itself should prove to be no pollutant, it is possible that many wastes might be converted into that gas, which would be stored permanently in the atmosphere. Even if carbon dioxide *should* prove to be a pollutant, techniques might be worked out to periodically "scrub" the gas from the atmosphere through precipitation. The gas would come onto the land and into the water in such a way that regulating measures could control its disposal. Under this proposed system, except for certain wastes which would not convert to carbon dioxide, there could be a general conversion into a single substance. The scheme also has the advantage of requiring no change in industrial practices. Air pollution would become fully accepted as simply another aspect of the technical employment of nature.

FUTURE CONDITIONS OF AIR POLLUTION

There is no need to assume that future conditions of the air can be projected by multiplying present emissions by the estimated increase in the number and size of polluting sources. This method would only point to a literally breathless America in 2000. Presumably even a nation which concentrates on increasing the gross national product will take corrective steps long before then. It is horrendous, however, to consider that the American culture has let itself come within one generation of this fate. If 1966 control knowledge were applied in severe regulations, for example, there would be a 75 percent increase in sulphur dioxide pollution between 1965 and 1980, with another 75 percent increase by 2000. Technology, however, appears capable of a maximum level control that would hold the increase to 20 percent by 1980. And there would be a 20 percent decrease by 2000. Assuming that man were to pursue all possible means known to him in the mid-60's, control would have caught up with sulphur dioxide emissions by 1990, and in 2000 the United States would be no worse off than it had been in 1966. Even so, some observers see only catastrophe ahead.

The automobile—that engaging status symbol and indispensable instrument of urban dispersal—is currently the chief source of urban air pollution, having pushed ahead of such classic ogres as belching chimneys. The air over the center city has become a public refuse basin for the private benefit of commuters who live elsewhere. Unless congestion itself forces abandonment of the car, conditions must grow worse. It has been suggested that all streets be put below ground, so that air pollution control would become a matter of mere tunnel ventilation. In lieu of underground streets, small electric cars could be used. These would be controlled automatically; they could be coupled or uncoupled on expressways and stored in stacks. They would serve very well, at least for slow, stop-and-go driving. In any event, there will be a restriction of vehicles that will leave no allowance for roaring up open lanes in a cloud of blue smoke. The peoples of Asia have not yet tasted what Dato Sir Alexander Oppenheim has called "the delights of autointoxication."

Oppenheim may be right in observing that "those who have tasted the nectar will not forego the disadvantages the automobile is known to bring." [3]

Meanwhile, under smoggy urban skies, some men maintain that air pollution is a subjective matter and that no disease has been directly related to it. They point out that the air pollution disasters so often cited—the Meuse Valley incident on the Franco-Belgian frontier in 1930; the situation in Donora, Pennsylvania, in 1948; and the half-dozen examples in London since 1950—are really very few. Besides, they produced fewer deaths altogether than a couple of good holiday weekends in the United States. Furthermore, the districts concerned have peculiar weather and industrial conditions that make problems quite likely. To stand in Armentières at high noon is perhaps to know why Mademoiselle left the place.

As a source of discomfort, smog may be a nuisance or an unaesthetic condition, but it is not a subject for very much concern. Some British studies show a "strong association" between chronic bronchitis and high levels of sulphur dioxide in the air and in sootfalls; and some California studies show "objective evidence" of improved lung function among emphysematous patients put on filtered, rather than on regular, Los Angeles air. But as the medical educator Eric Cassel has pointed out to some alarmists, "We have a cause, but no disease to go with it." [4]

ACTIONS TAKEN IN CONTROL OF AIR POLLUTION

Yet even discomfort and crises in aesthetics can produce action. Los Angeles—and there may be some portent in its having been called the City of the Future—had a smog problem as early as October, 1542, when Juan Rodriguez Cabrillo witnessed a thermal inversion that trapped the smoke of Indian fires in the valley leading to San Pedro Bay. Even with only Indians in the area, air conditions could deteriorate, since the area has a limited air supply because of mountains and air currents, and a high quantity of ozone, or allotropic oxygen, in the air.

Ozone attracted health seekers to the area in the 1880's. A light-blue gas, ozone gives, or seems to give, a sparkle to the day of anyone who breathes it. Nineteenth-century physicians regarded ozone as a great vivifier. But by the mid-1960's, medical opinion had concluded that even in minuscule quantities ozone was harmful. The very "sparkle" it imparts is damaging to the circulatory system. Medical doctors are exerting more and more pressure to have ozone deodorizers, ozone nostrums, and the "ozone parlors" dear to the old-fashioned naturopath banned.

Ozone's sparkling action is rarely noted now by Los Angeles residents. The ozone is still there, however, catching other pollutants and holding them in suspension. On a morning in the 1880's, an Angeleno might walk through his orange grove smelling the weak chlorine odor present in a light blue ozone haze and congratulating himself on the atmosphere, even if his eyes smarted and his breath came faster. In the 1960's, no Los Angeles driver jammed up on the freeway could say anything good about the air. After several years of improvement following the institution of air pollution control in the mid-1950's, the situation grew worse in the mid-1960's. Los Angeles, the City of the Future, is still seeking remedies, even asking furnace owners to burn gas rather than oil and auto owners not to use their cars during alerts. The situation in 1966 was worse than ever and deteriorating. Los Angeles, as Igor Stravinsky put it, had become "sunless as a mushroom farm." [5]

New York City's air is also heavily polluted. Los Angeles has about 176,000 tons of oxides of sulphur dumped on it in a year; New York receives 600,000 tons. The concentrations vary, from less than ninety-nine tons a year in part of Staten Island to over five thousand tons in parts of Manhattan and the Bronx. Simply to live in mid-Manhattan is like smoking three packs of cigarettes a day—and inhaling them. New York's air problems are not eased by what seems to be a vicious circle whereby air over the city is replenished from a pocket over the Atlantic, the latter source being recharged in turn from a pocket over New York City. Nature and man's economic structure alike seem to conspire against the human organism. In any event, New York serves as another example of the "range of resistance" provoked by resource use.[6]

Because of its great difficulties—or perhaps its greater awareness of them—California has led the way in auto exhaust control. Legislation in 1961 called for crankcase blowbys which, as of 1963, became standard on new American cars. By 1966, California required all autos and light trucks to have exhaust control devices. About 20 percent of the unburned hydrocarbons emitted into the air by vehicles comes from the vent in the crankcase which the blowby prevents from escaping. About 65 percent comes from the exhaust. The new devices will reduce this pollution by 70 to 80 percent. Simultaneously, carbon monoxide fumes will be cut by 60 percent. The last figure is no small matter, since the emission of carbon monoxide over Los Angeles has increased from about 2,700 tons a day in 1940 to around eleven thousand tons a day in 1965. The new exhaust control devices will cost about $40 to $50 for each car. The investment, quite apart from increased enforcement costs which such a program entails, will be a substantial one.

Even these requirements will not be sufficient to control pollution of the atmosphere by exhaust fumes. Pressure continues in Southern California and elsewhere for still more stringent and costly controls. The harm done to the atmosphere by the automobile has evolved gradually from the motor car's commercial appearance on European markets in the late 1880's. The Benz and Panhard proved to be forerunners of a social and economic revolution with demands upon the environment that have begun to be appreciated only since 1960. Since the problem has taken so long to develop and to be recognized, it is not going to be solved in one legislative session or in a single season of enforced controls.

COMPLEXITY OF THE AIR POLLUTION PROBLEM

Oldsters have often sagely observed, "Dilution is the solution of pollution." This concept was borrowed from water pollution experts by the controllers of air pollution programs. As a motto, it seemed to be a ready-made sanction for the urban sprawl that marked American city growth after World War II. If cities spread out the people would have cleaner air. Unfortunately, the adage holds true for neither air nor water.

As a concept in water pollution control, this maxim was about as valid as the other old saw, "A river purifies itself every seven miles." Both were folk sayings with a certain validity only if the amount of waste was small and its accumulation spaced out over a long period of time. Lake Michigan, which Chicago calls its "drinking-water ocean," serves as only one example. By 1965 it was showing signs of "dying before its time." A United States Public Health Service study, conducted between April 1962, and July 1964, showed what no one would have believed possible even ten years before—that this huge waterbody had been disturbed by colorless, odorless, non-toxic solutions of nitrogen and phosphorus coming from treated waste and agricultural run-off. The lake had been so enriched that the growth of algal blooms in the water and along the shore became explosive. The director of the study, Clifford Risley, predicted that, without drastic and expensive changes, "Conditions are sure to grow worse and more rapidly."

In this, Lake Michigan is typical. The list of America's great rivers, once used by poets to summon up a vision of grandeur—the Monongahela, Cumberland, Ohio, Mississippi, Hudson, Delaware, and Rio Grande—is now simply an enumeration of waters that are blackened with sewage, chemicals, oil, and trash. So far as water has been concerned, there simply has not been enough to make dilution the solution for pollution.

What proved true for the resource upon which the idea of dilution was developed—water—has proved equally true for the resource to which the idea was extended—air. Los Angeles, which has the lowest population density of any major city, has the worst air pollution problem. For this, there are three reasons: a) cities draw their air, like their water, from wide spaces beyond their limits; b) in the advanced stages of pollution, small reductions in intensity are so meaningless that the average effectiveness of pollutants is actually increased through their having been given more air individually, and c) the larger the area of city, the larger the polluted zone and the longer it takes to renew the air, with a greater chance of irregular wind directions slowing the exhaust and of photochemical reaction among the pollutants because the pollution is in a wider belt. The dispersing emissions cover a widening angle and the air turbulence increases the angle as the pollutants travel further.

Where air in layers is moving out of the city, the greater the distance between the stack and open country, the more smoke, grit, and chemicals must reach the inhabited levels. The air in that open country is the refuse area for the city; and the larger the city, the further from its source of air pollution will its air refuse area be. Urban sprawl simply increases the amount of truly open land needed to attain the degree of segregation of particles regarded as sufficient for purified air. The conclusion which this fact seems to demand is that air conservation, even when the auto exhaust fumes in a city of suburbs are not considered, is best obtained through the containment of urban sprawl. What seemed to be the easy "solution"—letting the conurbations simply grow—has proved instead to be a contributing factor in the growing problem.[7]

MAGNITUDE OF ENVIRONMENTAL POLLUTION

The problem—whether it concerns adequacy of water, air, soil, or some related renewable resource—is that the earth is constant and man is a being of incessant demands. Man is continuously converting "neutral stuff" into resources, and changing what have been valuable resources into "non-resources" once again. Still, it is obvious that the total demands being made upon the environment are reaching the point at which some radical shifts in resource management will have to be made.

Despite a 60 percent improvement in efficiency of treatment between 1940 and 1965, domestic and industrial wastes have raised the oxygen demand alarmingly. By 1980, waters that receive treated wastes will generate a demand which will be met only by an oxygen resource that all twenty-two river basins in the United States might yield in dry-weather flow. Every twenty years, American industry doubles the amount of chemical waste it discharges into water. Thermal pollution from power production increases at a rate of 20 percent a year. And solids draining from the land, largely as a result of erosion from agricultural use, are annually seven hundred times the urban-industrial contribution. Merely setting up the rough outlines of the problem, with endless lists of data, can confuse an observer to the point where he can hardly see how grave the situation is.

The nineteenth century has traditionally been called an age of production and the twentieth an age of consumption. Consequently, the former century is seen as having had a culture dedicated to work and frugality, whereas the twentieth is a time for leisure and expenditure. Whatever insights may be gained from this, the larger problem, so far as resources are concerned, is that in both centuries man has been a user more than either a producer or a consumer.

Mountains of junk demonstrate that modern urban industrial man does not consume autos, furniture, or appliances. That he does not consume even his food, fuel, and water is perhaps less obvious. He uses these things, extracts energy, changes the form, and then deludes himself into believing that the residues disappear. To push used matter to one side, to bury it, to flush it, or to blow it away on the winds is thought to constitute disposal. Men have assumed that there was a direct line from production to consumption to disappearance. Now it is evident that man, whether as producer or consumer, is part of a cycle. The residues streaming from his production and consumption do *not* disappear, and when they accumulate beyond a certain point, they very plainly demand reconsideration. Ideally, there should be an equilibrium or steady state existing between production and consumption on the one hand and the residues or spillover on the other. Unfortunately, production is ever increasing, while the capacity of resources into which wastes are dumped remains fairly constant.

The dire predictions made in 1960 by studies of the United States Senate Select Committee on Water Resources, we are assured, should not be taken as the sole word. The warnings are based upon several estimates: that the natural run-off in the United States is 1,250 billion gallons a day; that existing methods can recover only about 650 billion gallons of this loss; that by 1980 the United States will be using all of this recoverable water; and that by 2000 the country's needs will have risen to 1,000 billion gallons every day.

The question is, what precisely are these needs and how can they be estimated? Human demands upon water are variable indeed. An adult drinks from one and a half to ten quarts of water each day, depending upon such matters as climate, work load, and the like. The average American urban dweller, however, uses a daily minimum of from four to five metric tons, or about 720 quarts of water. No one really knows what even industry's needs are for water per discrete unit of production. Steam generation of one kilowatt hour of electricity may draw from 1.32 gallons to 170 gallons of water. To refine one gallon of crude petroleum may take as little as 1.73 or as much as 44.5 gallons; to finish a ton of steel, 1,400 to 65,000 gallons; to make a pound of artificial rubber, 13 to 305 gallons; or to blow a ton of glass bottles, 118 to 667 gallons. With statistics such as these, it seems bootless to talk about America's "needs" or "requirements" for water in 1980 or 2000, as if the use existing in the mid-1960's represented a determination of what industry had to have. Kaiser Steel Corporation quickly learned that its mills in an arid area of the West needed less water to roll steel than mills in Pittsburgh, and Israeli industry is always engaged in showing how little water any particular process really requires.

In the mid-1960's, daily per capita use of water in the United States for domestic, industrial, commercial, and agricultural purposes (including irrigation) averaged 1,800 gallons. In New York City the water consumption in non-drought periods of the 1960's was 1.25 billion gallons daily or, with a population of eight million, about 150 gallons for each person. Conservation measures in 1965 did cut that consumption by 25 percent, or to less than 125 gallons, but this reduction could not continue because it would be economically stultifying to the New York metropolitan area.[8]

London residents subsist on fifty gallons of water a day, those of Durham, England, on twenty-seven gallons, and those of Hong Kong on five, apparently without hardship. But Americans are not impressed by these illustrations. The United States has been wont to have higher water demands for such conveniences as air conditioners, industrial water coolers, and water-borne flush waste. A level of water use which seems extravagant to a Sicilian farmer might make most United States citizens feel they were in a state of crisis. The water flowing unheeded past New York City throughout its droughts has always been plenteous, if badly polluted. Use and re-use of this water would mitigate any drought's effect and permit New Yorkers to demand even more water, regardless of rainfall for several decades. The Sicilian farmer would pay more attention to the Hudson.

Americans sometimes seem to be as heedless in their treatment of air as in their treatment of water. It would appear most rational to regulate the use of air on the basis of the "air shed." This concept relies on the fact that there is no single air mass over North America for communities arbitrarily to cut out in chunks. Instead, meteorological conditions set wind currents and wind directions and divide the continent's air space into semi-contained areas. The land surfaces covered in any such sub-regions are mostly open and emit few pollutants to the atmosphere. The waste discharge, which creates the demand for the atmosphere to dilute it, to carry it off, and to replace it with pure air, comes from urban zones and at a few isolated points such as power plants.

Air, of course, is less manageable than water. There is no way to build reservoirs from which air could be released as needed in order to dilute and carry waste. Nor is it possible to speed up, slow down, summon, allay, or direct the winds and air currents that do much of the work of revivifying the atmosphere. But then industrial demand is reducing the water resource to a similar unmanageable condition. Some experts think that under the very best conditions, the minimal residues of the most efficient treatment works will still be so concentrated in the future in heavily populated and industrialized areas that streams will be used principally as sewers.[9] If such should be the result in a resource which can be stored, diverted, channelized, and released at will, what must happen to the air, which cannot be governed in these ways?

In air pollution, the problem is more complex than merely measuring the components of discharged waste. In the 1920's, when men first began to express concern, the problem did seem to consist of the presence of these contaminants. This had been the attitude from ancient times. The city of Sybaris in Calabria adopted about 700 B.C. the first zoning laws, confining industrial smoke and odors to a district from which they could be rapidly dissipated without annoyance to the rest of the city. In 1273, Edward I banned the burning of sea coal in the city of London to relieve air conditions that had deteriorated seriously even at that early date. Tradition has it that a Londoner was beheaded for violating the prohibition; Edward's queen had a violent allergy to coal smoke and fumes.

Recently, observers have realized that air pollution is an end product in a chain of reactions and transformations which occur in a varied context of interacting pollutants and physical influences such as radiant energy and humidity. It is no longer just a matter of alarm at the sight of thick smoke rolling over the city. Rather, the concern is focused upon the chronic exposure of individuals to low pollution levels over their lifetimes. It may even be that man is damaging the air permanently, by changing its very chemical composition. What happens once the contaminants reach the atmosphere is the subject currently beginning to receive study. The hope is that research will lead to some better solution than the capital punishment of polluters.[10]

THE PROBLEM OF WASTE REMOVAL

For all forms of waste disposal, there are certain immutable constraints which cannot be ignored. Among these are the facts that waste can be dispersed only in a receiving body, or concentrated for re-use, or disposed of in a way that is only slightly different from displacement. If waste is dispersed, it must be assimilated into air, water, or land, either by being carried off, altered, displaced, or simply held by the receiving body. If the waste is concentrated and cannot be re-used either in the waste-producing process or as a by-product, it must be disposed of the way sealed containers of radioactive waste might be dropped in the sea, buried in the earth, or shot into outer space. Because the limits for discharge of pollutants into the environment are currently not known, concentration and sealed disposal of the waste would seem to be the best methods to avoid both assimilative problems and any ill-effects of concentrating the waste before dumping. Unfortunately, the problem in such disposal is the limited availability of dumping grounds.

The earliest form of waste removal was hauling it away. What made many eighteenth- and nineteenth-century cities filthier than their medieval predecessors was their greater size and the larger quantity of filth to be hauled out of them. It was calculated that a scavenger with a horse and cart could not make a profit if he had to haul waste more than three miles from where he collected it. This caused a breakdown in private scavenging systems as the nineteenth century advanced. The bankrupt private collectors were replaced by municipal trash collection systems.

The gradual easing of the problem has been brought to a halt by the almost unbelievable volume of solid waste that must be carted away. Twentieth-century trash disposal systems are simply overwhelmed. In 1920, solid waste in the United States averaged 2.75 pounds daily per person. By 1965, it was 4.5 pounds and increasing at the rate of 4 percent a year. By 2010, this rate of growth would give a national daily average of 8.1 pounds per capita of routinely collected waste. The rate of increase is likely to be even faster; in Los Angeles, for example, per capita collected waste went from 4.5 pounds in 1955 to 6.5 in 1965. If all waste were counted, including that from agriculture and that which is directly salvaged, the average in 1965 already would have been 8 pounds per person per day. Probably 25 percent of the residents of municipal areas in the United States in 1965 were without any kind of public waste removal system and either had to pile it up on their own ground, abandon it on others' property, or have it carried away by private contractors. So far as getting rid of the trash is concerned, the crisis has returned to about what it was a century ago.

Open dumps violate aesthetics, pollute underground water supplies, provide breeding grounds for vermin and rodents, and raise a widespread stench. Beyond this, they can be a menace to public health through discharge of silica crystals during burning. Abandoned dumps, which can smolder underground for years, may periodically catch fire on the surface and release dangerous particles from poorly combustible materials. Even a sanitary landfill will have leached from every acre in its first year of operation about 1.5 tons of sodium with potassium, 1 ton of calcium with magnesium, 0.91 ton of chloride, 0.23 ton of sulphate, and 3.9 tons of bicarbonate. It is quite evident why lands near dumps are not prime residential property, although in the case of a well-run landfill there is no reason why adjoining property need suffer a severe decline in worth.

In the handling of solid wastes, there has been relatively small improvement since the Middle Ages. It is now carried in motor vehicles, and it is baled and compacted. But the archaic character of the work is evidenced by the extremely high injury rate among sanitation workers, which runs twice that of police and firemen and ahead even of stevedores, and by a higher rate of occupational disease among these workers than among other manual laborers. In solid waste disposal, 75 to 85 percent of the total cost goes for collection, with labor charges making up the major portion.

Composting, which many have regarded as the best solution, has proved disappointing because of the cost, the proprietary nature of many composting processes, and agricultural disinterest in the end product. As the garbage committee of the City of Houston, Texas, pointed out in 1964: incineration may pollute the air and requires a deposit for the ash; landfill requires low ground which may not be available and depresses surrounding real estate; and composting has competing proprietary processes and needs both research and development. Certainly very few cities will be able, as Houston did, to sign contracts amounting to $5.5 million in the research development program of a compost project for the city.[11]

Public authorities have not shown much interest in solid waste disposal. Only twenty-five states initiated any legislation on solid waste disposal during 1965, and of these only sixteen already had programs directed at the problem. Only nine states in that year authorized the formation of districts to operate area-wide solid waste disposal systems. A few counties have taken the initiative on their own to form such units, but they are exceptions. In 1965, the federal government had only six persons working on the problem; of the fifty states, seven had more than one man working on it, seven had one-man programs, and the rest either did nothing or had a single employee giving it only casual attention. In the presence of the almost geometric growth of solid refuse, such indifference cannot remain a standard practice. Regular refuse collection service for residents of urbanized areas is a responsibility that should be fixed by state law, because as the DuPont Company observed, "Control will become increasingly difficult and expensive as urbanization spreads and thickens." [12]

Sanitary landfills, incinerators, composting, open dumping, and other disposal methods are now better technically than their early counterparts, but too many American communities still use incredibly antique equipment. Many major cities delayed until after 1945 in retiring the horse-drawn, fly-blown, crusted garbage wagon, with its leather curtains usually open. Many improvements in the field have been about on a par with the suggestion the governor of North Carolina received in 1965 from a state women's organization when he asked their advice on how best to beautify the state: the trash trucks should be painted blushing pink!

Solid trash in most American communities continues to be collected, stored, and disposed of as cheaply as possible by incinerating and compacting it and burying the remains in the closest available ground. This ultimate dependence upon the land is what makes the problem acute, and not because of any harm which may be done to the land or to the air and water above, below, or near it. Rather, the developing crisis can be traced to the shortage of land within economic truck hauling distance. Any land at a distance over ten miles from the source of waste becomes, mile by mile, less desirable for a refuse receiving ground. When the twenty-mile range is passed, the distance is hopelessly uneconomic for hauling of trash by truck.

As for alternatives, one proposal is that all potential waste be made of burnable or shreddable material, so that in the future there would be no containers made of glass or metal and the shredded organic material would be flushed into the sewers. The disposal of this shredded matter, however, would pose a problem. Garbage disposals in the home have already increased the daily per capita requirement for water by one and one-half gallons. The proposed addition of shredded trash would call for an additional three gallons of water per capita daily.

Despite the risks, Los Angeles has begun shredding solid waste for sewage disposal, after first separating out non-organic matter. The remaining shredded matter is dumped into a sewer for transportation eighteen miles to a treatment plant. This is better than the Thope system, which would carry all waste in a granulated waterborne mixture, because the Los Angeles method does not require a separate sewage system and is limited to waste biologically degradable so that receiving waters need not be silted up. For the same reason, the Los Angeles plan is also superior to the Garchey system, which calls for a sewage system for the pneumatic collection of all wastes ground to a maximum dimension of sixteen inches. Unfortunately, in the Garchey method there would still remain the problem of disposing of non-organic waste, since it seems improbable that all such materials could be eliminated from the economy. But even if the difficulty of disposing of the non-organic junk is overlooked, the shredded material would never enter sewers which can hardly carry their present loads.

Other solutions would bring the solids to regional incinerators, like some built in France, which require no separation of garbage and rubbish. In them the refuse is crushed, unburnable materials separated out, and the rest reduced to an odorless confetti that can be used as fill. Los Angeles has lowered compacted waste into ocean depths of over three thousand feet where, once water-logged, it cannot rise. Experiments have shown that water-logged waste will stay down at shallow depths of fifty feet if not disturbed. Boston has hauled waste out to sea on Liberty ships, burned it, and dumped the ashes in the ocean beyond the reach of the tidal ebb and flow. It also has been suggested that solid waste could be chemically reduced to inert liquids with a consequent discharge of non-noxious gases in some disposal units and only a relatively small amount of waste matter going into sewers.

Whatever method is suggested, however, there remains the problem of a residue which must be buried, drowned, or scattered on the earth or in water or air for dissolution or displacement. A perfect destruction is not possible, and the effect that such residues must have on the receiving environment continues to be an issue. Maximum reduction of waste is important enough to be an immediate goal, but with production growing so rapidly, man must be constantly watchful to make certain the assimilative capacity of waters, the earth, or the atmosphere is not exceeded.[13]

The cost of managing waste disposal is already high. In 1965, public agencies in the United States had expenditures running at an annual level of more than $3 billion for the collection and disposal of solid waste. When to this was added the monies spent for solid refuse disposal by private persons and industry, the total expenditure merely to dispose of solid trash came to a total exceeded only by public investment in education and transportation, so far as public funds spent to defray social costs were concerned. Industrial waste is expected by the end of the century to have increased over 700 percent. By the year 2000, the waste to be dumped in the United States will be about 733 billion gallons per day. (This figure exceeds the total stream flow in the United States and is equal to two-thirds of the total quantity of available water in this country.) In 1965, the average for refuse produced daily by a single person in the United States was 4.5 pounds of solid waste, 120 gallons of sewage, and 1.9 pounds of air pollutants, of which vehicle exhausts made up over half. Clearly, some drastic changes in waste disposal must be developed.

ASSISTANCE POSSIBLE FROM RE-USE OF WASTE WATER

Even assuming that water consumption rather than water use figures is crucial to judging how adequate streams and underground waters are for waste reception and water supply, it is projected that between 1960 and 1980 the consumption of water in the United States will have increased about 50 percent. One source of hope is the belief that, even without technically improving ways to re-use water, the United States by the year 2000 will be using every day about 900 billion gallons of the 1.1 hundred billion gallons available.

This question of re-use of water will grow more important with every decade. The Chanute, Kansas, experiment, in 1956–1957, when the Neosho River went dry, is often pointed to as an example. Chanute simply re-cycled its treated sewage effluent through the water purification plant. At the end of five months, the water was faintly amber, with a frothy head, but residents seemed to suffer no ill effects. The Southern California city of Santee, with the advantage of geologic river beds in which to build settling lagoons, uses its sewage effluent for boating, swimming, fishing, and supplementary water supply. An even easier use, for that one-third of the United States with a limestone or clay soil, is to recharge aquifers by spraying waste water over the ground, so that the hard-to-dispose-of waste would serve to stop the falling of water tables without the municipality's having to cut back on pumping demands. Where water tables are unusable because of a naturally brackish condition, it has been suggested that waste might be injected into these permeable underground formations so as to dilute them into usability.

It would be a serious mistake, of course, to consider re-use of waste water as a solution that has not yet been widely adopted. A 1965 advertisement asked, "Would a surgeon scrub his hands in secondhand water?" The answer was that of course he would, and in water which had already been used again and again. For many years, the waters of the Ohio River have been used an average of two and a half times between Pittsburgh and Cairo. In 1965, about 50 percent of the population of the United States drew their water from waterworks; and of these people, about 60 percent were receiving water that had already been utilized at least once for domestic sewage and industrial waste. The foul taste of so much American water does not come from its being too heavily chlorinated, as many believe, but to its not having had sufficient free chlorine added to counteract the taste of organic waste remaining in the water. Quietly, without fanfare, the use of waste water for drinking has been increasingly promoted in the United States. Now that about half the people are drinking such re-used water, it can be expected that schemes to re-cycle waste will be even more ambitious in the future.

COMPLICATIONS OF NUTRIENT POLLUTION

One of the major problems with American surface waters is their eutrophic, or so-called "enriched," condition. This refers to the presence in the water of such nutrients as nitrogen and phosphorus upon which aquatic plant life relies. Needless to say, it is natural for waters to contain nutrients or they would be without life. Some allotrophic lakes have been found which, despite a crystalline quality, have so low a natural nutrient level that they are without fish.

Usually when pollution is considered as harmful to water, it is because of the direct toxic effect of wastes on aquatic organisms. In late 1965, an accidental chrome dump from a factory below Anderson, Indiana, alerted officials for an expected fishkill: nothing happened because in that stretch of White River nothing was alive to be killed. The chrome dump is the sort of harm most commonly envisioned by the public. Yet it is the demand for oxygen, whatever the source, that typifies polluted water and alters the effect of water character.

An example of the importance of oxygen can be observed in the results of thermal pollution. Until after 1960, the problem of what heat by itself did to receiving waters was seldom considered. It was known that heat prevented water from retaining dissolved oxygen, so that the effect of heat was the same as of some putrescent additive which demanded oxygen. Even with the knowledge of how heat cuts a stream's cooling capacity and waste assimilative ability, men did not really attempt to reduce thermal poisoning until the 1960's. When the temperature of water passes 70° F., the mortality rate of fish increases sharply. It is not necessary to boil a river to fatally disturb its aquatic life, nor is more than a steady seeping of nutrients required to produce an ultimately unbearable eutrophic condition in river or lake. In either situation, the reduction of oxygen is the crucial factor.

Because the process of eutrophication is one of enrichment, there is often a stage of tremendous growth in sheer quantity of fish within the affected waters. Sportsmen may not care for the quality of the catch, but in terms of poundage alone, an enriched lake may contain far more carp or catfish than it ever did bluegill or whitefish. As phosphorus, nitrogen, sulphur, carbon, iron, and vitamins come into the water, various plants respond with degrees of vigor related to the type of nutrient which is dominant in quantity. Sewage sludge is rich in vitamin B12, although bacteria can synthesize the same vitamin if they have themselves been stimulated by nutrients. Algal and aquatic growth can come directly from carbon dioxide and inorganic nitrogen and phosphorus; or such growth can result indirectly from organic material in the form of vitamins derived from the work of bacteria that have been stimulated by these same nutrients.

Aquatic growth is controlled by the limiting factor inherent in the amount of any one of these nutrients and by the overall bio-oxygen demand of all the living aerobic organisms in the water body. Phosphorus and nitrogen are the dominating factors for algae, with the phosphorus element being the limiting factor for most forms. This phosphate budget is the one largely used to describe the content of effluent and the change in water conditions, because it is easy to measure. But factors can change for aquatic plants in the same lake—from a phosphate need in the spring to a nitrate demand somewhat later, with carbonate, iron, sulphate, and other elements playing different roles at these times. Efforts to find a single rule by which to measure nutrient capacity of receiving bodies will always be frustrated. The situation is a dynamic one which follows the seasons and the bio-cycle of growth among the living things within the water.

Although an enormous amount of research has been done since World War II, scientific understanding of the complex hydro-biology of lakes and streams is very incomplete. Phosphorous run-off from fertilized fields may have no effect if the phosphorus is not able to assume an ionic form. A superb sewage plant that brings waste up to the nitrate level in treatment may by that fact provide a degree of enrichment not otherwise available. Bottom-dwelling insects may keep loose sediments stirred around, so that insoluble substances get worked up to levels at which they can serve as nutrients. The growth-death-decay cycle of the aquatic life will help maintain an enriched level in a lake; and once it reaches a level just short of oxygen exhaustion, the eutrophic process may be able to maintain itself with the noisome, unattractive aspects so inimical to recreation and the aesthetic sense.

Once in the water, nutrients become very hard to manipulate. In the mid-1960's, there existed no known process of removing nitrates or nitrogen compounds from water, and dissolved phosphates could be removed only at great cost by alum coagulation. Some observers think the best method is to encourage an algal growth that, having soaked up the nutrients, could then be harvested. This last solution sounds rather like the never-dying trust in the power of the Oriental carp to eat away all noxious aquatic weeds and pollutants. This hope brought the carp to the United States in the 1870's and to England in the 1960's; but, as the carp could not purify the streams, neither can the algae, since there is no practical way to harvest algae nor any present commercial use for it. Unless the various suggestions for synthesizing palatable foods from algae prove feasible, the use of algae itself to clear up the algal nuisance cannot be economically feasible. But it remains as a tempting prospect of solution.[14]

Whenever hydro-biologists are in a pessimistic mood that makes them wonder if polluted lakes can be saved, they think of the Red Lake in Switzerland. A river may be flushed clean, but a lake cannot. Therefore, if a river can be turned into a sewer, a lake can only become a cesspool. Considering the stilling of so many of America's wild rivers by dams and channelizing levees, it is rather optimistic to think of flushing these streams. Yet by drawing down on the reservoirs, man can produce a certain flushing in a river bed which is not possible in a lake. When conditions in the Chicago-Illinois River System grow intolerable, water can be diverted through Chicago's intakes to draw water from Lake Michigan and use it to rinse the fetid channels of the rivers. But for the excessively polluted southern tip of Lake Michigan, or for Lake Erie, many of whose beaches are permanently closed, even cessation of pollution would probably not help now.

Before the experience of the Red Lake of Switzerland, the theory was that if man stopped what he had been doing, nature would eventually return to its former state. This is the concept of the sere that is at the base of ecological thought about the functioning of nature. But when sewage was diverted from the Red Lake and the sere should have begun, nothing happened. Changes brought on by pollutants had established a new equilibrium which nature could keep going on its own. The Red Lake was a defeat for the optimistic view that for man simply to stop would be sufficient.

Some observers have refused to accept the Red Lake as a symbol of man's frustration. They argue that merely to divert the sewage did not halt the effect of human activity on the lake, because heavy run-off from surrounding fields continued. Furthermore, the lake was small and shallow, so it could easily maintain its enriched condition even though no nutrients ever again entered its waters. But even the optimists conceded that, once oxygen is exhausted in the deep levels and any lake has become eutrophic, there is a self-perpetuating tendency inherent in the condition. The limnologists, or lake experts, know only that all nutrients must be excluded, whether coming from industrial waste, municipal sewage, or agricultural run-off; that once the nutrients have been excluded, the return to the seral climax may be erratic and very slow; that further assistance such as dredging out sediments may be required; that techniques of nutrient absorption may have to be developed; and that, despite all such efforts, it may be impossible to restore a lake once a certain new equilibrium has been reached.

Dumps, landfills, septic tanks, waste ponding, and spray irrigation—each of them in itself an effort to accommodate the residues of human activity in the encompassing environment—contain concentrations of nutrients that are dangers to lakes even though they may percolate to the lake through underground layers. Earth filtration will not stop nutrient pollution, particularly when the soil itself has reached a high stage of enrichment. Indeed, the soil itself may be an important contributor of nourishment. The storm drains sweeping rain water off city streets are important conveyors of nutrients whether separated from sanitary sewers in their own autonomous system or connected to the sewage treatment plant which their overflow may flush out without treatment. In the first situation, they bring street silt and nutrients, whereas in the second they bring the waste of the whole city for an instant. In either event, the resultant problem is not to be simply solved.

UTILITY OF DUAL SEWERS FOR WASTE DISPOSAL

Prior to 1940, most sewer systems built in American cities were combined ones, in which both storm drains and sanitary lines led into the treatment plant. The reason for this was the belief that all waste should be treated and that the combined-purpose sewer would also handle illegal hook-ups which dumped sewage into storm drains. But with the improvement in the quality of treatment demanded and the growth in the quantity to be treated, the plants proved inadequate. Some cities regularly by-pass their treatment plants when the rains are heavy, but even infrequent use of the by-pass valve is harmful. Chicago gives 99 percent of its dry-weather flow in its combined sewer system a high degree of treatment. During the year, a mere 3 percent of the total sewage flow escapes treatment. But this failure occurs during the summer at the rate of about five overflows each month and accounts for up to 30 percent of the organic matter discharged by the whole system. Although these figures indicate that even a high rate of treatment produces a substantial quantity of organic matter in the effluent discharge, it is striking that so few failures to treat should produce such a disproportionate harm. If one assumes that corrective steps should be taken, the question of cost looms as a barrier to action.[15]

It has been calculated that it would cost $30 billion to completely separate storm and sanitary sewers on a gravity-flow principle and not much less if a pressure-type system were used. This estimate does not include the cost of disrupting commerce in cities while such an ambitious program was being carried out. The cost of holding tanks and impoundment ponds, particularly in cities with many discharge points, is quite high. In areas where receiving waters are subject to sharp seasonal drops in flow, these delay devices are the only choice. But building conveyance systems to them and cleaning out the accumulated sludge add to their costs enormously. To reconstruct treatment plants in New York City so as to delay flow for just fifteen minutes, while heavy suspended material was removed and the effluent chlorinated, would cost $600 million. New York City has a plan to protect city beaches with six storm overflow treatment plants around Jamaica Bay and other facilities which will cost $175 million. This so-called "marginal pollution plan" to protect a few beaches costs a sum amounting to 25 percent of the planned treatment costs, excluding sewers and pumping stations, for the entire city between 1931 and 2000.[16]

Gordon Fair has suggested a way out of many of these costs by using a system of underground holding tunnels through which the water would be drawn at a velocity that would keep matter in suspension. The waste would ceaselessly re-cycle until drawn to holding tanks on the surface. The movement of the waste, meanwhile, would serve to generate power. Fair's system is expensive, both in terms of initial outlay and losses to businesses during construction. Also, the suspended matter might clog the tunnels or, conversely, have a scouring effect destructive to the pipes. Whatever solution is proposed, the expenses will come high, even if no more were done than to enlarge existing treatment plants. None of the suggestions is certain to resolve the problem of run-off and storm drain discharge.

Adding to the urgency of the whole sewage problem is the fact that, in 1965, about 40 percent of the United States population were without sewer service of any sort and about 15 percent of the sewer users had no treatment of their sewage. This represents an improvement, most of which took place between 1957 and 1962, over what had been a rather consistent previous pattern from the 1930's to the 1950's. During the earlier period, about 50 percent of the population was served by sewers, and no more than 50 percent of the sewage involved was treated at all.

By 1963, about one-third of the population served by sewers had their waste given only primary treatment, in which passage of waste through a settling basin removes suspended solid matter. At the same time, just over half of the sewer users had their waste given secondary treatment, in which the filtered waste is aerated and then subjected to an accelerated form of bacterial degradation, additional filtration, and stabilization in ponds. Since 1963, a few communities, such as Lake Tahoe, California, have instituted tertiary treatment which includes spraying the waste over the ground for aquifer recharge and further filtration.

The present investment in sewers and sewage treatment plants in the United States is at least $12 billion. Merely to provide for population growth, the prevention of obsolescence, and the improvement of standards in this existing investment, an annual expenditure of $800 million a year will be required. To extend sewer lines to the suburban population would take another $800 million each year. Communities are hard-pressed to find funds for any of this, since existing sewer service charges bring in less than half the money needed for minimum maintenance and expansion. New York City's current sewer construction needs have been calculated at $1.25 billion, but in the 1965–1966 budget only $38 million was allocated to the job.[17]

In the presence of sewer costs such as these, with so much of the population either not served at all by sewers or having its sewer waste either go untreated or be subjected to very elementary degradation, the more sophisticated problem of what to do with storm drain water looks small in proportion. The same might be said generally of land run-off which reaches the streams without the benefit of urban sewer systems. That this assumption would be misleading is revealed by a consideration of the pollutants entering American watercourses, as classified by the United States

Public Health Service: a) sediments from land erosion; b) sewage and other wastes containing organic, oxygen-consuming substances; c) chemicals which act as nutrients for aquatic plants; d) organic chemical exotics such as insecticides, pesticides, and detergents; e) a wide array of chemicals produced by industrial processes; f) heat from power plants; g) radioactive materials; and h) drainage from mining operations.

From this list, it is clear that land run-off, the discharge of storm drains and drainage ditches, the waste sent through by-pass valves at treatment plants, and the material which cannot be removed by present treatment methods make up the bulk of the water pollution problem. Urban sewer systems are important, both for public health and for environmental amenity. Like water mains, they should be extended to more people. But though this is an expensive and a difficult business, the problem of environmental protection from wastes that cannot be brought to enter such systems, or that cannot be treated within the system because of expense or technical unfeasibility, is far more complex, difficult, and expensive.

IMPORTANCE OF COPING WITH ENVIRONMENTAL POLLUTION

A Libyan economist once noted that the purpose of planning in North Africa was to create for that region the sort of problems existing in Western Europe and the United States. The resource economist Erich Zimmermann, with a pessimism unusual for him, called this Euro-American condition an "economy of pleonexy"—that is, an economy built upon an ever-growing consumer demand, gross national product, and the spirit of covetous greed for material well-being.[18] Whatever moral issues arise when even an economist starts talking of spiritual values, resistances arising in nature wherever man converts some part of it to his uses are the particularly pertinent problems. Modern production economy must find a harmonious relationship in which the environment may assimilate human activity. Otherwise man must dominate his environment so that it becomes an amenable part of a larger artificial scheme of social and economic betterment. What cannot be tolerated is the continuing pretense that man's actions mean relatively little in the larger environs of the world.

Soil mining, exhaustion, and erosion made their first appearance on the tobacco plantations of the Virginia Tidewater in the seventeenth century, bringing that area to economic decline soon after the American Revolution. The reduction in fertility has been counteracted by government conservation programs and the abandonment of the land by rural poor who have fled cityward, but in these very "improvements" lie the next set of problems. Any human action to restore the land must alter the soil, the water, the vegetation, and the life cycle of wildlife dependent thereon. New and profound readjustments will be required in nature. Americans are even being told by social commentators that we should not accept a prospective urban-rural ratio in which 90 percent of the people will inhabit 1 percent of the country's land mass. We should aim instead at having at least 20 percent of the population living somewhere outside that alluring 1 percent of space.[19]

Wherever one inquires about man's place in the environment, there is a profound sense of disturbance and malaise. After twenty years of hard work in research, legislation, and law improvements, during which Los Angeles succeeded in producing the lowest industrial air waste emissions and the best auto exhaust control system in the world, the situation showed no overall improvement. The irradiation by sunlight of hydrocarbons and nitrogen dioxide produced ozone in great quantities, adding it to an already naturally ozonized atmosphere. The reforms which had been expected to resolve all problems have provided only the "small solace" that circumstances would be much worse if it were not for the control measures instituted.[20]

Water quality administrators have made about the same progress. Although they have not come up with any conclusive countermeasures their work has certainly kept conditions from being far worse. For one example, in 1939 water quality standards were promulgated for the Delaware River. In 1964, after many years of industrial growth and efforts to control waste, dredge out culm, and seal abandoned coal mines, it was estimated it would cost $250 million to make minimal 1939 standards operative. Despite yeoman work in the past, water quality in the mid-1960's was regarded as a "major policy gap" in the Delaware Basin.[21]

Environmental protection efforts in the United States have had to be very strenuous to do as much as they have. As for any return to pristine nature or even reaching a balance between environment and the demands made upon it—these seem as elusive as ever.

In the American culture there has always been the ambivalent double vision in which the country has been viewed as both "an unspoiled Garden of Eden" and "a land of machine progress." What we should now be trying to do—and perhaps are doing—is to create "the middle landscape" between these two views, in which we can "square the machine with the pastoral ideal." That is, we must either maintain an environment capable of assimilating the growing economy, or else create by artifice an environment in which what is natural continues its existence upon human sufferance. What cannot be continued, without serious consequences, is the present "processing of the environment." That course of action might well subject the life-cycle resources to a fatal conversion from which return would be impossible.[22]

6

Nature as a free good

Man's economic relationship to the natural environment has long been a puzzle. At times, nature has been like the dream of plenty which eternally recurs in folk myth. The witch's edible house in the forest looked no more delectable to Hansel and Gretel than the seemingly inexhaustible riches of nature appear in the eyes of some human exploiters. Like the children tearing confections from the enchanted cottage, man has taken nature's bounty without hesitation and almost without any fear of consequences. The lost children in the tale never pause to ask what a candy cottage is doing in the forest. In the same way, the exploiters of environment have never seen flaws in the vision of nature as a cornucopia. Either deity or some godlike human enterprise has created an abundance in nature. In either event, the good things are there for the taking without risk of harm or loss.

There have been other concepts, naturally. In some, nature represents chaos essentially incapable of total order. Man wages an endless struggle in which he cuts from chaos patches of substance that he subsequently organizes into order. The Currier and Ives print of a frontier farm illustrates this view: in the foreground stands the neat log homestead, the split-rail fences, the cleanly plowed clearing, while all around the backdrop looms the brooding forest primeval. Nature here is not a giver but a fierce, rich enemy from whom human wealth must be torn. And, in war, who worries about the enemy?

Other observers who display more insight and less pessimism see nature as neither donor nor adversary. Instead, the physical world is neutral and passive stuff waiting to be touched by the wand of human energy and purpose. Thereafter, nature responds as it is molded by the human will. Neither forcing its gifts upon man nor resisting his encroachments, nature is a kind of Galatea to be given any form that her Pygmalion, man, desires.

If these views seem poetic rather than economic, it is no accident. Human thought on the subject seems to have been embodied largely in such images as Ceres, goddess of the cornucopia, or Gaia, the brooding resistant earth-mother, or Galatea, the perfect passive image awaiting the call to exuberant life. To move from this kind of context to talk of nature as a fund from which withdrawals are taken and to which deposits must regularly be made, is a decided wrench. Yet this is what happened in the history of man's economic relationship to his environment. One warning proviso, however: the earlier images still command reverence and are invoked, even as the dry rustle of modern economic thought grows louder. It is very hard to forsake goddesses and nymphs for Keynes and anti-Keynes, Marx and crypto-Marx, or Adam Smith and pseudo-Smith. Even so, one must remember that, however appealing they may be, the Ceres-Galatea representations, like most myths, have the serious shortcomings of being inexact and of coming to us in an aura of divinity.

The dangerous thing about these ideas is that they present nature as something freely available to man. Insofar as this idea appears in modern economic thought, the same danger is inherent. Nature, under any of these views, provides free goods for the human economy which call for no payment by man, other than his costs in extracting them. The bounty includes both the renewable and stock resources.

The classic age of Greece and Rome, the thought of Asia from Shinar to China, the Renaissance and the Enlightenment, and much twentieth-century production theory have this view as their base:

nature represents the only free value to man in the economic world. As Thomas Jefferson pointed out for American history, capital and labor might be scarce in the early United States; but everything else—land and what lay on and within it—was present in abundance, merely waiting for a productive force to be applied.

ANCIENT VIEW OF NATURE AS A FREE GOOD

Massive irrigation cultures such as those of ancient Sumer, Egypt, and China might appear to be an exception to this. Water in the way they needed it was no free gift of nature. Faced with the need of governing the water resource, these cultures reorganized their social structures so as to be able to build the required huge constructions. In the Nile and Mesopotamian valleys, the need was for a vast system of irrigation to spread the river water over as much arid land as possible. Inhabitants of the Indus and the Chinese valleys had to anchor the rivers' courses, put up levees to protect the low-lying plains from the rising river beds, and irrigate. The water was not to be had easily; elaborate contrivances were needed to secure and distribute it. If anything occurred to disturb the distribution of the water, the civilizations so carefully built up utterly disappeared—like those in the Indus and Mesopotamian valleys—and scanty populations took their place.

Certainly water was not a free gift in these cultures; still, it cannot be said that resources were conserved or costs fully considered. Once the water had been brought to flow as these cultures thought it should, it was treated thereafter as equal to a free good. As for the other renewable resources, their treatment was never otherwise.

Whatever forests these cultures found available were ruthlessly cut. No one worried about damage to crop yields and soil by the salt deposits left through centuries of irrigation. Egypt was spared this concern because of the gentle leaching action of the regularly rising Nile, but the collapse of the irrigation economies of the Indus and Mesopotamia may have been due as much to the ravages of salt as to foreign invasions.

The Mongols, striking Mesopotamia in the thirteenth century A.D. at a delicate moment in the country's physical economy, destroyed an irrigation system that had no capacity to make a comeback. Other nomadic desert peoples conquering the region had acquired a system too viable for their ignorance to harm for long; but the Mongols seem to have reduced the population of the region by about 90 percent within a decade. Not until the Iraqi began using oil revenues to encourage agriculture in the mid-twentieth century did the area begin to revive itself. An atomic war could have done only a little more harm than the Mongols. As it was, the Mongols seem only to have hastened a fate which the native peoples had taken no interest in preventing.

The same indifference greeted the erosion of soil into China's Yellow River. For centuries, forests were lumbered off the hills at the river's headwaters, and the crumbly, loess soil was allowed to erode into the river in such quantity that the receiving sea was stained by it all the way to Korea. Yet no program to reforest those hills was begun until the middle of the twentieth century. If that program should succeed at this late date, it would be more astonishing than China's sending a rocket to the moon.

Taoist and Buddhist philosophy and the classic thought of Greece and Rome hold that man ought to live in harmony with nature. The same ideas can be found in Eskimo, Amerindian, and other mythologies which express an ideal of the proper relation of man to nature. But this never affected the Plains brave who thought nothing of eating ten pounds of buffalo meat each day, or the Eskimo or Aleut who consumed salmon in comparable quantities. The same prodigality manifested itself even among the more sophisticated Greeks who stripped the Attic forest. And the great irrigation cultures, ranging from Egypt to China, were equally heedless. The myths and ideals of a culture ought not of course to be confused with its economic practice. In the real world, nature remained something to be freely exploited.

When the state took over from nature as the supplier of water, divine monarchs and priest-kings were careful to keep their subjects confused. The masses, whose labor was required, were not to distinguish between water coming from God in a natural flow and water brought through artificial channels by some god in human form or by some human viceregent for God. Despite the enormous efforts expended to build the water systems, however, water was still treated as a free good.

In the largely subsistence peasant economies of the ancient irrigation cultures, little was done to maintain the water system, and the deterioration of the very basis of the economy was rarely noticed. What earlier generations had created was regarded in these ahistorical cultures as the equivalent of something natural. Where natural physical conditions were self-sustaining, as in Egypt and China, the worst that happened was economic stagnation and a steady decline in living standards. Marco Polo knew a far more prosperous China than the nineteenth-century bible missionaries found, and Marc Antony bade farewell to a richer Alexandria than the one which received Napoleon. But the cultures that lacked such physically sustaining conditions simply vanished. Babylon came to exist only as a kind of remembered El Dorado, and the Indus civilizations were completely forgotten until the nineteenth century.

Until the twentieth century, almost everyone regarded the renewable resources as free goods, and attempts at private engrossment were bitterly resented. Medieval European kings, for quite selfish reasons unrelated to conservation, shut out all unlicensed persons from the royal forests so that game could not be taken, fagots gathered, trees lumbered, or charcoal burned without payments to the Crown. Because of the extent of the royal demesne, the heavy payments demanded for licenses, and the severity of the forest police, the use of the forest was held in check and gave rise to much popular bitterness.

The forest was the absolute dominion of the medieval king. Robin Hood in Sherwood Forest was a symbol of popular resentment. In England, the royal prerogative was reduced to a vestigial remnant after the seventeenth century. Even that remnant was a source of great bitterness and proved to be one of the causes of the American Revolution. The Crown's marking choice American trees for the Royal Navy and trying to prevent settlement in areas west of the Proclamation Line of 1763 were intolerable constraints on what Americans regarded as freely theirs. As the liberal nineteenth-century historian Henry Hallam expressed these attitudes, the forests "were protected by a system of iniquitous and cruel regulations . . . which it became afterwards a great object with the asserters of liberty to correct." [1]

On the European continent the royal forests were dissipated as gifts from the Crown or swept away by the liberating economic policies of the French Revolution. Under the impact of *laissez-faire* thought, forests were for a time thrown open for free exploitation by entrepreneurs. The heavy cutting was so disturbing that the restoration of Crown forests or the creation of state forests became common policy from Scandinavia to the Balkans.

The new model, however, was not the old medieval preserve operated by and for the Royal Household, but the eighteenth-century forests of the German princes, operated as self-sustaining economic units. The German princes, who had resisted vigorously the idea of the forest as a naturally self-replenishing free good, established practices from which modern forest management, in one form or another, has developed. But the attitude that the forest is a free good of nature was common to the Levantines, to Greeks and Romans who denuded the shores of the Mediterranean, to Robin Hood and his merry men, to American frontiersmen, and to many persons in the twentieth century. The idea that the cut-over forest will make a quick regrowth on its own dies hard, and the model forests of the German princelings were considered by Americans as merely other neat examples of tyranny.

THE AMERICAN FOREST AS A FREE GOOD

The classic pioneer image in the United States has been of a simple man cutting down vast expanses of hardwood forest with an ax and using a cast-iron plow to open the loam left by deciduous trees. So strong was this image that, when pioneers reached the prairies, further settlement was delayed a generation: the hard soil required a steel plow, and the farmers believed that treeless ground would be barren. The hardwood forests were simply encumbrances to the early settlers. Once they were depleted, their slow regrowth made the natural return of these forests quite unlikely. When the woodlands of Indiana were being cleared in the nineteenth century, great log-rollings were held during which timber was burned at the rate of one hundred cords of wood for every acre. Oak, wild cherry, poplar, tulip, beech, black walnut, hickory, ash, and basswood were subjected to ruthless cutting and burning. The destruction was so rapid that some southern Indiana counties, first opened to settlement about 1800, were without any timber by 1875.

Demand for black walnut in the nineteenth century was such that this wood was often shipped abroad instead of burned. It became so scarce that by 1875 a single shipment of black walnut logs from Whitley County, Indiana, to Europe brought a price of $50,000. Since 1875, black walnut has grown so rare that in 1965 a single standing black walnut tree near Franklin, Indiana, after "fierce bidding" at an auction attended by buyers from the United States, Germany, and Switzerland, sold for $12,600 to a veneer company. This was the last such tree in private hands in the state. The four others remaining, all that are left from countless thousands, stand in the Pioneer Mothers Memorial Forest. When the tree sold in 1965 was a seedling in 1815, black walnut was a nuisance to be burned off the land. By the time it was a young tree in 1875, the fad for solid walnut furniture had induced widespread cutting. By 1965, with none of its kind left for sale in the state, the tree was sold to be microscopically sliced for veneer. Plainly, that which had once been a free good had become within one and a half centuries a priceless item.[2]

Economically, there is little reason to replace these slow-growing hardwood forests. If some acreage had been set aside, as was suggested by the famous 1867 report of the Wisconsin Legislative Committee on Forests, a steady cycling policy of planting and cutting would have been economic over the past century and would remain so into the future. (Germany had such a hardwood program, but the brutal tree-cutting policies of the Second and Third Reichs in World Wars I and II have rather spoiled Germany as the perfect example.) But to begin a hardwood tree planting program in the 1960's does not strike contemporary economists as rational. As Dugald Stewart observed concerning a Royal Commission suggestion in 1792 to plant oak that would mature in one hundred years, hardwood trees flourish best on prime agricultural land, and it is more economic for a country to leave overhead costs of oak timbers to foreigners or else find some substitute.

The "foreign" sources for any national economy are in scant supply at this point, but technology provides the economic solution missing in the past. Plastics made from the pulp of softwood trees can simulate any hardwood from mahogany to teak, and the genuine substances may be left, like purple wood, for artist materials—something quite outside normal channels of commerce. Aesthetically the substitute may be less appealing, but such synthesizing makes more economic sense than retiring good crop land and nurturing plantations of hardwood for over a century without cash return. Land of poorer quality could sometimes be used, and mixed plantings of hard and soft wood trees could bring in a quicker partial return. Even this might involve too much waiting for our impatient culture. When the time from building plat to housing blight is only thirty-five years, talk about setting out hardwood plantations to mature in the year 2100 does not sound practical.[3]

Forest management in the United States, therefore, is a matter of managing softwood. These trees grow rapidly, can be planted on poorer ground reclaimed from subsistence agriculturalists or earlier slash-and-burn lumbering, and find a ready market. One example of successful management is the United States Forest Service's North Central Region which in 1965 sold more trees to private loggers and harvested more trees from its thirteen national forests than ever before. The total sale was 591 million board feet for a high bid total of $3,630,000. Peaks in sales and harvests follow roughly a twenty-year cycle, with the trend toward successively higher peaks as the forests are enlarged and more closely managed. The previous peak, 32 million board feet smaller, was in 1946. Wisconsin forests, which in 1965 made up 18 percent of total regional sales, had as young forests composed only 2 percent of the 1946 total. Since about 80 percent of softwood timber is used to make paper, wood prices must be kept low. The forest service sells the trees as selective stands to private loggers on a high-bid basis. These buyers have the job of financing removal and may not move in to harvest until several years after purchase, so that dates of sales and harvests do not necessarily correspond.[4]

The unique Indiana black walnut tree sold for $6 a board foot, while these timber-farmed softwood trees in the same year were selling for 12½ cents a board foot. These stumpage, or standing timber, prices do not correspond, of course, to the finished board prices. The federal forest service has an appraisal system which follows private lumber sales to calculate costs at auctions of government trees. In 1965 in southern Wisconsin, aspen logs, cut from private lands, and delivered to the mill, were selling for about 3 cents a board foot. Since most of both private and government logs in the region go for paper, they can be low-quality timber with accordingly low prices.

Low prices have to be accompanied by cost-saving devices such as cultivation of single species, close planting, brush cutting of competing growth, and cut-off sweeps of managed stands. Without such practices, low prices simply accelerate forest destruction. Whenever forests are managed for income, of course, the results are tree farms rather than forests, since the growth is something nearly as artificial as a field of annual crops. The cut-off sweeps leave the ground subject to erosion until newly planted saplings can take hold. Cultivation of single species exposes the trees to rapid incursions of disease, which requires heavy spraying. Although brush cutting offsets the fire menace of close planting, it deprives wildlife of its habitat and simplifies both flora and fauna. Recent research has indicated that at least in the colonial period fairly accurate estimates were made of the character and quality of the American forest. Optimism seems only to have distorted the reports made later. From the eighteenth to the twentieth century, when the "Legend of Inexhaustibility" prevailed, timber was used up as if our forests were indestructible. Before 1900, almost nothing was done about conservation.

It does not take long to list early conservation measures in North America. In 1772, Albany, New York, passed an ordinance forbidding any person "to bring into Albany or the Manor of Rensselaerwyck any firewood under 6 inches in diameter for pine, or 4 inches for other species at the stump end." In 1805, making the first attempt at forestation on the North American continent, the Russians planted Sitka spruce on the naturally bare Aleutian island of Unalaska. Although the grove still exists, the experiment failed. In any event, no trained American forester even visited this plantation until 1901. John Quincy Adams set aside a live oak preserve in 1828, and Carl Schurz, as Secretary of the Interior in 1877, viewed the American forest with alarm even as the frenzied cuttings of the lumber barons seemed to find no end of timber to cut.

In 1878, Wisconsin created the first state forest, some part of which managed to withstand two State Supreme Court decisions on the unconstitutionality of such a concept. (The judges were not able to accept the idea until the twentieth century.) And in 1891, Benjamin Harrison set up the first national forest. Thereafter, interest in the protection of American forests grew apace.[5]

Meanwhile, the attitudes of many observers continued to reflect the old notion which is so hard to destroy: that renewable resources are free goods.

THE STATE AS PROVIDER OF FREE RENEWABLE RESOURCES

There are signs, however, that supporters of the "cornucopia" theory may be changing their position. An American businessman said in 1965, "The thing that bothers me is that people regard air and water as something that is free. When you pay your rent and your taxes, you find out how free they are. Water probably is one of the most expensive commodities we have." [6] When public monies invested in reforestation, restocking of fish and game, rebuilding of soils, preventing erosion, purifying streams, and controlling air pollution are combined with private losses due to pollution and depletion, and with private investments made to purify water and air or maintain soils and forests, only one conclusion is possible: there is nothing "free" about any of these goods. The businessman who calls them "expensive commodities" is absolutely correct. The free goods have moved into the cash economy.

This fact, however, can be obscured by massive governmental investment of non-reimbursable funds. The activities of the priest-kings of Sumer and of the divine pharaohs in Egypt were rather similar in scope and operation to some of the programs which modern governments are called upon to carry through.

A prime example of what such programs can involve is the proposal of NAWAPA, the North American Water and Power Alliance. The NAWAPA plan calls for the construction of a continental interchange which would: a) collect water from the rivers of Alaska, British Columbia, and the Yukon; b) redistribute the 178 million acre feet thereby collected annually to water-scarce parts of Canada, the United States, and Mexico; c) produce millions of kilowatts of power through the gravitational flow of the water down the face of the continent; and d) provide a canal from Alberta to South Dakota as an inland waterway connecting Vancouver with Duluth. Many bankers and industrialists have been quoted as saying that "the NAWAPA project [is] essential if our economic growth and standard of living is to be sustained."

NAWAPA would necessitate a treaty among Canada, the United States, and Mexico; a master plan for cooperation among twenty western American states and among the Mexican states and Canadian provinces; and "an understanding between private utilities and the Federal Government so that private enterprise would have a major role in NAWAPA and thus preclude centralized Federal control." Canada would have to be paid to release this much water, but Canadian cooperation is expected because of the chronic trade deficit which Canada has with the United States. Mexico, unfortunately, might have considerable trouble meeting payments unless it received the water under terms of a grant, subsidy, or payment in "frozen" pesos for further United States investment in Mexico.

The more optimistic supporters of the plan say that it can be carried out within thirty years and for a construction cost of $150 billion. The entire sum is to be supplied by the government, which would also have the job of maintaining most of the system's canals, tunnels, and channelized rivers. (It should not be overlooked that the amount of water to be handled within the system would be 58 Franco-American trillions of gallons of water every year.) Assuming that the sum of $150 billion is not too modest (which most engineers believe it is) and assuming that it can be financed at the 1966 prime lending rate of 6 percent (which no economist would regard as high enough), the annual funding charge at simple interest in the beginning would be $8.25 billion. Maintenance would involve the prevention of bank slippage, the removal of silt from all channels, the building of conduits from main channels to users, and the disposal of used water by injection into aquifers, transportation to the sea, or return to the system's own main lines. Without considering purification and waste treatment costs, these maintenance expenses ought to run to a sum comparable to the initial construction costs of the central system.

Since in 1966 many industries, such as petroleum, wanted water for as little as 2 cents per thousand gallons, since water in the New York reservoirs was valued at 12 cents per thousand gallons, and since desalted water usually cost $1 per thousand gallons at the plant, it is apparent that the costs per gallon of water delivered at the tap by NAWAPA still cannot be calculated. Like the delivery of desalted ocean water, this project lacks economic feasibility if current competitive alternatives are considered and if NAWAPA is expected to recover the bulk of its costs from the ultimate sale of the water. It would be much easier for NAWAPA to endure "centralized federal control" of these projects than to satisfy any federal expectation of reimbursement.[7]

Irving Fox, a teacher of regional planning, has argued that unless desalted water can be provided for less than a nickel per thousand gallons, desalination will not be of much significance to the world economy. Most proponents of desalting projects, however, think in terms of a cost of 35 cents per thousand gallons at the plant. Though the sale of by-products brought a few plants close to this cost in 1965, the goal was still elusive. The average cost in the world's desalination plants by 1965 had dropped from $5 to $1 per thousand gallons. In water-hungry and relatively prosperous parts of the world, this might not have seemed an uneconomic cost, especially since there is the prospect of lowering it.

Elath, Israel, where the well water has a dissolved salt content of sixteen hundred to two thousand parts per million (as against the United States standard minimum of 250 ppm), has been pleased to convert water at $1 per thousand gallons by a flash distillation process which has proved widely popular elsewhere. Any source can produce the heat: atomic energy, as at Riverhead, New York; natural gas, as in Kuwait; garbage, as in Hong Kong; or the desalting process itself, as in Elath. Under Elath conditions, even a rival vacuum-freezing desalting installation, which produced water at a cost of $1.50 to $2 per thousand gallons, has been considered a success. In that city, the available sea water from the Gulf of Aqaba has 42,000 ppm of dissolved salts, compared to the Atlantic Ocean's level of 20,000 ppm. The Aqaba water has to be desalted to a 20 ppm content, which is comparable to the level in some American cities that draw their water from tidal streams. Next, Elath must mix the desalted water with the brackish local well water to obtain a solution with several hundred parts per million of chemical salts.

Such water is not especially palatable or healthful and its industrial uses are limited. The Elath economy has been built around the peculiar quality of the water as well as around the potentially available quantity. The greater costs in the industrial use of this relatively salty water and the hardship it imposes on the inhabitants have been reckoned with in the Israelis' plan. Still the final calculation has not been regarded as so high that Israel must cancel construction of a southern port and a harbor for the newly settled Negev. The situations in Kuwait and Hong Kong may be as extreme as Israel's, but other regions have highly competitive alternatives if the economics of supply are considered.

An inescapable side effect of desalination is the salt, which must be disposed of somehow. It takes about 3.5 gallons of salt water to make one gallon of very pure water. Every quart of sea water has an average of 1.5 ounces of salt, so that a 150-million-gallon plant, which would supply only about 12.5 percent of the non-drought demands of New York City, would produce about 23,000 tons of salt every day. In very dry desert climates, this residue might be piled on the ground, or dumped into some sterile receiving body like the Dead Sea, or injected into brackish aquifers or into unoccupied permeable underground layers. But it cannot be dumped into the ocean or its concentration will kill all marine life within a wide area. In such large amounts, it probably could not be diluted so as to become harmless. The residues might be used as a fuel, though for that purpose the amount might be too small. Or it could be simply burned.

The desalting industry denies the existence of any serious salt disposal problem. It claims it can build a 150-million-gallon desalting plant which can produce water at less than 35 cents per thousand gallons, with a residue of only 7 percent salt which can be discharged into the ocean without harm. This may be true, though no such plant exists to test the hypothesis. Even if one assumes that the claim is valid, the fact remains that even harmless disposal of salt residues will have to be calculated into the cost. Salt residue disposal may not be the enormous problem which some have foreseen, but it will probably remain a cost factor unless the salt can be made into a valuable by-product, either as a source of energy or through commercial sale. Simply to ignore the salt residue as a trifling spillover effect would certainly be uneconomic and perhaps even tragic.[8]

Desalting costs have been calculated as "total cost to the economy," since the allocation between power and distillation elements has not yet been calculated. Furthermore, whether the cost is $2 per thousand gallons, as at the vacuum freezing plant in Elath, or $1 per thousand gallons, the supposed world average cost in 1965, or 35 cents per thousand gallons, as in industry's claim of what is currently possible, the charge is an unallocated cost at the production plant itself. Americans are certainly not accustomed to such expensive water. In 1965, the average American family spent $3 per month for water and $15 per month for alcoholic beverages. It took a thousand gallons of water to produce 10 cents worth of irrigated crops in the same year. New York City drew its water from the mountains at a cost of 15 cents and sold it for 12 cents per thousand gallons. It has been proposed that the drier south Gulf coastal area of Texas supplement its supply by bringing in water from east Texas at 5 cents per thousand gallons.

It is true that many low-cost examples are based upon subsidized water supplies. Americans generally expect their water to be cheap, even if some agency of government must sell the water at a loss. Yet even the lightly capitalized private water companies in the United States, which provide for only a small portion of the country's water needs, are able to turn nice profits, pay better salaries for engineers and other technical talent than public agencies, raise loan capital more quickly than public administrations, and pay a variety of taxes—simply by selling water at the consumer's tap for prices of less than 25 cents per thousand gallons. This price is for water that has been filtered, chlorinated, and delivered to the consumer and not for water standing in the water companies' tanks.

It is estimated that for delivery of desalted ocean or brackish water, an additional charge of 20 cents per thousand gallons should be added. Currently, most water is conveyed to consumers by gravitational systems, which hold costs down because reservoirs stand in river uplands. Desalting plants, however, will have to be built on estuarine land or in sumps above brackish aquifers. This means that desalted water will have to be continuously pumped throughout most of the delivery system, with resultant expense for power and pumping stations. Because of the pumping and the higher initial cost of desalted water, it would be cheaper to deliver fully treated water from the St. Lawrence River to a consumer in Manhattan than to supply the same consumer with desalted water from a plant at the edge of the city. Even if a technical breakthrough provides desalted water at prices that currently would be competitive, other technical changes will permit fresh water to be transported more cheaply from lightly populated remote regions than any desalted water that could be supplied.[9]

It seems plain that proponents of continental water transfer schemes and water desalination projects do not believe that both are compatible or needed. When a smaller diversion scheme than NAWAPA, the Feather River Project, was pushed through in California, many observers believed that by its completion date, desalination would have rendered it unnecessary. It has been said that northern California in the 1960's had 70 percent of the state's fresh water, while southern California had 77 percent of the state's "need." Southern California, which is sure of ever-expanding "needs," has currently taken a "needy" attitude in its requests for the Columbia River waters guarded by rather hostile neighboring states to the north.

Arizona is in an even worse condition than southern California. By 1965, Arizona residents were pumping an annual average of 2.5 million acre feet more than could be replaced naturally in the ground. As early as 1940, Arizona planners privately had admitted that the state could not grow as it wished without large quantities of water from very distant sources lying outside the Colorado basin. Even if Arizona's total claim on Colorado River water were recognized by all other rival-state users in the basin, the overdraft on underground water pumped still could not be met. For Arizona's future, huge volumes of water must either be diverted from the Pacific Northwest and Canada or imported in equal amounts and in desalinated form from the Pacific Ocean, or from the Gulf of California, or from brackish interior aquifers.

Costs for either water transfer projects or desalination are enormous. In the mid-1960's, however, it seems that the United States will try to pursue both policies. The Federal Water Resources Council has spoken of creating "strategic water banks" set up in major river basins. All reservoirs, whether built primarily for water supply, power, or recreation, would be coordinated, so that water could be shifted within the basin to fill depleting reservoirs or to hold back an encroaching salt front in a tidal river. Ultimately, these basins in turn would be coordinated so that interregional transfers were also possible. And, within the limits of continental geography, there would be a national interchange system for water roughly analogous to the national power grid for electricity.[10] Even if NAWAPA should never be built, transbasin transfers of huge quantities of water are in the planning stage in California, Texas, and other parts of the American West. These transfers will probably be effected by 1975. If the federal government should be drawn in, expenditures will rise astronomically. Considering that up to 1965 the United States government had spent $21.5 billion on "water development" in the American West, it seems highly possible that the federal government will become further involved. The reluctance expressed by Congress in 1964 to encourage transbasin water transfers will probably crumble under sufficient political pressure.[11]

As for future desalination projects: in 1965, the United States was planning to have 100-million-gallon plants in operation by 1970—this despite the fact that only fourteen-million-gallon plants were supposed to be operative by 1968. On October 4, 1965, the United States, Mexico, and the International Atomic Energy Agency agreed to carry out "a technical and economic study of a large-scale nuclear seawater desalting plant to produce fresh water and electricity for the arid regions in lower California and Sonora in Mexico, and California and Arizona in the United States." The United States told the First International Symposium on Desalination that it would like a common international fund set up to deal with the world-wide development of the earth's total water supply, including that portion which would require desalination. If this one should prove to function in the manner of other similar international funds, the contribution of the United States would not be less than one-third of the total sum subscribed, and the American share probably would run higher.[12]

Even without plans to make desalination a major concern of the government, federal involvement has gained a momentum since 1955 that makes large-scale expenditures, simply to carry out plans prepared by 1965, a certainty. In both desalination and transbasin water diversion, a study program, once translated into field conditions, tends to become a positive public program that appears to have been consciously adopted. It proceeds forward steadily, with the massive thrust of any government effort.

Easy solutions to the water problem simply do not exist. Federal intervention for regulation or financing now seems necessary. In the United States, water use grew from forty gallons per capita daily in 1900 to 150 gallons in 1965. For such growth in use to continue, for the total consumption of water to increase as well, and to maintain the capacity of lakes and rivers to dilute waste, elaborate proposals to desalt and to make complete distribution of surface water at public expense have been made.

These projects would certainly be expensive, and water transfers inevitably precipitate disputes between states or larger areas. For these reasons, there have been proposals to re-use water as many times as possible, to pump underground water without mining it, and to clean up the pollution in surface water bodies. Yet these alternatives also require heavy investments of public and private monies; for they will not succeed if undertaken on the cheap. In short, money must be spent all along the line.

GOVERNMENTAL ACTION AND LAND VALUE

The American tradition of plenitude in natural resources is undergoing a transformation. As a 1965 White House Conference report said, "The luxury of gradual, almost unconscious, adaptation to urban growth has moved out of our reach." The present economic situation concerning land illustrates the urgency of resource problems.[13]

Throughout most of the country's history, land has been in plenty on the market. For a time in the eighteenth century, and again early in the twentieth, rural land was valuable enough to create constraints upon buyers. But after the collapse of rural land values in the 1920's, economists began to feel that land was growing progressively less important. The farmstead had a social significance during the Depression as a refuge for dispossessed, unemployed city dwellers, but few of these people ever became contributing elements in the rural economy. As late as 1953, economists still believed that rural land values were in a downward spiral from which they would not soon pull out.

Events quickly disproved this assessment. Between 1953 and 1965 farm values rose 58 percent, the rise between 1958 and 1965 having been 50 percent. The vested interests of farm landholders in these values, the larger part of which had been supported by publicly financed farm programs, are now major obstacles to the reorganization of extant farm programs which have become obsolete. In the mid-1960's, inflated land prices discourage young men from farming.

Under such conditions, the ambitious, landless, cash-embarrassed rural youth of the 1960's does not tie up his capital in land purchases. Instead, he executes leases with cash payments. Having calculated his land costs in advance and having ascertained how government support regulations would put a floor beneath the market, this lessee is quite different from the sharecropper of southern fiction. Whether these lessees will care any more about soil values than the Erskine Caldwell type of tenant farmer is doubtful.[14]

Rural land has an inherent soil value which has not previously been a factor in the market. The site, and not soil conditions, has conferred value on urban land. Suburban growth has changed this criterion. Some suburban land planners recently have begun to study soils in order to determine drainage courses, the suitability of ground for septic systems and wells, and the best means of managing those public limitations on private land development which have evolved since 1945.

Traditionally in the United States, private enterprise has managed the use of urban land, with any avowedly public purpose playing very little part in the layout of municipal areas. The huge systems of streets, sewers, and mains laid out in American urban centers between 1800 and 1930 took on forms which met specific requirements of land developers, street railway speculators, utility companies, and urban political machines. After 1945, movement to the suburbs accelerated. Pressures similar to those that had created the nineteenth-century American cities led to creation of regional cities that had only the unity of contiguity. This meant that huge costs were passed on to local government when unimproved streets were dedicated and houses and apartments were constructed in areas unserved by sewers, water lines, schools, and other public services. Inevitably, local governments resorted to enormous increases in real property taxes, special assessments and service charges, and improvement bond debts.

The soil survey is one means which some communities are using to reduce excessive levies. Such surveys can suggest how well a previously rural zone will adapt to urban conditions. Surveys, generally made at public expense by governmental agencies, are intended initially for use by those agencies. They have been employed, for instance, by boards of health as aids in field inspections of ground for which development plats must be approved. With governmental agencies using the surveys to determine requirements, suburban developers use the surveys to reach their own decisions on the direction and density of land use. Planners are sympathetic to the surveys, which can prevent the kind of expensive mistakes made after 1945 and the pitiful errors currently being made in relation to soils and urban growth in California and Alaska.[15]

Houses in the Los Angeles area have been built on hills where the spontaneously combustible mesquite grows and where fire insurance cannot be obtained at any premium. When the mesquite is stripped off, any rain causes slippage of mud into the valleys, with gross destruction to houses both on the slopes and in the bottoms. In an area subject to earth shocks, urban site values are such that builders continue to affix houses to shifting gravel hillsides by means of precarious stilts, cantilevers, and cables. There seem to be no effective public restrictions, and such unstable lots retain a high market price. The same kind of seemingly impossible situation prevails in Alaska. Ground beneath the hills in Anchorage, as the earthquake of 1964 revealed, was quick clay, which during severe tremors turns to liquid so that solid layers atop it simply slip off. Needless to say, this discovery did not persuade men to stop building in the danger areas. Instead, builders have called for a nonreimbursable federal project to pump into the ground substances that will fix the quick clay.

Soil science had been developed in the Ukraine in the 1880's by V. V. Doukochaev. But until 1963 it had not been used as an aid to an integral part of urban planning and engineering. Soil inventories first had been made in the United States about 1905. The basic soil survey is meant to reveal the properties inherent in the soil and, hence, can be used either for crop projections or to predict the problems of urban land development schemes. Except where land has been exposed to extraordinary disturbances, old soil surveys remain valid and need only be re-examined. These inventories are predicated upon the existence of soil patterns which allow the surveyor to avoid step-by-step examination of the ground and keep survey cost down to about 50 cents an acre. Only the top six or seven feet of soil are studied, with emphasis on determining what the natural soil condition was before human activities affected it. In downtown and urban renewal areas, consequently, the knowledge of soil surveys has been largely useless. In such zones the soil engineer, with his deep borings and detailed reporting, has been used. The soil surveys have proved most useful in areas in transition from rural to urban use or in highway construction.

The publicly financed and conducted soil survey is intended to serve general planning and zoning, to set limits within the natural pattern of specific soil conditions, and to detect local natural conditions that can be remedied only at great expense. By using soil surveys, planners hope to come to economic terms with natural conditions instead of going directly against them. Soil permeability, with its percolating rate, determines land potential for a septic tank field. Where soil surveys have been available, there has been an average reduction of 27 percent in septic tank development. Zoning maps for farm or vacant land about to be developed have also incorporated survey material. In certain areas, for instance, standing water and bad drainage make construction inadvisable. Knowing about such areas before development has begun, the planner can reserve the area for non-building use. Once development gets well under way, the discovery of problem areas is not so easily resolved.

The United States Soil Service and the Housing and Home Finance Agency have become quite interested in soil surveys for planning purposes. Land that is unsuitable for building can be set aside for parks, recreation areas, and arboretums. It is not always enough, of course, to know merely that certain lands cannot be used for *building*. Consider the small Wisconsin town that put its football field in a drained peat bog. The peat bog cracked under the lush grass cover, and during the first game several players disappeared in the crevices. The match was called on account of unexpected hazards. A building might have been lost forever.[16]

All this recent use of soil knowledge has been in areas peripheral to built-up urban land in an effort by government to avoid some of the public costs that economic activity has imposed in the past. Cities have been constructed in improbable places highly unsuitable for construction, and have flourished there. In our time, some men believe that Venetian palaces and the Leaning Tower of Pisa soon may collapse because they stand on soils where they never should have been put. But no city in history has yet proven eternal, and most of man's metropolises have been quite transitory. Currently a hundred-story skyscraper is being built on the swamplands of Chicago. Urban real estate values will make its construction inevitable even if it should prove more difficult to build than the Leaning Tower of Pisa.

LAND VALUES AND EXPENDABLE SURPLUS

Urban planners have not been concerned until recently with soil composition, and only a few suburban developers have shown interest in it. Consequently, printed accounts of soil values have been written in the context of agricultural use. Americans have seen too much building on flood plains, exposed beach dunes, swamps and clay sumps, shifting desert sands and slipping mountainsides to be impressed by talk of inherent physical properties in soil. Indeed, the urban mind believes that if enough public money is spent, there is no reason why "derelict lands," which have been abandoned in a shattered state by strip-mining operations, cannot be reclaimed despite the problems of acid-impregnated water tables, smoldering culm, slag heaps, and hillocks of sterile earths.[17]

For economic purposes, rural soils can be divided into four classes. The basic one is the matrix, which maintains itself and which, like urban soil, derives its economic value from location. The matrix is practically indestructible, though activities such as strip mining and road building will accomplish this. Almost as permanent in soil economics is the conservable flow element. It represents that part of the soil which should return future revenues that will greatly exceed any present costs of conserving the element. After this in importance comes the revolving fund of nutrients that are removed from the soil by crops and livestock raised on the land and which are, like an inventory, economical to renew. The least permanent part of the soil is the expendable surplus. This includes elements which have a value while being liquidated, but which it does not pay to renew, and also self-renewing elements which are not worth the cost of conservation. If topsoil is five feet deep and plant growth can use soil only to a depth of three feet, then to the economist the top two feet are expendable surplus which can be permitted to erode off.[18]

The same attitude has been held toward the primary forests of North America which, from an economist's viewpoint, have been principally expendable surplus in terms of their standing timber. The problem is that something which has once been expendable can later become economically conservable. The change in man's behavior which should accompany the natural change simply does not take place. Instead, the old ways persist until even the matrix is ground up.

In southern Indiana and Ohio, both the primary forests and the secondary growth that replaced them were lumbered off in the nineteenth century, and by 1933 many counties in that region were economically decrepit. Yet no private efforts at reforestation were made, although nearby markets existed that needed wood for furniture and paper manufacturing. State and federal forests were gradually created at public expense after 1933, and in just one Indiana federal forest, the harvest increased from 1.5 million board feet in 1956 to 6.5 million board feet in 1965. The growing forests generated considerable employment, since in their newly flourishing condition they were able to support a returned wildlife and a large recreation program. In those same nine years, the Bedford, Indiana, office of the United States Forestry Service increased its personnel from four foresters and three clerks to thirty-three persons, which included fifteen foresters, three engineers, a wildlife biologist, and a landscape architect. Values of lands being steadily added to the federal forests moved from an average of $7.19 an acre before 1950 to about $30 in 1965. And with more money budgeted for land acquisition because of increased need for recreational parks and because the accessible wood supplies have nourished the local woodworking industry, the price of this slashed, timber-gutted, farmed-out, eroded, and exploited land will continue to advance.[19]

Yet without the capital poured in by state and federal governments, nothing would have been done. When resources are in the class of an expendable surplus, their cash value per unit is low. The result is that an exploitation undertaken without a set maximum extraction is not regarded as waste. The trees, or soils, or fish, or whatever else is being exploited are taken without regard to their ultimate destruction or spoilage. Because the market price is low, many units have to be taken in order to bring a sufficient gross return. This sets up a circle in which the number of units taken must be large because of the low market price; the large number of units delivered to market drives down the already low price; the lowered price means more units must be sold to maintain the gross return; and so on—until, for some reason, demand greatly exceeds supply.

This change to a demand that exceeds supply may come, as in the timber markets in World Wars I and II, because of a sudden spurt upward in total requirements. In such a situation, the effect can be destructive of the remaining forest resources. Under the psychological stimulus of patriotism, as in England, or of totalitarian plunder, as in the German occupation of the Slavic peoples' forests, effects on the resource can be very harsh.

Only when the supply of timber is shrinking before a steady and persistent demand do economic forces usually request that measures be taken to stop the trend toward ruin of the resource.

This has occurred in England, whose forests were revived after both world wars through government encouragement, and in much of the United States through heavy investments of public monies in federal, state, and county forests. The investment had to be public, for earlier profits from the forest had usually been dispersed. Because of the low unit price during the period of surplus, much of the gross return had been used up in operative costs or to maintain the smaller entrepreneurs. Whatever larger profits had been made had tended to drift to other regions and into other investments.

Some reinvestment in timber through reforestation has been made by a small but significant number of timber and paper companies in the United States and by the landholding families in Europe who have never done more than license timber-taking. Yet even these private investments are often the result of public finance programs. Tax rebates, lowered assessments, special rates, depreciation allowances, outright exemptions, and subsidies have all been part of governments' agreements with private industry. Private investment in reforestation has grown, but without massive initial public investments and their steady public maintenance, the reversal from the expendable to the conservable would not have taken place or been kept up.

The difficulty of preserving French reforestations in Morocco since 1956 has demonstrated this. These man-made forests may go the way of the original forests which fell before Roman axes and were nibbled away by the teeth of Arabs' goats. The popular attitude in Morocco is still that forests are expendable surplus if the gross national need requires them to be. If the United States position on expendable surplus has changed significantly, the more enlightened attitude has not altered concerning timber until recently. Many owners of private timber lands have no doubt at all that trees are expendable. As a result, apprehensive ecologists have been calling for federal timber-cutting regulations to cover private loggers operating on private land. By the time such regulations are authorized, there will probably be little private timber left to manage.

If a stable society of private timber ownership, management, and exploitation can be formed, so that the resource can be approached as conservable, then heavy cutting can be permitted, and regulations can serve to encourage rather than to discourage timber. Such, at least, has been the Scandinavian experience. The American forest, however, has never been controlled by a representative stable group. The United States tradition has been to move into a district, lumber it off, depart with the profit, and leave the deforested region for Heaven and the public treasury to restore. The justification, insofar as it has ever risen above the purest self-interest, has been that an expendable surplus must be converted to cash so that agricultural ground may be cleared, or cheap housing made possible, or employment created, or some other national interest served. Then, in the future, conserving steps would be taken within the economy to counteract whatever mistakes might have been made during the earlier period.

This tradition does not acknowledge the resistance to "costly conservation practices" which still exists. The sharp rise in land values since 1958 has been attributed, in part, to federal farm subsidies. It has also been traced, however, to popular belief that costly conservation practices which originally were regarded as crucial to yields are superfluous. Many agricultural producers now believe that conservation techniques have been superseded by developments in chemical fertilizers, soil stabilizers, and plant growth stimulators. Their practices cut back on the quantity of conservable flow-elements in the soil, and increases either the expendable surplus or the indestructible matrix. If these chemical additives actually do all that has been attributed to them, a considerable portion of the soil elements now painstakingly conserved will either be allowed to erode away or else be disregarded as part of the matrix whose function it is merely to serve as fundament for the cash-producing soil layers.

This determination of the soil market in the 1960's may be wrong in terms of physical soil qualities. But if it is not valid, its flaws can be determined objectively only after the event. For current prediction purposes, it is necessary to rely on what is implicit in market prices. The market continuously seeks the lowest maintenance costs possible on renewable resources, tending always toward traditional treatment of them as free goods. Nor can one overlook the possible attitude that if calculations on the size of soil surplus have been wrong, the government will restore the difference, at public expense, to the equivalent of a free good.

THEORIES OF SOIL VALUE IN LAND ECONOMICS

From the beginning of economics, there have been two views on soil values. The first is that of Thomas Malthus, who believed that soil is perishable and irreplaceable and not to be regarded as either permanent or expendable. The opposite position was assumed by David Ricardo, for whom soil was a man-made and humanly renewable resource as indestructible as a clever dry-goods merchant's inventory. Unlike some other economists, Ricardo was not indifferent to soil maintenance, but he took a sanguine view of human providence's ability to sustain the land. It was this sanguinity that caused him to argue that the best resources are used first.

Unfortunately, as Ricardo's near-contemporary, Henry Carey, the early American economist, pointed out, it is the poorest and not the best resources that are first exploited. This was true for stock resources such as the bog iron of New Jersey and the Seneca oil or petroleum of upstate New York which was skimmed off swamp pools. It was even more true of the agricultural soils in the East which were either exhausted at an early date or driven from the market by cheap western grain after the Erie Canal was opened. For these lands, at least, the optimism of Ricardo is not justified, though in an economic sense the opening of the better lands keeps the deficiencies of poorer soils from mattering very much to the total economy. Lands which in Ricardo's view ought never have gone into production, fade quickly from participation in the market. Only as they accumulate do they have a noticeable degrading effect on the economy and, indirectly, upon the market. At that point, in the natural course of politico-economic pressure, the Appalachian Regional Commission is set up to make all well again.

Yet if Ricardo's view permits too easy an optimism, Malthus takes a stand which is too severe and inflexible. It has been this economist's fate to be perpetually misunderstood. The exquisite irony in Leo Tolstoy made him give the name "Malthus" to the capitalist with whom the virtuous people around Anna Karenina will not associate because he speculates for his selfish advantage without regard to the suffering and destruction he causes. For the real Malthus and Karl Marx, alike, the urban industrial society developing around them was destructive of the resources of air, water, and soil. Indeed, the real Malthus would probably have joined with Tolstoy's good people in refusing to have social intercourse with his rapacious, parasitic, and destructive fictional namesake.[20]

However, soil is more dynamic than Malthus believed it was, and working it has other effects than simply to make it weak. Topsoil that has come to be below the root levels is incapable of further improvement, as it is safe from any erosion. When roots are permitted to penetrate this layer, natural soil-building mechanisms are called into play which convert subsoil to topsoil. For this reason, many soils in western Europe are probably in better condition today than they were in Neolithic times. Soil management expertise consists of cooperating with extremely capable soil-building forces in nature, and human participants should not take too much credit.

Because natural soil conditions differ so much, the rehabilitation of "worn-out" soil has rarely been an economic success. This is soil which ought never to have been cultivated originally, and to make it regularly fruitful is to work against nature. Once the effort to maintain such poor soils relaxes, they decline to their original state. In lands that are better constituted, however, conservation is amply repaid, as in western Europe, since it is always cheaper to keep up such soils' fertility than first to liquidate good soils and then rebuild them. To "conserve" here means to retard depletion, to determine the rate of depletion, to encourage natural soil-rebuilding ability, and to husband in the soil's economic development any physical characteristics which cannot be reproduced.

Virgin soil possesses a chemistry of stability and a dynamic equilibrium in its living parts. Breaking it with the plow interferes with its natural perpetuity, but allowing the ground to go fallow permits the seral function of nature gradually to restore the soil to its primary condition. At least this is true if the matrix of the soil has not been broken too badly. Once the matrix has been seriously disturbed, the pessimism of Malthus would apply to soil conditions as much as to population growth—if his assumption of population growth near the biological maximum is maintained. Malthus, like any other economic prognosticator, can be only as sound as his factual assumptions. His very narrow view of scarcity in soils, matched by his view of scarcity in resources generally, has not been widely applicable because of technological innovations, the dynamic character of the renewable resources, and a greater number of market dimensions than he had foreseen. But when events produce physical conditions like those he predicated— whether it be population growth in Bengal or soil destruction in Bechuanaland—the dark view of Malthus acquires a real pertinency.

THE ECONOMICS OF MAINTAINING
RENEWABLE RESOURCE VALUES

Because in conservation man must work with nature, the task of keeping up a renewable resource like soil is much more complex than maintaining a man-made structure. Natural and human creation are not analogous. Any structure made by man, though it may acquire a patina of age, will deteriorate in time. All man's efforts at maintenance can do no more than delay the process of decay. When man forces a soil to produce more than its constituents were naturally designed to do, the soil acquires an artificiality, which is subject to deterioration and requires careful maintenance. Insofar as it is a soil whose inherent constituents make high productivity possible, the soil has a renewing capacity which gives conservation measures a dimension beyond that of mere maintenance.

Renewable resources have been classified economically in terms of the speed with which each category can be renewed. Each of these classifications has a liquidation value. But, considered socially over the longer course of time, such a liquidation value is lower than the embraced value. Unless institutions prevent or discourage conservation of renewable resources, the owner of a renewable resource is wiser to forgo the immediate cash return of liquidation and to allocate the renewing use over time as productively as possible.

Institutions which permit renewable resources to be effectively controlled by someone with a low equity encourage liquidation of their conservable elements, no matter what these flow resources may be. When individuals are permitted to engross such values, to convert the long-term worth of these entities into a present cash value, to dissipate or depart with the cash, to leave the gutted remnants to the concern of government or society at large, and to share no part in the costs such actions entail upon the general economy, the result means an anarchic organization of economic values.

The present value of any renewable resource falls well below future liquidation values, and as liquidation approaches, the value of the remaining resource increases. Incipient exhaustion in some resources might divert economic attention and lower the market value of the remnant. The renewable resources, however, are so crucial to man that any regional depletion immediately raises the value of the unliquidated supply. Because of this, a present liquidation hurts the distant more than the near future, and an expenditure for conservation yields benefits which extend far into the future.

Some resource destruction may be necessary to create a future value on the basis of which it will be economic to initiate conservation efforts. Forest products, for instance, are increasingly scarce and more valuable because demand exceeds supply. At this point, therefore, it would appear wise to encourage programs of reforestation, to bring the cutting of trees into balance with their replacement by regrowth, and to create tree plantations with regrowth and cutting cycles running from twenty to one hundred years, depending upon the species planted.

This present need for reforestation should not suggest that the vast cutting and burning programs in North America during the eighteenth and nineteenth centuries were entirely uneconomic. Because hardwood trees prefer the better soils, their clearance was necessary in order to make agricultural settlement possible. Their use for lumber, and the prodigal cutting of the even more abundant poplar and pine, made possible cheap and rapid city development within the newly settled areas. Through clearing growth and draining fields, human settlement helped eradicate the malarial fevers which had become endemic to so much of North America. All of this, coupled with the industrial revolution, created the late twentieth-century economy within which the trees left standing held a value far beyond anything which trees had possessed in the previous century.

The same economic patterns hold true for soil, even though scientific methods of use have so greatly increased production from it. While there are murmurs concerning the toxic or biologic effect of many chemicals, the need for ever larger supplies of food acts to quiet these fears. If cattle were not thriving and growing fat on supplements of hormone, current demands would require a growth of one-third of a million head per year in addition at current demands. The sharp limitations that the federal government has put upon use of this hormone (diethylstilbestrol) indicate that it involves risk. Still, it, like other chemicals, must be used to enlarge food production in a world of accelerating population. Though farming has been mechanized, its basic structure has changed little since neolithic times. This failure has helped drive up the market value of soil and increased the environmental pollution through the necessary use of biocides and fertilizers.

Both soil and land value could be on the brink of another decline if world agriculture should depart completely from man's traditional agricultural practices and substitute the synthesizing of food. Already synthetic substances are being used for animal feed in the United States. Coal, wood, natural gas, and petroleum—the latter two being preferred—can be used as sources of amino acids for protein supplements. Special cultures of micro-organisms growing on controlled substrata can biosynthesize millions of pounds of food at low prices. Nitrogen can be drawn from the air and hydrogen from the water. In short, the synthesizing of food can almost entirely replace the animals, plants, and soil upon which man has previously relied so much.

If such a conversion should prove feasible, famine would have no physical basis. Malthusian fears would not become relevant until world populations had passed fifty billion. Engineering problems and public prejudice against so profound a threat to present vested interests may delay these changes. However, the triple pressures of technical advancement, advancing food costs, and population growth are not likely to be stopped by such brittle fabrications as the private value of land, though the public treasury may still be asked to underwrite that value if it is lost in a synthetic food revolution.

Synthetic production of food might already be a reality if agriculture had not been so successful at increasing enormously the yields from conventional food sources. This does not mean that the synthesizing of food will not eventually replace agriculture, or so alter it that the economic effect on resource values will be the same as if agriculture *had* been supplanted. Once the world converts from agriculture to biosynthetics and synthetics directly derived from minerals, everything that has been said about the economic value of conserving soils for their direct worth will become suspect. Just as game may become entertainment in a social forest in the future, or hardwood trees rarities in arboretums, so soils may become important only for the raising of the traditional foods as "luxury" items. An Idaho potato may someday be the truffle of synthetic cuisine.

SCIENCE AND THE ECONOMICS OF THE LIVING ENVIRONMENT

The synthesizing of food would simply compound the artificiality of the human environment and reinforce the attitude that nature is something to be entirely controlled by man. The prospect of such a change can only discourage use of conservation techniques on soil. These, after all, would represent a present expenditure or sacrifice made *without* hope of future benefit. If technology should make soil, animals, and vegetation obsolete as sources of substantial cash income, the public attitude will obviously put them right back in the category of free goods, unless some other argument can be made for their protection as integral parts of the living environment. In any event, the argument that sees them as mere luxuries will be very appealing.

Traditionally, the renewable resources have been regarded as free goods anyway. Economics and science have often encouraged that viewpoint. *Laissez-faire* economics in the nineteenth century taught that market demand for timber would provide by invisible laws the incentive to plant trees. This, of course, was not true.

Perhaps technology can by synthesis render the renewable resources superfluous and prove thereby to be more soundly predictive than *laissez-faire* economics. But it is dangerous to depend upon such a development, and whatever may be true for soil, animals, and vegetation will not be equally true of air and water.

Certain of the renewable resources must retain their economic and physical utilities into a very distant future, despite technical revolutions. Artificially produced air and water may be technically feasible today for use by astronauts. But, barring some catastrophic polluting event that simultaneously would leave a wealthy and highly technical civilization surviving, the artificial substitutes for naturally fresh air and potable water will remain highly uneconomic on any comparative scale. Also, though man may cut all agricultural ties that have bound him to the soil for four hundred generations, that time has not yet come. The internal, conserving economics relative to soil and vegetation cover hold firm.

Even more important: there is reason to believe that artificial controls are not economically, physically, or biologically wise. Assuming that the biologists who consider the world a vast interface of life systems, too grand for absolute human governance, are right, soil and vegetation will retain a primary physical and a marginal economic significance that would require a continuing program of conservation measures perhaps as urgent as if there were no prospect of food. Then, technological change will not replace economics but will simply require new adjustments, and the need for conserving renewable resources will probably remain vital.

The saddest result of science and technical change, Utopians to the contrary, would be the news that they could make the renewable resources the truly free goods which man always has wanted nature to provide. Technical changes could give man a dominion in which many of the renewable resources were economically superfluous. Such resources would be committed to destruction until perhaps irreparable physical harm had been committed upon the whole life cycle. Partial control over some of these resources may be in effect, but further regulation is not yet possible.

Until man controls nature totally, the economic decision in resource use must be considered the most effective. Though for brief periods their values may have been quite marginal in certain economies, renewable resources have never been free. On a planet for which a population of from thirty to fifty billion is predicted within six generations, and for which an urban industrial revolution on the Euro-American model is also prophesied, there can be no change in this fact. Not even the most arcane technology can make the supply of air, soil, water, game, grass, and trees truly free.

7

Calculating resource sufficiency

EARLY ECONOMIC VIEWS OF RESOURCE SUFFICIENCY

Although many principles in Thomas Malthus' and David Ricardo's work have been rejected, one of their opinions has been tacitly accepted until recently. In that view, as demand increased, the supply would grow correspondingly scarce. Malthus' position was quite rigid, assuming a monolithic supply that would be uniformly depleted. More experienced in commerce, Ricardo assumed that supply was composed of resource levels of steadily poorer quality to which demand would turn in succession from best to worst. But both of them had no doubt that in such a process prices must steadily rise and exhaustion loom. (Ricardo believed, however, that the supply would last into some distant future.) But both theories fail to recognize that technological innovation might so alter relationships that resource values would decline relatively rather than increase.

At the time Malthus and Ricardo wrote, the industrial revolution was functioning with many of the old tools and concepts. Henry Carey had asserted that the poorest quality resources were being employed first. Ricardo, however, realized that economically, under then current conditions, the best level of resources was being exploited because it was easy to reach and use. Once that level was exhausted, the search for more distant and difficult sources would be costly and seemed to justify Ricardo's quiet pessimism. His was good advice for the early nineteenth-century investor in mining properties. But events thereafter took a sharply different turn, and the overall pattern in the Western world has been a steadily falling cost in units of mineral extraction since about 1870. The rising demand has been present, except during brief depression periods, but technology has forestalled the rising costs which the early nineteenth century assumed would be the unavoidable consequences of the market's growing needs.

The average real cost of output has kept up a steady decline, with only temporary remissions, since 1890. Automation in industry can only act to strengthen that downward trend. In both agriculture and mining (though less so in the former), labor costs and capital per unit of output have both declined. In relation to other costs in the economy, food, clothing, shelter, and artifacts are cheaper than they were in the second quarter of the nineteenth century. Technical innovations and the availability of credit, along with a wider layer of affluence in the society, have made possible a choice of food, clothing, shelter, and artifacts at popular prices not previously considered possible.

The fact that the Vanderbilt family could not duplicate Biltmore or The Breakers today at any price has obscured the general real fall of costs. What was a comfortable American working class home in the Midwest of 1865 would seem to be, a century later, impoverished shelter. Without laboring the point or lauding contemporary economic practices that may be deficient in other respects, it is evident that Malthus and Ricardo have been made false prophets on this point by changes in technology, credit institutions, and the general economy which they could not have foreseen.

CHARACTER OF VALUE IN THE RENEWABLE RESOURCES

Technological development has caused some twentieth-century observers to insist on a return to Malthus' view of resources as essentially monolithic, subject to uniform rules relating to real costs. These economists see the renewable resources as no different from either stock resources or any economic entity entering the marketplace. It is argued that, since New York City has no difficulty organizing its supply of food through the invisible hand of the market, the city's water supply could be handled just as easily if the market were permitted to operate. Considering how complex a planner would find supplying the range of food, clothing, shelter, and artifacts to New York City which the market almost absent-mindedly provides, problems of environmental pollution and the conservation of natural resources would not seem to be any more challenging to a market operation.

If all resources were subject to uniform cost factors, this claim might constitute the case. But a historical study seems to indicate that the renewable resources, like water, wildlife, trees, or air, have rising values in terms of costs. For these renewable resources, the predictions of Malthus and Ricardo about rising costs seem in process of being borne out.

Statistical evidence on renewable resources is much harder to find than data for other aspects of the economy. The limited evidence indicates, however, that increasing relative prices characterize forestry, fishing, and water resources. In areas as diverse as the Alaskan salmon fisheries and public grazing lands, the costs of the resource and its relative price have risen, unless a deliberate government policy has kept open an unrestricted access or depressed the price so as to subsidize the industry.[1]

The occupation of the good sites for hydroelectric power is driving up the cost of electricity from this source. Quite apart from the disastrous effect the proposed Rampart Dam in Alaska is expected to have on migrating bird life, spawning fish, or game populations, and the fact that local foreseeable economic conditions indicate that the electric power will have a "dubious saleability," the most striking criticism of the project is that Alaskan coal and natural gas interests could probably supply the same amount of electricity for less than the "conservative" estimate of the Rampart Dam's cost, which is $1.5 billion. Since 1953, the vaunted Tennessee Valley Authority has been compelled more and more to turn from water to coal as the source for its power, with the result that cheap public electricity is bought through ruthless strip- and auger-mining of coal and the destruction of highlands, the siltation of streams, and the deterioration of other regions. Some claim that the Rampart Dam would be as much an enemy for much of Alaska as the TVA has been to the Cumberlands.

Soil could be kept in a highly productive state through organic agriculture and biological pest control, but this would require a labor cost that makes chemical fertilizers and biocides cheaper. In fact, if the change from agriculture to synthesizing for food production is made, it will be due in part to the rising cost of soil and soil utilization which, as compared with food produced, has proven most keen in those areas resistant to changes in agricultural practice such as have taken place in Western Europe and North America. But even in these areas the cost of soil maintenance is rising.

In the renewable resources of trees, fish, water, and soil, evidence indicates that rising demand has produced rising relative costs and prices, contrary to what has been true of the general real output. Technical innovation may reverse this exception, bringing it into line with the other economic developments which have refuted Malthus and Ricardo; but until this conformity occurs, to treat renewable resources in the same manner as other economic elements is a serious miscalculation.

EXAMPLE OF AIR AS AN ECONOMIC VALUE

What has proved true for other renewable resources, the accumulating evidence shows, is also true for air. Air pollution has been an intermittent problem for several hundred years. In 1635, William Harvey, who discovered the circulation of the blood, declared that sudden removal of an aged person from his customary clear country air to the smoke-polluted air of London could prove fatal. In 1661, John Evelyn noted what has since been commonly observed, that broncho-respiratory infections are more common and more severe in polluted than in unpolluted air. Since the seventeenth century, scholars, novelists, and poets have continuously commented on the grimy, unhealthful character of polluted air, with its unaesthetic, apparently unhealthful oppressiveness. The first rail commuter services began functioning in the United States in the 1850's, and the automobile made mass flight from the city possible for the millions who desired the facsimile of that elite suburban living which had been enjoyed by only a few hundred thousand persons in earlier years.[2] Unfortunately, the automobile, with its use of the gasoline-combustion engine, has served not only as a vehicle for escape and freedom but also as the new primary source of air pollution.

The old soot- and solid-particle pollution of the "black city" of the nineteenth century was tightly confined. The newer pollution of burnt hydrocarbons is far more diffuse and affects whole regions rather than a few municipal districts. In the later twentieth century, it has been a sometimes invisible, usually odorless pall that has settled on areas as extensive as the shores of San Francisco Bay and the Los Angeles metropolitan complex. Indeed, some biologists are more apprehensive about the chemical elements in the air which human senses cannot perceive than about the overtly obnoxious ones.

At the moment, it is difficult to know the precise scope of the menace. Careful studies of persons habitually inhaling aromatic and halogenated hydrocarbons, ketones, esters, alcohols, and glycol have failed to show irreversible damage. The potential toxic effect is high, but little physiological damage has been noted, and even that condition has cleared up when the user has been compelled to cease his inhalations. The commonest method for these experiments is to put the aromatic substance and the user's head in a plastic bag, which is removed when the user reaches euphoria, unless asphyxiation intervenes. Obviously, this is an intense exposure, and, since users become tolerant, steadily heavier and more frequent exposures are required. Although these exposures are more severe than any that would occur in even a Donora-type inversion, the harm to the user rarely exceeds a general condition of mild malaise which quickly disappears once the inhalations are stopped. For persons compelled to breathe the exhaust fumes and hydrocarbon smog of large cities, this is rather encouraging, unless one remembers that the "common mild reversible symptoms of malaise" among these habitual inhalers include muscular incoordination, amnesia, depression, hallucinations, weight loss, low blood pressure, digestive disturbance, membrane irritation, renal difficulties, and edema.[3]

Yet, statistically, the higher the rate of air pollution—other factors being as near equal as possible—the poorer the degree of pulmonary function. Though man has been using tobacco for several hundred years, deaths from lung cancer and emphysema have taken a pronounced upward spurt only recently. Granted that diagnosis has improved and that many previous deaths from these diseases may not have ben identified, the interesting point is that the increase in deaths from emphysema seems to concentrate itself in areas of greatest air pollution. In the United States, the death rate for emphysema has gone from 8 per million in 1950 to 67 per million in 1962, and it grows steadily higher. Although the evidence is all statistical rather than clinical, it appears that fewer pulmonary, broncho-respiratory, circulatory, and even digestive disorders occur among persons who, up to age thirty, live in regions with pure air than among those who do not, and that the rate of mortality and incidence of illness rises sharply after a Donora-type inversion. Clearly, with only statistical evidence, other explanations could exist. Still, the figures indicate that air pollution is probably debilitating to a pronounced degree, and that if chronic exposure persists, even though the pollution grows no worse, evidence of damage will begin to accumulate in large quantities.[4]

Estimates of harm done by air pollution to property are just as unclear and uncertain. Vegetative damage by photo-chemical smog, ozone, sulphur dioxides, fluorides, and ethylene has been observed in over half the states. In 1965, it was said that air pollution damage to property in the United States exceeded $7.5 billion, although no one knows how this figure was reached.

Some observers would measure air damage to property by the book values of investments in facilities and the accounting costs of resources used to control pollution. Others would judge it by the damage that air effluent discharges cause to vegetation and structures, so that crop losses, building repairs, and the great investment needed simply to do business under conditions of air pollution become the measures of its cost. Still others speak of the harm which one sector of the economy does to another through air pollution as being the excess of the cost of the resources needed to eliminate the damage. Each system of cost analysis is related to the others, but the resultant figures would differ considerably. Beyond this, however, all the systems of cost analysis here depend upon facts that are presently either non-existent or extremely difficult to gather. The precise extent to which corrosion from air pollution reduces the life expectancy of a structure is nearly impossible to calculate.

Yet it seems certain that air damage to property is extensive, even if lower residential property values in center city areas are excluded because so many other factors are at work. Pollution is a real source of trouble and expense to users who depend upon a supply of pure air for their businesses. Although in the past contaminated air seemed to be an aesthetic problem of concern only to sensitive souls like D. H. Lawrence, the incursion of burnt hydrocarbons and other chemicals into the atmosphere since about 1920 has created an aggravating problem of insults to human, animal, and plant organisms and injury to structures that threatens to become economically intolerable. It was one thing when air pollution simply turned Notre Dame de Paris black, but when it caused the stone to slough off, the matter was rather different. After 1960, the aesthetic nuisance had become an economic hardship.

The Italian League Against Air Pollution and Noise was told at its 1965 Siena convention that increasing use of petroleum for heating was causing an upsurge in air pollution which would not soon be halted. Changing economic conditions had produced huge blocks of heated apartments in the suburbs of burgeoning cities in northern and central Italy, and the oil they used was high in sulphur content. Switching to a different fuel, or changing to oil with a lower sulphur content, or desulphurizing the oil used have all been rejected as economic possibilities to reduce air deterioration. An international symposium on air pollution at Venice in 1965 was warned that there existed "a precise relationship between air pollution and lung cancer." But even with that threat before them, the Italian experts agreed that they could do little beyond agreeing upon the risks and costs of air pollution from burnt hydrocarbons. Their conclusions, in the presence of the economic pressures and dislocations that would ensue from an effective prohibitory program aimed at hydrocarbon burning, were no more certain than those reached elsewhere in the world.[5]

No place in the world has done more to control air pollution than Los Angeles: the use of coal as a fuel has been forbidden; open burning of refuse and leaves has been prohibited; industrial effluent discharge has been brought to low individual plant levels; more auto exhaust controls have been instituted than anywhere else in the world; and probably the most sophisticated air pollution control administration in the world has been set up. Yet Los Angeles still has one of the most severe air problems of any major city in the world—possibly surpassed in seriousness only by London and Tokyo-Yokohama. With its first daylight dimout as early as September 1943, Los Angeles can take comfort only from the assumption that conditions would be incalculably worse if the steps taken between 1955 and 1965 had not been made. The Los Angeles experience has not been very encouraging to air control experts, some of whom argue that, because it and similar programs are based upon unsound economic premises, failure is almost inevitable.

ECONOMICS IN THE CONTROL OF AIR POLLUTION

Beginning with the thirteenth-century English legislation forbidding the burning of sea-coal within London, air control programs have all been predicated upon the idea that air pollution is unnatural and that every man has a right to pure air. Very little direct thought has been given to the beneficial aspects of air pollution. Thoreau might confess to enjoying the odor of smoke from a passing train, but few artists have had a good word to say about smoke-laden air, aside from some who have glossed over the problem by praising "progress" and the possibility of some future utopia.

Business, of course, has treated air as it has always treated water: air was something freely given by nature to be used as the economic interests of the moment indicated. Air and water might be used to drive, to clean, to cool, or to receive as sewers, and all such uses were regarded as beneficial. They ceased to be so only when someone else's use of air or water interfered with their driving, cleansing, cooling, or sewering properties. At that point benefits became costs; and the state was asked to intervene in order to make punishable and prohibit activities that had become harmful. A single plant emitting black, noisome, irritating smoke over an isolated area is rarely bothered by control regulations. It is the concentration of effluent dischargers in one area that causes legal intervention, even though individually they may be petty polluters compared to the undisturbed isolated plant.

Air has been called an open access resource, comparable to open range with unrestricted grazing, high seas fisheries without treaty limitations, or public parks without access control. Various restrictions on these other sources have evolved over the years, but air has been offered little protection.

Air is a resource that should be considered not as something wild but as a part of what Jeremy Bentham called his Ministry of Domain. Air belongs within the public tenure, as do public parks or the grazing lands of the American West. An invasion or seizure of air is as much a trespass as crossing the White House rose garden, uninvited, while the President is holding a press conference.

In a sense, non-polluters who draw in air for economic advantage can be said to have pre-empted part of the public domain from those who wish to use it for waste disposal. Economists measure costs and benefits by exchange value, which is their way of communicating and mediating differences between rivals. Quantitative judgments as to whether improvement of air quality is worth a certain cost at a particular time and place can be made under this method.

Physical quality itself is not what most concerns the economist, and data drawn from the physical condition of the environment are not the bases of his calculations. Economic science is concerned with the operation of the market and the allocation of costs and benefits within market terms. The health of humans, the well-being of animals and plants, and the purity of the environment are all aesthetic externalities unless they are reflected in the market. The accelerating demands of modern industry increasingly provide that reflection, however, and the function of the economist is to see that all benefits are jointly maximized so that the losers from the process may be reimbursed by the winners.

This concern over compensating losers is not due to a rejection of Adam Smith but to the fact that, without it, whole industries may be regionally extirpated in the way that chemical pollutants have affected the bald eagle and the peregrine falcon. An example of this is the conflict over air uses in Polk and Hillsborough counties, Florida, between the phosphate industry which wishes to emit effluents into the air, and the citrus and livestock industries which need pure supplies of it. These two counties, which produce 75 percent of the phosphate rock in the United States, have enough, at the present rate of withdrawal, to last for three hundred years. They also produce citrus crops almost equal in volume to the total citrus output of California, Texas, and Arizona. Since 1941, a major cattle industry has also developed to supply the southeastern United States with much of its beef.

The phosphate and citrus industries co-existed comfortably for sixty years, but by the 1950's there was clearly a scarcity of pure air in the two counties. The sudden difficulty was due to the phosphate industry's switching, after 1945, from the production of superphosphate to triple superphosphate because of the demand for a stronger fertilizer. Increases in railway bulk freight charges also compelled the industry to treat the phosphate rock at the mine site. The new treatment process in its drying stage released to the air, in gaseous form, the 3 to 5 percent fluorine by weight which is in the Florida phosphates.

After 1950, the cattle in the area began suffering from fluorosis, and the citrus trees showed a chlorotic condition attributable to gaseous fluorides. Since cattle get fluorine toxicosis from grazing, their response would be greater than that of an animal merely breathing the air, in which toxic content is less concentrated. Citrus plants, ordinarily, are only moderately susceptible to fluoride damage. In these counties during the winter, however, the temperature inversions which occur two nights out of three reduce the air's cleansing capacity. Winter is also the peak production period for triple superphosphate, since 70 percent of the sales are made between January and May, for spring application.

If left unrestrained, the phosphate industry clearly would have produced a gradual reduction in and perhaps even extirpation of two other economically important industries. Obviously, it was not possible to close out the phosphate industry. Florida authorities, by creating the Polk-Hillsborough Air Pollution Control District, have tried to strike a balance. At a cost of $16 million to the phosphate industry between 1959 and 1965, fluoride emissions were cut from 33,000 pounds per day in the winter of 1961–1962 to 13,000 pounds per day in the winter of 1963–1964.[6]

The cost of this control to the phosphate industry has actually been higher than this cost would indicate, since the program has necessitated the building of more modern plants, one of them costing $20 million. And, although the situation is improved, even more stringent measures must still be taken which will require still larger expenditures. In the face of this, one large corporation closed its phosphate subsidiary on the ground that changes in treatment were "not economically possible." [7] The perfect compromise among the area's industries had not been reached by the mid-1960's.

The problem of air pollution—and of water pollution, too—lies in the failure of the market to allocate the resource among those using it. Where the costs and benefits of emissions have been completely separated, one of the two situations results: either offsite parties must bear all the costs while the emitter enjoys the benefit, or pollution control compels the emitter to bear all the costs of purifying the discharge while the user of pure air enjoys all the benefits. It is argued that there is no justice in making the emitter bear all purification costs.

After all, the very triple superphosphate whose refining in Polk-Hillsborough counties has caused such damage to local farming operations was, in its finished condition, probably needed by the same farmers as fertilizer. Some experts therefore believe that the permit system is unfair to phosphate refiners. It gives existing treatment plants one year in which to cut daily fluoride emissions to six-tenths of a pound for each ton of plant capacity. Any new plants can emit only about half that amount of fluoride. Failure to comply can mean a shut-down until abatement equipment is built to meet this physical standard of value. This seems harsh to those who believe the approach is discriminatory.

Air has two capacities: it supports life and it can act as a vehicle for waste disposal. Ideally, there should be enough relatively pure air to sustain growth and enough other air to absorb undisposable wastes. Any institutional organization which thrusts the burden entirely upon either the receiver or the emitter should be considered economically unsuitable. Persons with this economic point of view want to allocate the air's two capacities so that the life-and-property-supporting dimension would be exchanged against the waste-disposal dimension until the benefits and costs to emitters of waste and receivers of purified air might be brought into an economic balance.[8] In Polk-Hillsborough, this would mean that both the phosphate industry, on the one hand, and the citrus and cattle industries, on the other, would have to pay charges to the air pollution control district.

In one sense, government has tried to meet this issue for any of the renewable resources through taxes, subsidies, competitive bidding for resource acquisitions, licenses which are transferable in the manner of titles, and zoning. Each of these is meant to spread the burden of waste emission. Water rates and sewer service charges which include payment for treatment costs; special assessments to build sewer mains so as to prevent septic tank overflow into water supply tables; maintenance of pollution control agencies out of the general tax fund—these are all common devices presently employed to ensure an equable sharing of cost and benefit in the use of those renewable resources which have so commonly been regarded as free goods.

Institutional devices have yet to succeed in defining air rights or in dividing responsibilities for a jointly used, presently indivisible resource. Air has no cash value in itself, but when economic activity begins to add to air content or draw upon it, air-related industries can calculate its precise value to them through their production and earnings. To individuals, air may appear to be a free good, but in a situation of intense use of air by industry and agriculture, it becomes extremely scarce in economic terms.

Government can help through tax policies, zoning, and what the economists call "royalties." Pollution control equipment, and even all combustion equipment that meets certain standards, can be exempted from taxation. Otherwise, taxation acts as a penalty upon those making improvements. Fast tax write-offs, when permitted, act more or less as subsidies. Any subsidy should be direct, explicit, and specific. It is difficult to adjust subsidies to the differing needs of various airsheds.

It would perhaps be even better to measure the tax rates so that the lowest fall upon the least noxious fuels. The cheaper fuels and highly sulphurous oils should be most highly taxed of all until the price differential is greatly reduced or even eradicated. The same sort of relation exists between taxation and the base price of whiskey and tobacco, except that natural gas and refined oils offer a better alternative than anything which exists for alcohol and tobacco. For this reason, air conservation would call for low or no taxes on cleaner fuels, at least until competitive pricing with the aid of tax policy had driven the dirtier fuels off the market. Needless to say, this assumes a sufficiently affluent society which can absorb the cost of the cleaner fuel and not resort to political resistance or offer the ultimate economic barrier of withdrawal from the market for fuel of any kind.[9]

LEGAL RESTRAINTS IN THE CONTROL OF AIR POLLUTION

Economists themselves are a little dubious that tax policy can carry the brunt of air conservation. Generally they prefer what they call royalties, although they would not substitute these for all regulation, and they might even agree that requirements of physical quality might compel the total banning of some sources of pollution. This, as a last resort, would be used sparingly. In an attempt during the winter of 1965–1966 to eliminate noise, solve certain traffic problems, and prevent further harm to the fabric of ancient buildings by auto exhaust emissions, Rome simply banned the auto from parts of the city. Noble as the purpose might have been, the order had to be rescinded under massive public pressure.

Economists will admit that royalties, with their reliance upon a system of costs and prices, may not always offer true indices. But the easier alternatives often offer no more hope of ultimate success. The royalty scheme, at its ideal best, calls for a full metering of all benefits received and costs assessed, with the charges being collected from the beneficiaries so as to provide compensation for those hurt. Because full metering is rarely possible, an alternative is to sell a license to the polluter, the price being determined by his ability to pollute the air. Some physical calculations would have to be made to determine how many licensed polluters the atmosphere could bear. There would have to be some scheme encouraging competitive bidding for the licenses, or the first licensees would acquire pre-emptive rights to the whole airshed. But even though the system would have to be flexible to respond to changed conditions, it would also require some strict qualifications, or the licenses would become either political prizes or privileges too flimsy to support much investment.

This system would require a government-operated measurement and monitoring service, probably financed out of the license fees. This system would lead to a steadily more complete metering of available air and regulation of the purposes to which it was being put. Various classes of licenses might also be issued, ranging from those allowing pollution under any conditions except a smog crisis to those giving more restricted permission. Licenses might also be issued on the basis of the hours of the day or seasons of the year during which emitters would be putting waste into the air. Wind directions, the frequency of inversions, or the expected response in the air to certain emissions could all serve as bases for different kinds of licenses.

Unfortunately, until all emissions can be measured, any licensing system would have to depend upon a substitute for measurement— and that means guessing at the atmosphere's capacity and what reactions would probably occur when the emitted chemicals came together. Then, too, if the price for the license were set properly high, and if the bidding were kept properly competitive, and if the license were not allowed to become a preemptive, freely-alienable property right, and if the greater knowledge of air conditions that must accumulate meant ultimate changes in the license, then licensees would be under every economic inducement to use their licenses to their fullest extent.

Even proponents of licensing and royalties are certain this will not produce optimal air conditions—at least until the knowledge of the air pollution control authorities equals the competence of the emitters. In the interval, reliance on licenses alone, or even upon licenses primarily, could produce an even more profound deterioration in the atmosphere of those airsheds which serve most of the population.

In this early period, licensing might be combined with zoning. Today, as in ancient Sybaris, the best location for noisome industry is downwind from the greatest concentrations of population. Downwind land zones, if available, could be provided in every airshed. In lieu of such zones, outlying locations might be used. A more practical alternative would be a belt of industry built around the city, so that the level of pollution in the skies over the city itself could be kept even and—presumably—low.

Power sources might be removed completely from urban areas. Instead of bringing the coal or slurry to the power plant, the power plant could be set up in the coal fields, most of which are remote from population centers. Tax rebates, or low assessed valuations, or similar tax advantages, could be made available to encourage these removed locations of power sources, on the basis that any loss suffered in tax income would be offset by the rise in valuation of properties freed of smoke pollution. This would mean an even heavier reliance upon the national power grid, with the concomitant risk of massive power failure. But air conservation in any single region is furthered by the removal of pollution sources rather than by scattering the sources throughout a region and thereby merely diluting the pollution.

The tighter the confines of one urban area, the easier it is to cope with impurities in the air. Zoning techniques therefore ought not to operate as further inducements to urban sprawl. It would probably be wise socially to impose heavy taxes upon vacant, low-priced land located in close-in, underused districts. This would encourage the maximal use of such ground by waste-emitting industry and prevent it from oozing out over the countryside. Yet, once again, the tax policy would have to be buttressed by a tight zoning program that shut industry into these special enclaves and did not permit waste emitters any escape into the open countryside.

From an economic point of view, it would also be wise not to exempt established industry from newly adopted standards. Favored treatment of this kind discourages the location of new industry, puts any newly located industry at a competitive disadvantage with the exempted old, and provides no incentive for the exempted industry to improve itself. "Grandfather" clauses in any proposed air purity code encourage a history of air mistreatment. Similarly, a prospective nonconforming user of land will grab whatever he can before a new zoning code can go into effect and ban such uses in the area. Once the air purity code is adopted, persons benefiting from "grandfather" clauses have every economic incentive to keep and exploit them as long as possible. Economic practice should be something the very opposite of "grandfather" clauses. If the older practices or outmoded equipment cannot be outlawed, penalizing taxes should be levied in order to provide external encouragement to change.

The problem, of course, is not purely economic. Emitters who have established strong economic positions as they polluted the air usually feel that they have also built up pre-emptive rights which ought not to be taken from them. Legally, air pollution, like water pollution, cannot become a vested interest protected by the due process provisions of the federal and state constitutions. Pollution has been subject to the police power of the sovereign, and efforts in the United States to regulate nuisances to air and water can be traced at least as far back as the town ordinances in the seventeenth-century colonies along the Atlantic seaboard. The barrier to reaching established air polluters is not a legal or constitutional one. It is rather the sense of injury, usually held with moral fervor, however much unjustified, that gives urgency to political opposition to any retroactive effect which proposed air purity codes might have.

ROLE OF SPECIFICITY IN CONTROLLING RENEWABLE RESOURCES

Many economists believe that renewable resources are hard to control because property rights are not well defined. Instead, there is recourse to legally fixed standards which are arbitrarily imposed by institutions operating outside the economic processes. As the sole solution to any problem, legally imposed standards must fail. Gordon Fair has charged that ". . . standards are for the lazy person, and this is the only justification for them because we have so many lazy people in the world. Ordinarily, we don't need standards; we use a rational approach to each individual problem and this is the *ideal* in the long run, rather than trying to evolve a very complicated set of rules and regulations that govern every possible situation." [10] What bothers many economists is that the standards, designed for flexibility, are uncertain. Institutional regulation is also characterized by a general arbitrariness and by its reliance upon administrative fiat.

The resource economists, who are extremely critical of physical quality standards, prohibitions enforced through the criminal law, and administrative regulations backed up by state power, are trying to make all resource uses specific. This means that "all services and costs accrue to and may be marketed by a particular individual or firm" which is using the resource for economic advantage. Specific use is a means of preventing what economists call "external diseconomies" or "spill-over effects," which are the results of treating certain objects as "free goods" to be worked into the market process without cost to the one profiting by their use.[11] What has to be done is to create constraints that will make each business concerned with using renewable resources act as if it were a monopoly whose profits had to absorb any harm to the location in which it was operating.

For example, if one thinks only of the damage produced by air pollution, he is underestimating the value of air as a waste-disposal facility. In dollar terms, as opposed to general environmental harm, the costs of treating pollutants equal the present value of any expected returns which users of pure air must forgo because of the pollution. Savings in costs to the polluter equal the present net returns coming from the increased economic utility of their capital facilities and the present values of any increased expenditures which will not have to be made. It is "the present values of expected net returns accruing to or forgone by emitters and receptors" during the lives of their capital facilities which represent the true worth of the emission of waste into the atmosphere. The problem is to relate emitters and receptors of aerial pollutants to each other and, by an air pollution control program, to internalize what had been externalities.[12]

This situation occurs under our present legal system, but in a very uneconomic way. In Polk-Hillsborough counties, Florida, shrewd speculators have deliberately bought land that was highly polluted by fluoride dust, and have actually planted citrus trees, which promptly responded by showing heavy damage. In these counties, "phosphate" land sold for $1,500 to $2,000 per acre at 1965 prices, while high-quality citrus land sold for $4,000. But the speculators, by threatening to initiate well-conducted law suits, produced settlements from the fearful phosphate companies that brought prices of $8,000 to $15,000 per acre for the damaged land. Plainly, these were cases of the receptors turning diseconomies against the emitters who had created them.

So common has this type of pressure become that many emitters in rural areas are buying square miles around their plants and then blithely dumping waste into the air above their own land. The land is often leased to farmers, with covenants protecting the lessor from poor crops which may be garnered by the lessee. It is truly misleading to say that air is a free good, as far as the emitter is concerned, when the emitter must often pay large sums to persons harmed by wastes or, if this liability is to be avoided, must either install expensive waste-control equipment or else buy up and vacate large adjacent tracts.

One proposition that appeals to those who want to internalize what would otherwise continue to be "spill-over effects" comes from Adam Smith: "It seems not unreasonable, that the extraordinary expense, which the protection of any particular branch of commerce may occasion, should be defrayed by a moderate tax upon that particular branch. . . . It should seem equally reasonable to lay a particular tax upon a particular branch of trade in order to defray the extraordinary expense of protecting that branch." [13] This does not mean a revival of the poll tax as a levy to be paid by every human being in his capacity as an air receptor. But in modern economic conditions, with the emission of waste a necessity, the theorists of specificity think it is dysfunctional to the economy and the consequence of outmoded traditions in the social order to put all the costs of air purity on the receptor, or the emitter, or the general taxpayer alone.

The present law of property defines both the space on or in the ground and up into the air to which the landowner can claim title and from which he can exclude trespassers. From Sir Edward Coke in the seventeenth century to Welf Heinrich, Prince of Hanover, the noted twentieth-century authority on property in space, landowners have owned a diminishing cone to hell and then again to heaven. But the rights which may exist in water percolating through soil or in air flowing above the ground have not been settled.

When there were ample supplies of water and air, this deficiency in the law of property scarcely mattered to either the market or the court. But once the supply became short, it seemed time to develop property and tenure concepts that would link users to each other as well as to the resource. Under present rules, emitters may buy ground in order to acquire air for receiving waste, but individual receptors can scarcely buy up the privileges of emitters. Some collective action might organize the receptors within an airshed so that they could buy emission rights. Given the modern pressures for industrial production, even action on such a general level lacks practicability. It would be more profitable to supply rights for the use of the air's waste disposal ability at charges varying with quantity, time, and location and to find some means of recouping from receptors a part of the benefit that comes their way when otherwise polluted air has been purified.

RELATIVE WEIGHING OF QUALITY AND MONETARY CONTROLS

In this process of specifying and internalizing total economic costs incurred in the use of the renewable resources, it is not necessary to speak only in pecuniary terms. The language used in the market merely simplifies the cost-benefit analysis. If market language is available, it becomes fairly simple to specify what variables are not functioning efficiently, to determine what kind and degree of change will be needed to produce a proper functioning, and to evaluate the various means of achieving the necessary modifications.

This quest for specificity underlies the suggestions of Yevsey Liberman and Sun Yeh-fang, the Marxist economists who have risen to prominence since 1960. As the state planning organism previously functioned in Marxist systems, every part of the economy lacked specificity; internalization of costs by particular units was discouraged, with profound resultant spill-over effects; and every element within the economy came close to being the traditional "free" goods of the renewable resources like air and water. Liberman's purpose has been to alter this, so that specification becomes possible. It is highly doubtful that this process is any more a "return to capitalism" within the general economy of the Soviet Union than United States attempts at the institution of specificity in renewable resources mean a "turn to socialism."

Market-related terms or conditions need not be used to attain this specificity. S. V. Ciriacy-Wantrup, whose work in resource economics goes back to the 1920's, has stated that renewable resource conditions can be judged "in terms of the direction of changes, the relative speed of changes, and their sequence in time." It is true that among economists, Ciriacy-Wantrup gives an unusually high importance to "quality requirements of individual uses" as constituting "the most economical approach," and that he has a low opinion of what he has denounced as "narrowly conceived pecuniary costs." As he sees it, the dumping of waste upon the renewable resources of air and water for disposal is not only a "real external diseconomy," which even rigidly market-oriented economists use as a term, but it is scarcely an act to be considered "beneficial" in the eyes of an economist to whom physical quality has been of primary importance.

After all, "real" for him means "those externalities that are not merely income transfers among sectors of the economy through offsetting increases and decreases of values due to price changes." This in turn means that any resource analysis "must focus on the *structure,* the *functioning,* and the *performance*" of the quality of institutional organization of the renewable resources.[14] "Real external diseconomy" becomes something more extensive than the relation between savings to emitters of waste and losses to persons who must utilize the deteriorated resources that result from the discharge.

Theoretically, this would seem to separate the expert who emphasizes physical quality from the economist who is trying to arrive at specificity through internalization of costs and reliance upon the market mechanism. But in practice, when the constraints that both viewpoints regard as necessary are examined, a layman might be excused from finding the differences fewer than he expected.

Advocates of maintaining physical quality in the environment have concluded that there are five major alternatives which would give an economic incentive for reducing demands upon the renewable resources. The first of these would prohibit completely certain production processes, either to eliminate them or to encourage the affected business to develop improved versions. The next alternative would be the requirement for each industry to set up certain administratively determined treatment and disposal facilities to cope with waste. Related to this is a next point, which would impose quality standards upon the treated wastes from industrial processes, leaving business interests to decide what methods can best meet these standards. The fourth alternative would be for a public agency to gather and treat all wastes at the emitters' expense. (The amount of the charges would depend upon studies of the effect which quantity, quality and timing of individual discharges have on costs of collection, treatment, and disposal.)

Concerned as they are with preserving the physical quality of the environment, these four alternatives emphasize public constraints rather than private or local initiatives. The fifth suggestion, which so concerns economists with a different orientation, is more of a salvage operation for private firms than a technique strong in its own right. Incentives would be provided by public support of tax relief, rebates in royalty payments, loans at favorable rates, and direct grants upon condition that recipients engage in pollution abatement.[15]

Even the economists who support this last approach regard quality factors as necessary preliminaries to effective market operations. Four of these quality variables whose adjustment lies behind the effectiveness of monetary market control are: a) the total volume of pollutant emissions; b) the time intervals during which these emissions would be allowed to take place; c) the rate of emissions in any single interval; and d) the timing of the release of initial emissions associated with any particular production program.[16]

Practically speaking, if one uses air quality as an example, these quality requirements necessitate government monitoring and information service that would keep track of the discharge of every emitter and the needs of every receptor within at least key airsheds. It would also require an administrative agency with the power to alter these variables as changing physical conditions might demand. Some facilities would be ordered to reduce their use of air. In other situations, wastes which were causing a deleterious "mix" in the atmosphere would have to be cut off until chemical conditions in the air permitted their release. And, of course, the public agency would possess the power to levy contributions from receptors so that all burdens for air purity would not fall upon the emitters.

In some respects, this is a constraint upon private activities greater than those foreseen by the economists who emphasize physical quality rather than monetary market techniques. In all other respects, the emphasis upon government's role in the latter approach is at least as great. The two positions are similar because the spill-over effect of individual action so overwhelms the public in both an aesthetic and an economic sense that governmentally imposed quality controls must be stepped up. Even economists with the greatest faith in the market's ability to allocate benefits and costs in the use of renewable resources equably think that pollution problems are another matter and tend to qualify the extent of market maneuvers by permitting them only so long as "third parties" are not hurt.

In their relative weighing of physical against monetary controls, economists are restricted in their suggestions: only a limited number of physical methods for pollution control are, or ever can be, applicable to any kind of pollution of the soil, air, or water. As set out by the Committee on Pollution of the National Academy of Resources–National Research Council, these methods are:

1. *Recover and Re-use*—recovery of used air, water, or land for re-use and/or recovery of pollutants themselves for beneficial utilization.

2. *Waste Treatment*—modification of contaminants in a waste or separation of contaminants from a waste, plus disposition of the residues in non-pollutional fashion.

3. *Product Modification*—deliberate introduction of properties into materials which may eventually become environmental contaminants to reduce their pollutional effects or to enhance their controllability.

4. *Process Change*—modification of the process in which a contaminant is used or created such that the contaminant is not released or its release is reduced.

5. *Elimination*—prevention of a contaminant from entering the atmosphere by eliminating its use or generation.

6. *Dispersion*—distribution of a waste discharge over a

larger area of the land or into a larger volume of air or water.

7. *Dilution*—artificial augmentation of the volume of the environment used to assimilate waste.

8. *Detention*—temporary hold-up of the production or the release of discharges for later gradual release or for release at a more advantageous time.

9. *Diversion*—transportation of a waste to another location for discharge.

10. *Environmental Treatment*—treatment of the air, land, or water itself to remove pollutants, to diminish their effects, or to eliminate or inhibit their generation.

11. *Desensitization*—desensitization of pollution receptors.[17]

Whatever is done by public administrators must fit within this listing. And economists, in their search for specificity for the renewable resources, must also accept these physical constraints.

LACK OF AUTONOMY IN USE OF RESOURCES

Within the physical constraints, however, it is possible to relate the users of renewable resources to each other in economic terms so that the quality of soil, water, or air may be preserved or restored out of funds from the proceeds of a resource's use. Few industries only emit waste into the environment and few only draw in pure quantities of a renewable resource. Overwhelmingly, modern industry, including agriculture, is both an emitter of waste and a receptor of the renewable resources which have received the waste. Commonly, both a physical and an economic reciprocity exist between the units in any economic system.

One of the oldest explicit cost internalization schemes for renewable resources was founded on this interrelationship. Usually called the *Ruhrverband,* it is composed of three organizations for controlling the water quality within the Ruhr industrial complex: the *Emsgenossenschaft* (founded in 1899), the *Ruhrverband* (1913), and the *Lippeverband* (1926). Under this plan, emitters of waste and receptors of water alike take a part in bearing the charge of water quality, though it is through their emitting function that even receptors of water are most likely to be affected.

Pollution of the human environment raises important issues concerning either property rights, or the relations between social and private sectors of the economy, or the distinctions between a public and a common good, or the making of decisions without confidence in the basic data, or the setting up of efficient administrative and physical quality systems. But the fundamental thing in each of these choices is that pollution establishes a technical link connecting the economic units—factories, stores, and households—in society.

No one unit is independent of the others, because the waste disposal needs of each affect the range and character of the opportunities of all other co-existing units. It is this imposed unity which is economically so frustrating. Like Yevsey Liberman in Russia and Anthony Scott in Canada, the American economist Allen V. Kneese maintains that ". . . independence of economic units is an essential element in producing the desirable results often attributed to the operation of free markets. Consequently, an essential element of the pollution 'problem' is that the damages of waste disposal . . . are in most instances external to the polluting unit." [18]

Whether or not they participate in the costs of improving those qualities, all individuals in the economy share in the benefits of environmental quality. Consequently, every individual is strongly motivated to avoid bearing any part of those costs. This kind of roulette precludes development of a market for the control of pollution's effects on the general environment. It also explains why the value of renewable resources lying in the common sector of the economy is rarely calculated within the costs of specific economic units.

This generalizing factor has compelled the economists to search for some systematic specifying means of evaluating external effects of production practices. The search has become increasingly urgent because much pollution has subtle effects upon the environment. Since 1940, to be sure, a great deal has been done to undo the effects of man's heedless treatment of nature in the preceding century. The thousands of new persistent chemicals entering the market at the rate of over four hundred every year, however, are contaminating the supply of reasonably pure elements within the environment.

It seems certain that in this area, despite isolated improvements, the past market failures will grow radically more serious with time's passage. Even as the ideas of Lord Keynes, with their emphasis upon the growth of gross national product, have reached a popular peak, there are economists who say that the gross national product "does not and cannot possibly measure everything that is relevant to our feeling of well-being, [since] many of our activities of production, movement, and consumption do . . . inflict unwanted penalties on others." [19] They argue, instead, for publicly imposed limits or constraints that would restrict the cost-minimizing effects of individual economic units. This means they insist that some cost factors be built into the fundament of the gross national product so that it will not continue unchecked in its devouring the human environment for the annual material betterment of the cash-computable economy.

CALCULATING INTANGIBLES IN RESOURCE USE

It is true, as the market economist Jerome Milliman has observed, that "No intangible has infinite value. All intangibles have costs. The least that can be done is to specify and to make very clear to all concerned the cost of obtaining the intangible. . . . Such considerations may reduce the common tendency to consider intangibles as exceptions to economic calculus." [20] Yet the market alone has never solved the problem of intangibles, even in the nineteenth-century atmosphere of *laissez faire*. And it is unlikely that public preoccupation with the growth of the gross national product can accomplish much more than the unconstrained nineteenth-century market mechanism. Indeed, there is some risk that at this point the doctrines of Lord Keynes might persuade government to subsidize individual economic units by providing renewable resources as if they were free goods. For Lord Keynes and for Karl Marx, there is a certain fusing of "public" and "common" goods where the supply of air, water, soil, trees, game, fish, and grazings are concerned. Because they are so uniformly necessary to individual welfare, these resources become something to be freely supplied to the economy by public action.

The work of many general theorists is notably deficient in its understanding of and stress upon the importance of specificity in the management of renewable resources. These theorists have been like Malthus in predicting the imminent exhaustion of resources, or like Marx in arguing that governmental organization of resources in the environment will produce a final resolution. Life cycle resources, unlike "stock" substances such as coal, seem to have risen in cost, as Malthus predicted—but they are nowhere near exhaustion, nor need a world population of even fifty billion people exhaust them. If renewable resources are organized on a public basis—either Marxist or Keynesian—they can be enjoyed more evenly throughout the economy. But both Russia and the United States know that further work must still be done.

Whether under a state or private capitalist system, the need for increasing the gross national product means that free goods will be ruthlessly seized upon by every successfully participating economic unit. Resource quality must inevitably suffer. The worst that could happen in the past was the "stranding" of some region because its resources had been abused. Under present conditions of demand, however, the consequences will not be limited to a few places like Appalachia or the loess hills of western China.[21]

RESOURCE CONTROL THROUGH THE USE-CHARGE DEVICE

The successful operation over three generations of the Ruhrverband has demonstrated to resource economists that the uniform demands of pollution can be specified. Otherwise, the possibilities might have seemed merely academic.

Where life-cycle resources are concerned, the making of decisions rests upon a single fundament. This is so remote from the cost-analysis of the individual decision-maker that the decisions, whether of capitalist corporations or of giant socialist trusts, appear to be highly decentralized. (The giving and receiving functions of the environment are of course external to the decisions which are made.) At the same time, governments throughout the world are investing more and more of their general tax monies in renewable resources. Some economists, however, seriously doubt that these investments operate any more efficiently than the neolithic efforts on behalf of giant water systems along the Nile or in the Plain of Shinar.

All contemporary economic systems seem to be predicated, either immediately or ultimately, upon the allocation of resources in such a way that individual wants will be satisfied to the maximum extent. Welfare economics seems to be the goal of late twentieth-century state planning. In some systems, of course, the "ultimate" participation of individuals in income distribution and the fruits of technological capability seems uncomfortably remote. In any event, the fulfillment of these goals can be prevented, or their balance subsequently upset by the spill-over or spattered effects of resource use. To avoid these, it is necessary to devise some sort of a system under which costs and benefits to the total environment will become internal to the decision-making process of the individual economic unit.

Under the Ruhrverband scheme, the effluent charge imposed upon every emitter of waste enables the emitter's managers to internalize costs into a single decision-making unit. By fully recognizing the overall resource costs being incurred in the production process, managers can equalize both external and internal costs at the margins of economic activity. This means the adoption of a system of discharge fees that is based upon the quantity and quality of waste discharges and upon the creation of an administrative agency to collect fees, enforce the rules, and monitor the environmental conditions. Neither engineers nor economists engaged in management of life-cycle resources have given enough thought to balancing the costs of alternative approaches by concentrating on an analysis of the alternatives' marginal utility. But the Ruhrverband system of effluent charges offers a sound alternative to the treatment of renewable resources as free goods.

In order to provide some way of reconciling conflicts in the ratings or the evaluations that have been chosen by the individuals composing the economic system, an economic system has to rate and assign value to its multiple ends. Even though it may never be possible to obtain the precise unit value for every beneficial use of water, a system of trade-offs would obtain an optimum pattern of users and net benefits. The claim has been made that the establishment of quality standards is "the most convenient and inexpensive manner" of coping with the environmental pollution problem. Senator Edmund Muskie has insisted that the most important task is to establish a floor of minimum quality standards, "because at the present stage . . . the floor is dropping too rapidly. We want to put a floor in before we get to the bottom." Few economists would deny the utility of such constraints, but fewer still, with the Ruhr-verband success before them, would regard constraints as the sole, or even the best, approach to control.

An Environmental Pollution Panel has advised President Johnson that a charge should be imposed on polluters as a way to insure "individual rights to the quality of living" and to reduce such pollution of the environment as excessive noise, unaesthetic abuses of the landscape, and the sullying of the atmosphere and water resources.[22] British water pollution control legislation of 1963 has ordered the creation of effluent treatment districts to be financed out of waste charges imposed on industry; and each district is to collect and treat all water-borne waste within its region. The difference of the British system from the Ruhrverband is that the German example is permissive and merely allows a district to be created if local sentiment desires it. Until 1965, when a similar project was begun on the Neckar, the Ruhrverband had not been copied elsewhere in Germany. There is some doubt that the compulsorily formed districts in Britain would work as well in other countries.

The suggestion of a "polluters' tax" that would solve every sort of problem in the allocation of resources ignores the essence of the Ruhrverband idea. A general polluters' tax would involve more than creation of regional authorities to consolidate the varying aspects of managing the renewable resources. An accompanying program of charges to be imposed on polluters, beneficiaries, and other local interests would be unavoidable. Otherwise the program would simply have created another powerful pressure group for raiding the general fund. Even in the Ruhr, industrialists are vigorously fighting any effort to set up a charge scheme for air quality similar to that for water. Without simultaneous institutional efforts at quality control, a polluters' tax would accomplish very little.

Charges to be imposed on emitters, after all, should be carefully calculated in terms of damage done to receptors and probable costs of better disposal. The charge should provide a real incentive for both municipalities and industry to treat wastes sufficiently in relation to the ability of the resource, to seek the best processes whereby any "spill-over" costs can be internalized, and to locate potential sources of waste where they will inflict minimal damage on the environment. Just as the average decision concerning business costs is subject to the price of labor, material, and the factors of distribution, so the semi-automatic subsystem of administered prices on waste discharges would be considered in the decision-making process of operating units within the economy. The impact of the particular industrial practice upon the general environment could thereby internalize any cost or benefit to others. And treatment of any aspect of the environment as a free good would cease.

THE PROSPECT FOR RENEWABLE RESOURCE SUFFICIENCY

The fears that beset Thomas Malthus, David Ricardo, and John Stuart Mill were, respectively, that there would be a consumption of resources; that there would be steady diminution, level by level, of the better resources; and that there would be a deterioration in the quality of living. From the ecological writings of George Perkins Marsh in 1865 until the present, there have been economists, conservationists, biologists, and general social reformers to assure the modern world that any of this is not, or need not be, so. A few anti-Utopians have argued differently, but the general atmosphere has been optimistic.

Despite the prevailing optimism, there are some biologists who think it is "curious" to end upon a hopeful note; who think, in short, that it is "whistling in the dark" to believe it is possible "to retain the advantages derived from the use of chemicals and other technological innovations, and yet to limit and control their use so effectively that all dangers can be avoided." [23] If such fears are not paranoid, or if they are so accurate that nothing can be done except to wait for an irreversible toxicity to reveal itself in the human condition, it would be wise for man to continue his efforts at reconciling the modern economy with its total environment. Otherwise, in a bizarre fashion, the pessimism in Malthus' analysis may be borne out.

Or, if that prospect proves too dire, the deterioration in the quality of living which John Stuart Mill feared in his darker moods might prove an inevitable accompaniment to the increased material prosperity made possible simultaneously by technological innovations and introductions of new chemicals. The chemicals may bring genetic disaster to a world which, ironically, has grown utterly dependent upon the very sources of man's self-caused physical and biological illnesses. In that event, the world will have proven neither wiser nor more fortunate than the high school boy who said, "I don't worry about smoking three packs of cancer-sticks a day. By the time they get to me, science will have a pill to cure it. In the meantime, oh man, does it look like I've got guts!"

8

Legal concepts and renewable resources

DISTINCTIVE INTERESTS IN RENEWABLE RESOURCES

Biology, it has been argued, makes economics the foundation upon which all social institutions are raised. Since the mid-eighteenth century in Western Europe, North America, and, increasingly, the rest of the world, the material arts—embracing science, technology, and market organization—have developed in a way which has substantially altered man's economic and technical relationships to the biological community and his physical environment. The material arts have flourished at such a pace that a pronounced time lag now separates them from those social arts which are concerned with cooperation, human relations, and government. While technology and economics have been approaching the point of so affecting the renewable resources that some biologists fear irreversible harm to the human environment, the legal institutions that might help to find some sort of balance have not kept pace by developing any corresponding level of sophistication and power.[1]

From the thirteenth century on, air and water, under Anglo-American law, have been resources held in public title to a considerable degree. This public right is most evident in water law, since rights in air as atmosphere were analogized by doctrines governing control over water. The public has held continuous title to water percolating through the soil, running off the ground surface, or flowing in streams. It was agreed in thirteenth-century England that by natural law both air and water, together with the right to use them, were the common property of all people. Public superiority in claims to these renewable resources has remained fully recognized by the law until the present time.[2]

In connection with navigable streams, the public right has been extended even further through the sovereign's title to the stream bed, the banks below high-water mark, and the materials therein. With game the only exception, ownership of other life cycle resources has accompanied transfer of land title as an incident of conveyancing, so that growing trees, crops, and soil—which of course might be removed by the former owner—ordinarily go with the land's title deeds. From the late fourteenth to the early twentieth century, publicly held resources have been viewed with increasing casualness, and the public has been notably indifferent to privately held resources. Under such attitudes, it was highly difficult to claim that the public had more than nominal common interest.

In Anglo-American laws, the property-owner maintained and developed his ascendancy up to 1900. After the decay of feudal rights, one who held land in freehold had absolute right to cut trees, turn soil, and dig gravel on his ground. If the water on his land flowed in a non-navigable stream, he owned the bed and banks, with full right to exploit the materials in them. And, whether the streams were navigable or not, he had the right to use the water as long as he did not change its natural condition. The flowing water itself might belong to the public, but owners of the banks had the right to exclude others from the area and therefore prevent access to the water.

The property owner exercised dominion and control over all fugitive elements entering his close—wild game, fish swimming in streams, water percolating through the ground, or rain water running across the surface. Of equal importance was his right to exclude from his land all others who might wish to take any of these things. Except for that which might be closely held by the sovereign, publicly held resources, on the other hand, came to be regarded either as wild things which any man might appropriate if he could exercise exclusive control over them, or as something common, to which every man had as much right as his initiative might entitle him.

ENGLISH LEGAL HISTORY OF RENEWABLE RESOURCE CONCEPTS

Prior to the fourteenth century certainly, and perhaps as late as the seventeenth century, private interests had not held a superiority in renewable resources under English law. The Royal Demesne had covered a wide expanse of the country; and from it game-takers were excluded and the cutting of trees was strictly controlled. Beyond the Royal Demesne extended the Royal Prerogative, which exercised a powerful control over rivers and game outside the limits of the King's own lands. The overwhelming mass of inhabitants in rural England held very limited rights to any land they tilled. At any time prior to the seventeenth century, royalty, nobility, gentry, and Church—representing about 3 percent of the population—held all of England in freehold tenure or something much like it, while about 90 percent of the populace carried on the rural economy under servile titles. These percentages are extremely crude, but they indicate the sharp restrictions to which the workers of the land were subject. One factor which both complicated and alleviated conditions was the common land, which existed for the joint advantage of both free and servile title-holders on nearby ground. Common land made it possible for the rural economy to subsist despite the burden of feudal or royal restrictions upon the other land.

Many authorities would argue that these common lands were not subject to overlordship even by the Crown. These lands may have had their origins in the remote common "allod" of invading Anglo-Saxon tribes. On the other hand, they might have been the unassigned remnants of property to which the various thrones of the Anglo-Saxon kings had once held a superiority that had never been specifically granted. Origins of the commons are especially hard to determine since all explanations must use words and concepts anachronistic to the periods described.

Economically, the explanation for the common lands lies in the agricultural practices of pre-seventeenth-century rural England. This complex of techniques, called "champion husbandry," required regular cycling of the land to provide for fallow periods. This cycling developed because of the shortage of draft animals, the prevalence of subsistence farming that made each manor self-sustaining, the limited variety of crops available, and the short supply of fertilizers. With its stress upon crop rotation and mutual effort, this tradition economically discouraged the servile tenant from establishing a large, independent unit in his own or family name. To do so would have cut him off from help by his fellows, limited him to the resources of his own plot, and exposed him to the full consequences of his servile state.

The servile tenant's advantage under champion husbandry lay in limiting his personal holding and in expanding the common holdings as much as possible. His greatest profit would thereby be derived from various classifications of common rights: "shack," covering the grain he gleaned or the cattle he fed; "turbary," for the fuel he cut from the peat bogs; "estovers" for the wood he picked up; "piscary," for the fish he took from the pond; "digging," for the humus he dug from the soil; "fowling," for the birds he snared; and so on. From the bottom of rural English society up through the yeomen, who were the highest servile class and who simultaneously might hold land under servile and freehold tenures, these common rights were economically vital.[3]

Whether champion husbandry and the common rights acted as agents of conservation for renewable resources is extremely difficult to determine. And it is just as hard to establish a conservation function in the sweep of the Royal Demesne, the Royal Prerogative, or the reserved rights of overlords under the feudal system. Plainly, conservation was not the intention of any of these institutions. But, being status-oriented, they were directed toward preservation of existing situations and the prevention of any change. The King, after all, held onto the Royal Demesne and the Royal Prerogative for the same reason that a feudal lord guarded his claims or a servile tenant clung to his common rights: these were the contemporary means to wealth, power, and place.

These institutions probably *did* have a conservationist effect. The Crown's regulation of exploitation within the Royal Demesne certainly limited the loss of resources. Game was an abundant staple in the English diet until about 1725. Trees were available for charcoal until about 1750. The critical shortage of oak for ship timbers did not occur until the turn of the nineteenth century. And native wood was available for pit props and building well into the 1800's. Some of these resources may have remained available because of the exclusivity of the Royal Demesne, and some because the demands of feudal families in asserting their rights over resources were stable. Nevertheless, the availability of plentiful life-cycle resources during the eighteenth and nineteenth centuries was due more to the fact that demand developed later than to the application of any earlier use restrictions.

Even under pressure from growing economic demand, the Royal Prerogative, until the early 1800's, did stand firm against encroachments upon the public interest in water and timber. Dams, weirs, sluices, wharves, and other alterations which private ambition built as encroachments on the waters were ordered ripped out. The Crown buttressed its own authority against invasions by the Church, secular lords, and boroughs upon the public claim to water. The same self-interest motivated the lord when he enforced restrictions against his vassal or tenant, and the villein or yeoman when he acted in concert with others to prevent any participant in a common right from destroying it or making it a source of personal aggrandizement. The static, unprogressive, subsistence-conscious pattern of pre-seventeenth-century English economy, and not specific legislation, produced whatever conservationist effects there were. From roughly 1700 on, English society created an economy of a completely different kind. Older economic practices simply could not cope with new problems.

Why, after all, did the ancient English restrictions upon resource use and abuse perish, and why were their remnants swept away after 1830 with an enthusiasm that also infected the Continent and, for a time, the rest of the world as well? The explanation lay in an economic change that began at least as early as the fourteenth century. The creation of markets for produce, the growing importance of cash and credit as media of exchange in lieu of barter and oath, and changes in agricultural techniques themselves—these introduced stresses which the old institutions, premised as they were upon a static subsistence economy, could not resist.

Disaster also played a part. The Black Death in 1348 swept away the humbler class of English royal servants—the water and forest guardians—who never seemed to regain their earlier numbers. And the plague also destroyed the population base for the old patterns of rural underemployment. Unlike plagues in our own time, such as the Spanish influenza of 1918, the Black Death ravaged mankind enough to lower production and to drive up wage demands, thereby encouraging all the other pressures for the institution of a cash economy. And on top of this came the Revolution of 1399, after which the Crown was so beholden to the nobles that the Royal Prerogative shrank inexorably. All the Tudor efforts a century later to revive the Prerogative and the feudal dues could not bring back the old system.

Plagues and wars, however, were not the decisive factor. The growth of the wool trade, which required large tracts for grazing and flocks for fleecing, was less spectacular but more important. It drew England into international trade on a far larger scale than any known before, and it provided the upper classes with an easy source of new wealth predicated upon their ability to free expanses of land of tenants. The result ultimately was the extinction of the yeomanry during the eighteenth century, the creation of pronounced rural poverty, and the accumulation of an unemployed city rabble —refugees from rural conditions—for the new industries that came into being after 1750.

All yeomen were not destroyed by this process. Changing agricultural implements and techniques, such as better plows and introduction of new crops during the sixteenth century, had taken the economic incentives out of champion husbandry. They had also made it seem possible to specify cost-benefit ratios to a degree not previously attainable by the individual farming unit. Then, too, markets existed where crops could be sold for cash. Under these new market situations, self-sufficiency was uneconomic in comparison with alternative behavior that involved crop specialization, sale of crops for cash, and purchases in the market with this cash of everything a farmer needed but could not produce within the limits of the farm's specialization. Opportunities developed for investment of cash surpluses, and these gave the individual farmer an incentive to make profits. Only persons who could not function competitively were left to practice champion husbandry.

The great nobles at the other end of the social spectrum also faced a choice between country and city life. Those noble families who from the sixteenth century on chose to use their estates for cash income, to invest in trade and industry, or to participate in banking, city real estate, and foreign investments, are the families who now retain ascendancy in the Establishment. The old nobility who kept to their estates, despised trade, stayed aloof from finance and industry, maintained their retainers, and clung to the traditional ways, had sunk into eclipse during the eighteenth century. Their descendants survived as the doomed heroes of Gothic novels, like Houses of Usher crumbling in an industrial landscape.

Confronted by major changes in the economy and social structure, those at the top and at the bottom of society had the most difficult decisions to make. With limited capital, the lowest classes faced infinitely harder conditions than the nobility's, once the upper class disentangled itself from tradition. The gentry, though they were associated traditionally with Norman chivalry, seem to have made the transition from a subsistence to a market economy with less difficulty than the classes above and below them in the social structure. Perhaps the connections that the gentry had formed with the wealthy burgesses of the town—as early as the reign of Henry I, if the childhood of St. Thomas à Becket was in any way typical—helped ease the transition.

AMERICAN PROPERTY CONCEPTS BEARING UPON
RENEWABLE RESOURCES

What clearly emerges from all this background is that the be-
ginnings of a modern economy had been established in England
by the time British settlement began in North America. The Royal
Demesne had shrunk to a few parks.The Royal Prerogative was
in a decline, and when the Stuarts attempted to revive it, Charles
I was sent to the block. And the concept of land possessed in
common right had so declined that it did not even cross the
Atlantic.

Some facsimiles of commons' concepts might be said, however,
to have been created in the colonies. Common pasture rights in
the village green were directly in the tradition. In the Body of
Liberties of 1641–47, the Great Ponds—those of ten acres or more
—were declared to be subject to common rights, except for those
previously reduced to private dominion within Massachusetts Bay.
Beyond these particular examples, which were of little economic
importance, the more important effect of the commons' concept
may have been its transference, by analogy, to treatment of
unsettled public lands.

America's settlers never really thought that the Indians had a
valid claim to these lands, although legally great care was always
taken to get a *de jure* waiver of Indian rights, through treaties
with them as dependent nations. The prevalent view was really
that all land unsettled by colonists and frontiersmen was in a wild
state. This meant that any game wandering in the virgin forest and
any vegetation growing therein could be taken by any settler.
Logically, it meant also that the land itself could be pre-empted
by settlers, although this practice was rejected as unlawful by
royal governors, proprietors, chartered land companies, and the
early administrations of the United States. However, the fact that
something very much like pre-emption had to be recognized by
the United States in the Morrill Homestead Act of 1862, precisely at the time when the earlier patterns of settlement were
drawing to a close, indicates that land pre-emption had long been
close to the popular consciousness.[4]

Pre-emption, of course, is simply the most extreme form of

the theory that the public possessions were wild things waiting to be reduced to dominion and control. This attitude underlay the nineteenth-century rash of statutes and constitutional provisions which declared that the new states of the American Union were not successors to the King as Lord Paramount, that all land was retained in freehold by the people, and that there could be no reversion of it to the state. These statutes were meant to prevent any revival in some new form of the Royal Prerogative or the feudal restrictions upon the enjoyment of land tenure. In the 1780's there was even pressure to insert in the new constitution a prohibition against preventing the citizen's hunting and fishing as he pleased.

Such a suggestion and the attitudes which it reflects should not be taken as signs that Americans favored a general system of common property rights. American farmers, from the beginning, were overwhelmingly tied into a market economy. There was little interest in self-sufficient communities that employed a subsistence economy. Isolation was always a temporary phenomenon; the American farmer made great efforts to remain tied to national and world markets. American colonists in the seventeenth century had a more sophisticated commercial law than the British; the London borough custom, with its flexible market-orientation, was more the model for American commercial, contract, and property law than the antique, lumbering common law of England. Champion husbandry was never imported, and all efforts to import a feudal system of land tenure failed.

There was, of course, a frontier tradition of mutual help, but it was nothing like the mutuality that had existed on medieval English manors and persisted, anachronistically, in many parts of the country into the nineteenth century. On the old manor there had been a legal *right* to mutual help: the individual could *demand* this help from others and could *compel* other tenants to share any common right provided by manorial custom. Also, the tenant could *enforce* his rights before the manorial court or, if arbitrarily denied relief there, could bring the royal courts by writ of right to require the manorial court to deal fairly with him. The new American environment was hostile to the continued maintenance of such practices.

The marked difference was that, on the American frontier, aid was *given voluntarily*. A man denying this help to others might suffer social ostracism, but he stood in little peril of legal action. Furthermore, other men in the community had no claim upon the proceeds of his land, and he had no claim on theirs. Taxes aside, every title to land in the United States acquired an economic and legal autonomy that had been substantially absent in England prior to the fourteenth century and probably had not become the prevailing pattern there even in the 1600's.

While settlers in America guarded their individual land rights, popular opinion still insisted that public possessions were the common property of all the people. With the individual landowner motivated to acquire in his specific title as much property as possible, and with the collapse, after 1776, of an effective public superiority over natural resources like water and trees, the pressure would tend to be all toward treating the public possessions as something simply waiting for private taking. The United States did not reassert effective control over the public lands and the resources within them until well into the twentieth century.

Earlier, private use of resources on public lands had sometimes been carried on under the nominal cachet of such federal legislation as the Pre-Emption Act of 1841, the Swamp Land Act of 1850, the Mining Act of 1866, or the Desert Lands Act of 1877. But the more common course probably was to take what was desired without legal sanction.[5]

Certainly miners in the western United States between 1848 and 1870 were hardly concerned with the protection of the public lands, or navigable streams, or common property rights. When panning for gold had proved too laborious, hydraulic mining was introduced in the 1860's. No one, apparently, worried about the effect this would have on fishlife, stream flow, bank structure, or land erosion. Instead, jets of water were blown into gold-bearing, gravelly earths alongside mountain streams; and, after the gold had been filtered out by screening, the residue was allowed to wash down the channel or silt up the stream bed near the mine works.

The extraction of gold has long ceased to be an economic activity in the United States. But even though the hydraulic miners have not operated for a century in many western watersheds, the damage their work inflicted upon some valleys is still so shocking it seems as if the miners had just laid down their equipment. After an intervening century, nature still seems unable to restore the valley. The gold extracted has long since entered the national capital investment, but nature has not been reimbursed.[6]

CHANGE IN AMERICAN RESOURCE-PROPERTY CONCEPTS

Until very recently, private users of public possessions in the United States have been able to enjoy their profits without having to consider resource destruction as a cost. Instead it has been conventional to regard the private use, appropriation, or pre-emption of public possessions as progressive, economical, and shrewd. Efforts at conservation by public authorities, which occurred spasmodically before 1900, were considered reactionary, tyrannical, or plain foolish. In an era of acute capital shortage and booming industrial demand, the enterprising private operator was expected to exploit public resources. Any other attitude would have meant an endorsement of economic stagnation.

Attitudes must change, naturally, as economic conditions are altered. Champion husbandry and a system of property founded on shared title were not socially or economically workable in the America of the seventeenth and eighteenth centuries. Similarly, by 1900 there was no economic justification for private persons' treating public possessions like fugitive, wild things that it would be wasteful not to appropriate to a specific private control use. An unchecked appropriation of public possessions had now become wasteful. As a result, there have been steadily tighter controls over public lands under federal authority. The old view that the natural law is for air and water to be "common to all" requires further refinement.

Changing economic and technological conditions had simply made renewable resources too valuable to be treated as something common, available for every man's use as he chose to employ them. In the presence of economic, technical, and biological controls which were possible in the late twentieth century, the validity of such legal concepts as "fugitive" minerals, "ferae naturae," and "wild" land had become questionable. Except as legal fictions which might help settle private contract, tort, or property suits, they were doctrines that had lost the physical data upon which their very formation had rested.

In the mountains of Pennsylvania, there is still unsurveyed, unclaimed, untaxed land that might be called "wild." Under the floor of the sea there are still domes of gas—a truly "fugitive" mineral seeping through the pores in the permeable rock layers. It is possible to buy a ticket that will take the traveler to some remote place where he can be attacked by an animal *ferae naturae*. But these are exceptions and oddities upon which general rules of public law cannot be based. Even if the ancient legal writers were right in thinking that air and water were resources common to all the people, the time had come by the mid-1900's to reassert the public interest, to better allocate renewable resources, and to depart finally from the traditional viewing of them as free goods.

NEW PROPERTY INTERESTS IN RENEWABLE RESOURCES

Since 1945, many American states have attempted to reassert public superiority by creating statutory water-use permit systems of various types. These statutory systems are by no means all inclusive. Many state schemes apply only to specified water uses or sources and often exempt uses established prior to the start of the permit system. The criteria upon which permit legislation is based are very general, normally stressing public welfare considerations.

The states have been cautious to limit the rights which these permits confer. Rights are often of uncertain duration, effect, and scope. More important, the permits frequently provide little protection against interference by other permittees, the state itself, or water users who do not have permits. Some lawyers doubt that the permit gives any property right to its holder. Because they often involve heavy capital investments which are intended to be permanent, water projects tend to be financially inflexible. The flexible, revocable, and insubstantial permits issued under the average state statute are therefore paradoxical, and it is very hard to build firm economic structures upon such a foundation. But the states have been approaching the problem gingerly and have shown great reluctance in the overt creation of specific, alienable private property rights in the public and common possessions that comprise the renewable resources of air and water.

One of the reasons for this caution is the "riparian doctrine" which anciently governed streams under the English common law. A basic presumption in the common law, at least after the seventeenth century, was that the only persons with any interest in a flowing stream were the owners of land along its banks, and that the law's primary job was to divide the stream's use among them. Anciently, this meant that the riverside owners—the riparians—were entitled to receive the waters of the stream in their natural state. However, with the rise of the market economy and industrialization, the American states received this doctrine in one of two ways: either all riparians held correlative rights in the stream's water and in the water's quality, or every riparian on the stream was entitled to reasonable use of the water as it flowed past his own land.

In the arid western American states, the riparian doctrine seemed unsuitable because of the short and intermittent supply of water in the streams. The miners by their custom established the right of appropriation, whereby the first person to apply a quantity of a stream's water to his own uses became entitled to that quantity, either absolutely or proportionally. The riparian doctrine had usually limited the use of water to the watershed or an even more restricted base, and most jurisdictions had interdicted the sale of stream water to non-riparians if the stream were lowered by the withdrawal.

The very nature of the miners' needs made a change necessary. While the appropriator would have to acquire access rights to the stream, he was not otherwise concerned with bank location. What mattered thereafter was to establish clearly the quantity of water appropriated and not the uses, whether in or out of the watershed, or whether the withdrawal was near the source or the delta of the stream. In its purest or "Colorado" form, this doctrine became established in the Rocky Mountains and Alaska. A variant, the California form, permits the continuance of some riparian rights and has become the law on the West Coast and in the Plains States from Texas north.

Some experts claim that the appropriation doctrine was borrowed by the miners from some other legal system; but it seems more likely to have been the result of the miners' peculiar needs, with perhaps a little intellectual stimulation from the *laissez-faire* economics of the mid-nineteenth century. The appropriation system puts great stress on initiative, foresight, and priority, and it is put under greatest stress when an insufficiency of water excludes junior appropriators, who often are a majority interest. Their *lack* of initiative and foresight, or their inability to have gotten first to the water, leaves them highly vulnerable to climatic changes in stream flow.

It seems especially unlikely that the miners were influenced in the formation of the appropriation doctrine by the Indian and Mexican water law in the West, as some authorities have alleged. Common right, mutual help, and proportional share systems typified the water associations among the settled Indian tribes and Mexicans. The Mexican associations, formed under Spanish law that had itself derived the common rights rules from Visigothic and Moorish codes, and the Indian practices, which had been in existence in agricultural valleys of New Mexico and Arizona long before Spanish settlement, had little place for an individual property right in water. Although some still survive, these Mexican and Indian water associations in the American Southwest have meant little in the development of any American law, the possible exceptions being some procedures employed in western water districts and the pueblo water rights of those western cities which had their origin in eighteenth-century Spanish missions.

Most of the appropriation states have set up a mandatory permit system in order to protect the public interest in unappropriated waters. The advantages of a mandatory system range from bureaucratic convenience to a rearrangement of property rights in water. The absence of official records under a voluntary permit system can compel private claimants to enter into expensive litigation, which can delay or prevent proposed private water projects. Mandatory permits make it possible to see if appropriations remain in use, since, unlike rights under the riparian doctrine, appropriative rights can be maintained only on a basis of continuing beneficial use. Under a mandatory permit system in a state having the appropriation doctrine, state officials have an easier job of "policing" the water resource. Whether or not this is welcomed by private persons with water appropriation claims, the appeal is very strong to state governments in a period of ever greater economic demands for water.[7]

It would be misleading, however, to conclude that a permit system allocating surface water resources is limited to an appropriation doctrine jurisdiction in an arid region. It is possible to treat public rights as property in humid riparian states and at the same time to prefer those public rights to private riparian interests. As a powerful tool for protecting public rights from private encroachment, private riparian interests might have burdens impressed upon them in the fashion of a servient tenement, so that activities by the holders of these interests would be incidental to the enjoyment of the public rights. The problem, whether under the riparian or appropriation doctrines, is currently more in the establishment of a clear definition of public rights than in determining the private claims in those public possessions.

The scope of property in the public sector has been in fairly active formation since 1945. It is true that the definition of the full scope of public property will come in conjunction with the fixing of private interests in the renewable resources. But the latter can scarcely occur until the public rights to these same sources have been firmly established. Yet in the interval, if a permit system in water rights should be considered helpful, the jurisdictions governed by the riparian doctrine are not shut out from setting up a requirement for permits. Riparian states have been slow about setting up overt water preference priorities, but legislation reaching this end in other ways has long been on the statute books. However, indirection is becoming a method of the past, and systems are being set up that more openly go about the business of establishing individual priorities in water supplies.

New Jersey, for certain watersheds, has authorized permits to regulate surface water supplies. Florida and Wisconsin allow state administrators to issue permits under which water can be transferred to non-riparian uses, with Florida permitting diversion only if "this does not interfere with reasonable uses existing when the diversion, capture, storage or use began." Arkansas and Virginia issue permits to store water during periods of high flow. Their statutes define the extent of the protection offered the permittee against actions by the state or by third parties to remove or alter any impounding structures or to collect money damages, and the permittee is told where he may use the water, what minimum downstream flow is required, and what special limitations may be imposed because of navigation demands. Indiana also has impounding permits for "waters in excess of others' reasonable needs"; similarly narrow are the Michigan permits which allow to riparians the non-consumptive use of impounded surplus waters of local governmental units.

As long ago as the early part of the twentieth century, states enacted statutes providing for the establishment and maintenance of lake levels and minimum stream flows. As a part of such legislation, permits were required for persons whose activity might interfere with these levels. The tendency of such statutes was to keep up water levels for the benefit of uses which do not depend upon withdrawal of the water, such as the support of aquatic life, recreation, waste carriage or absorption, and navigation. The old milldam acts, going back to 1714, had a similar effect, as have statutes that require miners to obtain permits to use streams for mining purposes or operators of high-capacity water wells to get permits if these wells draw upon an adjacent stream.

Some states have tried to meet peculiar local problems with special statutes. New York has long had a statute to control water levels on Long Island, though this has only a peripheral interest in stream water, and Florida has an act permitting the formation of local water regulatory districts with boundaries that are contiguous with hydrologically separate areas. These Florida local authorities "without impairing property rights" may control "the apportionment, limitation, or rotation of water uses or the prevention of unreasonable or non-beneficial uses or the initiation of new uses, and the modification of existing uses and facilities." Other states have created a variety of special authorities, such as conservancy, watershed, or irrigation districts, while local units of government, under enabling statutes, have set up joint commissions to accomplish similar purposes.

This sort of administrative device, combined with the work of many specialized state agencies, has reduced the severity of some water problems and has enabled existing water law systems to continue functioning without basic change. Riparian owners seem to have raised no objections to these new statutory and administrative limitations upon their rights. The restrictions have been accompanied by substantial benefits for the riparians' economic and physical land interests. There has also been the implied pressure of eminent domain which would cover easily the condemnation of such riparian interests if their owners should be obdurate. The carrot and the stick have eased the public property interest in water into a dominant position.

Ohio, for example, permits landowners and water users to form a water conservancy district which, in effect, becomes the depository of any new or improved water rights. The individuals who form the district reserve the water rights they had at that time, but only to the extent they existed without later district improvement. Water rights created by the district, with the district's founders having priority of purchase, can be aliened for terms up to fourteen years, and it is plainly intended that, after a lapse of years, the district will have the common title to all the economically valuable water rights in the area.[8]

In this manner, under modern forms of business organization with their greater flexibility, something like the common right of the medieval manor or the Indian pueblo has been evolved. Opposition to a frictioning away of the full extent of vested private property rights is stilled by rewards and the implicit threat of condemnation until, eventually, no one considers there are private rights to be asserted. Gradually, in the renewable resources new property rights for the public interest are coming into existence, and, because of the way it has been occurring, the change has been relatively smooth.

LEGAL DEVICES FOR PROTECTING RENEWABLE RESOURCES

Considerably more protective legislation has been enacted in the United States than has yet been used. This is an old gambit. When there is doubt as to the constitutionality of a statute, either because it seems to disturb vested property rights or to be too vague, court litigation is postponed until administrative experience over the years has filled the hiatus of vagueness or created a new network of property relationships which the courts are too reluctant to disturb. Under present statutes, some of the hardest questions have not been answered because the administrators have avoided putting them to the court. Sometimes, half a century has passed before administrators of the renewable resources have dared trust the courts with the enabling acts of these administrators.

Persons who own an interest in renewable resources and who are affected by the law are encouraged to arrive at non-litigated agreements with the administrators. Occasionally this is done on the basis of an opinion of the state's attorney general, but generally it results from no more than an administrative determination to settle out of court in private agreement some specific statutory problem. The administrators, despite the rather nebulous character of property and rights to legal protection in renewable resources, have not been anxious for more certainty. The line between a valid exercise of the police power without the duty to compensate for taking property, and an invalid expropriation which must be rescinded or paid for in a proper eminent domain proceeding, is a cloudy one enveloped by a great deal of historical haze. Content with private proceedings carried on outside of court, administrators have pushed for no greater certainty; neither have those private persons who are either riparians or appropriators.

The impact of extant rules, as they relate to the developing economy and its associated changes in water use, seems to have been absorbed into workable economic decisions by entrepreneurs, investors, and private property owners. They, too, have not pushed for court decisions or basic reform by statute, but, like the public administrators, they have stayed content with the administrative arrangement. What threatens the permanency of this arrangement is not a present dissatisfaction but a future inability under the present "nebulous" system to cope economically with the accumulation of scientific, technical, economic, or other knowledge or theories concerning the law and the use of renewable resources.

EXAMPLE OF LEGAL LIMITS IN GROUND WATER USE

It is the growing demand upon renewable resources which has moved countries in Europe and states in the United States to overhaul underground water law and institute a system of use permits. Technical progress in well-drilling and growing economic activity after 1945 have caused huge consumption of underground water which, in some places, threatens supplies for agriculture and municipalities. This has produced a consciousness of the need to protect the quantity and the quality of underground supplies. And out of it has come legislation that tries to take into account all interests in, and measures involving, the aquifers, by regulating them on a regional or hydrological shed pattern.

Both the Anglo-American common law and the European civil law recognize that ownership of the surface includes the ownership of such renewable resources as the soil, springs bubbling through the soil, and water percolating through permeable layers. But legal restrictions upon the owner's use of this water have become common. Especially in the drilling of new wells and in running high-capacity pumpers, even countries purporting to have absolute property rights in groundwater for landowners of the surface have set up zones in which the "absolute" rights suffer a sharp limitation.

In Europe, the owner of the water-permeable underground layers, like the owner of riparian rights in Anglo-American law, can use the groundwater on his own property for his domestic, agricultural, and other needs so long as other users in his hydrologic shed are not injured by his actions. This arrangement resembles the correlative rights doctrine which prevails over underground water in several American states, except that some European countries have pushed to the logical end of such a doctrine by requiring all such uses to be declared, recognized, and recorded in an official Water Register. Gradually, these registrations have been supplemented by state restrictions on water use.

More important recently in Europe have been the regulations imposed on individuals and public, collective, and private enterprises, limiting the use and withdrawal of water and requiring the obtaining of permits. Under this permit system the determination of water conditions and requirements puts a heavy demand upon the technical and economic planning services. In conditions of absolute water shortage, the permit issuers are compelled to set up priorities of use which are similar to those adopted by many American states; that is, domestic use and municipal supply come first, followed by agriculture, industry, and such uses as those for mining, power, and recreation. The most complete regulations of this sort, more strict within certain hydrologic zones where water supply is short compared to demand, require applicants to file a plan and, if a permit is granted, to keep a technical journal and submit a report on the work done.

Some American states, such as Wisconsin, have had similar regulations for many years. This legislation's effect has produced much improved private wells, and the margin of safety has not been improved in only statistical terms. In 1964, over 8,700 private wells for human use were drilled in Wisconsin, and very few were in any degree unsafe to health. In addition, if these wells should need to be rebuilt or enlarged, the drilling has been done in such a way that improvements could be safely carried through.

In a manner rather similar to the regulations of many American states concerning oil and gas wells, some European countries have permit systems which require water wells to be spaced a certain distance apart, depending upon patterns of surface ownership, so that every landowner is assured at least one well. The systems also require permittees of artesian wells to keep them shut down when not in use and to control the pressure under which the water flows from the ground. European permit coverage also regulates efforts to recharge underground water levels, build surface drainage, store gas and petroleum products, work mines and quarries, or carry on building operations that would affect the quantity or quality of water below ground. This has even gone so far as to prohibit within certain favored zones a variety of activities which affect underground water supplies, such as the storing of gas and oil, drilling and excavating, the use of fertilizers, or the formation of dumps capable of polluting underground water levels.

Previously, the reputations of both Europe and the United States as humid areas had permitted lax legal attitudes toward use of underground water. But the change in technology which made possible enormous drafts of water, and the demands of the economy which rendered those drafts needful, have compelled changes in legal attitudes. The growth of public limitations on private interests has been the result of these social and economic changes.[9]

PRESUMPTIVE PROBLEMS IN LEGAL REGULATION

That public property interest in the renewable resources has assumed a greater role is now accepted in both the United States and Europe. This role has to be played at the expense of specific individual resource users, whether they are the private corporations typical of the United States and Western Europe or the public trusts and collective farms common in Eastern Europe. Problems in administering this public power arise from certain presumptions upon which the rule is based. The presumptions are a mixture of economic and technical opinions which are advanced by some writers almost as if they were conventions upon which action must be based. But even though they represent conventional thinking, such views have not gone unchallenged.

The common presumptions are quite general, viewing the public domain as certainly including all water and air which can be employed by individual economic units only under state licenses. The public domain does not specifically include other renewable resources, such as trees, grass, soil, or wildlife, but, clearly, there is a public superiority over these that can regulate their care and protection. For this reason, the public authorities have the right to investigate, to limit uses, to establish protection zones, and to set the terms according to which individual economic units may employ the resources. In setting these terms and limits, the public administrators must have the power to set up general plans, which are based upon precise observations and measurements of variations in the dynamic changes that occur in the renewing character of flow resources. In turn, the general plans have to set down the remedial measures which investigation has shown to be needed and to provide for continuing verification of how the plan has functioned.

These presumptions are so general as to be difficult to criticize; still they seem open to both economic and technical objections. Those economists who have been promoting specification of the value of the renewable resources and internalizing all use costs must be dissatisfied. First of all, they would not regard incorporation into the public domain as being in itself a satisfactory change. Rather, if it were accompanied by only an indeterminate license system, the change would be regarded as a reactionary step that would destroy the chance at economic specificity. These economists would regard the change as intended to move the affected renewable resource firmly into the area of free goods to be commonly exploited without effective restraint.

Economists of this group would prefer, regardless of public or private ownership of the renewable resources, a use permit system in which the permits would specify the user's rights, and which would be alienable, would be officially recognized by their being recorded in a public register, and would have the surety either of perpetuity or of a term. Apart from this requirement, so far as these resource economists are concerned, the title to the particular renewable resource could be vested in the state, and the holder of the use permit could be a collective farm or a state-owned factory. Specificity of the use and the cost of the use of the renewable resource concerns these economists far more than the individual, capitalist, socialist, or state character of title-holders and users of the resource. Merely declaring that a renewable resource is in the public domain, these economists feel, obscures the needed specificity and is either mere rhetoric or an unfortunate dedication of another free good, so-called.[10]

Where technical difficulties are concerned, many specialists in underground water supplies doubt that it is possible to have the sort of broad-scale knowledge presupposed about the renewable resource. The more experienced administrators are chary of a law requiring that certain potential (or even actual) activities would not affect other resource aspects before a permit could result. Barring actual extensive tests, it is impossible, for example, to know in what watershed underground water may be located. Human activity does not draw equally or evenly upon renewable resources. There is a cone of effect around the core of the particular activity. While it is possible to project from this data what the overall effect might be, the results are very uncertain. In such renewable resource sciences as ecology and hydrology, there is nothing like the precision of knowledge which so many recent laws presume. Even experts operate in a very large area of technical ignorance. If fairly enforced, law which does not recognize these gaps can only slow up the granting of permits to a tremendous extent and make the process defeatingly expensive.

DIFFICULTY OF CLOSE REGULATION OF RENEWABLE RESOURCES

Defects in the conventional presumptions concerning renewable resources in much post–World War II legislation are revealed in some recent regulations of underground water supplies. Underground formations are so structured that only a very detailed survey can produce the sort of profile upon which the administrator could base the decision to grant or withhold a use permit for pumping water if he must consider the effect on the whole underground supply or the possible draw-down on surface streams. Acquiring the detailed information needed would exceed in cost what any country, other than one with acute and persistent water shortage, has been willing to spend. Further investigations and data accumulation are taking place, but these studies move slowly, and no country in Western Europe or North America has a sufficient quantity of data upon which to base a detailed use permit system for underground water.

One of the most influential systems of control that presumes the economic wisdom and technical ability of absolute administrative dominion over a renewable resource is the highly sophisticated Polish method of underground water regulation. Under the

Polish procedures, the administration of underground waters is in the office of the national geological survey. Every permit issued to drill a well must include data as to the likely effect the proposed well will have upon the water levels tapped and upon any surface streams drawing upon or sustaining the underground water levels. All Poland is therefore considered in terms of its hydrological sheds. The well permit system must work within the physical operation of these sheds.

Florida has a system organized very much like the one in Poland. Floridian law also authorizes the setting up of water districts on the basis of hydrologic sheds. Being a peninsula, Florida has a simpler underground water organization than the one required for the continental land mass of which Poland is a part. Underlying Florida are two huge aquifers or permeable water layers—the Floridian, supplied by rainwater from the central highlands, and the shallower Biscayne, in the southeastern part of the state. These aquifers are on a gradient, with the greatest depth of the aquifer (as opposed to the width of or depth in the aquifer itself) being at the southern end in both layers. Because of heavy pumping to sustain irrigation and recreation-based cities, the counter-pressure which the aquifers have maintained against the ocean has been reduced, with resultant water invasion of the aquifers. For this reason, the Florida legislature has taken action to regulate pumping from the aquifers; and, because of the simplicity of the aquifers (except in the very northern part of the state), the legislation recognizes hydrologic sheds as the physical basis of the system.

But what worries underground water administrators is the apparent sophistication of the Polish-Floridian type of legislative systems and the nature of the burden they impose upon permit applicants and operators and the organizers and managers of local water districts. An Eastern European water specialist was quite dubious about the Polish system: "First of all, I think it is not universally applied there; that is, permits may be required for municipalities, factories, and the larger farms, but for the smaller users, I think the full requirements of the law are waived. For us, it seemed too complicated a system, requiring too many trained people, too much information, that it imposed too many duties on the economic units which would want well permits. For us, so sophisticated a system just did not fit within the requirements of the national plan as it affected water conservation. We were impressed by the Polish system, but we decided against following it." American administrators had a very similar reluctance to set up systems as elaborate as those contemplated by the Polish and Florida legislation.[11]

Most underground water specialists believe that the crucial factor is not close regulation but the area's rainfall. When rainfall drops off, the water tables fall, stream volume declines, crops wither, municipal demand rises, and the pumps have to work harder. Even suspension of pumping allows nothing beyond the maximum rise in water tables that percolations from precipitation make possible. It is different when aquifers are connate or where recharge is impeded by geologic conditions. In such situations, pumping up the water is the same as mining it. But in continental land masses in which the rainfall regularly reaches twenty inches or more a year, there are enormous quantities of underground water that it is not presently possible to calculate.

In most humid areas, falling water tables are more an inconvenience and a cost to the well operators than any sign of peril in the resource. Because there is more water available below ground than above it, and because underground water is not subject to the sort of pollution which affects surface streams, ever greater numbers of well drillings will occur and the volumes of water extracted will continue to increase under these economic conditions.

Present well pumping, although it represents a tremendous growth since 1945, is small compared with its probable future dimensions. And, whereas the renewable aquifers have not been physically imperiled or perhaps even much lowered, the pumping has prevented them from building up to that maximum from which the excess could flow into the surface streams. This condition has already lowered the flushing power of the streams and kept the marshes from full supply. Conservationist forces have been led by this, and by problems of salt water invasion, aquifer pollution, and even the exhaustion peculiar to some areas, to push for close pumping regulations. Some humid states have had high-capacity well permit systems since 1945, but that experience is not especially pertinent. Because of the lack of firm data on subsurface conditions and because the economic demand has made comparatively slight inroads upon underground supplies, permits under these statutes have been far more liberally granted than will be the case in the future when the demands begin mutually to conflict because the supply will then be inadequate to them.

Knowledge has a way of appearing when it represents an economic value. Then sums can be budgeted to make the surveys, to extract the knowledge that will provide a physical basis for the economic allocation of use permits. But what worries underground water resource administrators in the 1960's is that statutes will be drawn which assume such knowledge when the data are actually not known, when the technology to extract the facts has not been fully developed at the level of field operations, and when there is no economic pressure that would provide for investments in the needed technology and investigation of pertinent subsurface conditions. Statutes could, of course, prompt that very investment; but this will occur only if enactment of the statutes does not run too far ahead of an alteration in economic conditions that will support an elaborately developed use permit system.

Of course, many conservationists believe that high-capacity wells used for industrial, municipal, and corporate farm purposes are harmful because of the physical alteration in the hydrologic shed which their operation can scarely avoid causing. Aquifers, streams, marshes, run-off, and the unconfined waters percolating through topsoil all form the unity which constitutes any particular watershed. Each is physically connected with the other, and modern economic usage makes such demands on the totality that even in humid areas there is a drying up of the watersheds. Marshes have disappeared; run-off and topsoil waters are more quickly consumed; streams have less volume; and the drafts upon aquifers are steadily growing.

Countering this destructive process has been the non-consuming character of many uses. The water has therefore not been destroyed. Yet rarely has the used water been injected into aquifers, drained into languishing marshes, or sprayed upon the soil. When it has been poured into surface streams, used water generally has contained such burdens of silt and waste and chemical nutrients, or been so thermally polluted, that the streams can scarcely be said to have been refreshed, even though their banks may have been brimming.

The general conditions in the overall character of many hydrologic sheds are causing conservationists to push for close regulation of pumping draw-down on aquifers. This pressure comes despite the fact that up to the late 1960's the average aquifer in North America and Europe had not been put under a demand heavy enough to give rise to economic rivalry for its content. Still, given the potential demand, the conservationists' fears are not foolish.

The foresight present in this position on pumping is recognized by underground water administrators. What the administrators want are assurances of adequate investment in the accumulation of needed geologic data. If this investment were forthcoming, administrators would not be so troubled by the prospect of issuing permits on the basis of complex fact analysis.

In some parts of the United States, because high-capacity wells are pumping toward a combined physical and economic crisis, the investments may be made. In Arizona, water is being mined. With only 1 percent of the rainfall replenishing the aquifers, with 70 percent of the water used in the economy coming from aquifers, with water being pumped at the daily rate of fifteen thousand acre-feet, with every test used showing the water tables dropping and the content of the aquifers decreasing 2.5 million acre-feet annually, and with demand growing despite conservation measures, the American Southwest is pumping itself into an underground drought. In central and west Texas, although the aquifers can be replenished, pumping has been running far ahead of either natural replenishment or artificial efforts. In Florida and on Long Island, salt water invasions because of heavy well pumping have been a persistent and resistant problem. In Wisconsin, the ever-recurring hope of pushing agricultural settlement northward has been revived through the success of irrigation in the Sand Lands which run straight north along the glacier line. Conservationists claim this is adversely affecting stream flow in the area, though they have been unable to prove their case sufficiently to induce the state of Wisconsin to slow the pumping rate.

Even if, on a national basis, the United States is not yet at a crisis stage on underground water, a sufficient problem exists to be legally recognized. The underground water administrators ask only that, in the effort at improvement, too great a burden not be put on existing skills. Otherwise, efforts meant to provide total coverage might end up providing practically no coverage at all.

SIGNIFICANCE OF LAW FOR THE RENEWABLE RESOURCES

Technology can produce the answers that modern society, for political or economic reasons, believes are worth investment. The administrators in charge of conserving the renewable resources, through long experience, have some idea of the share society will allocate for protecting, reviving, or equably sharing any aspect or part of these resources.

The President of the United States may say that concern for renewable resources enjoys the same dignity in the 1960's as other national interests.[12] But if history is a guide, when a conflict arises over investment allocation, the protection of renewable resources is subordinated to the expansion of the gross national product, national defense, and social welfare. Tensions present within society always have been attended to as they seemed nearest the needs that society regarded as most important. It would be premature to assume that the equable allocation of the renewable resources among competing economic uses had become primary national concern in the economy. And legal process that would push beyond economic demand in order to protect physical quality will almost certainly be threatened with the risk of failure.

However, constant effort must be made to enlarge the scope of possible control. Given the nature of the fulminating demand upon the renewable resources since 1700 and the prospect for its further expansion, the matter cannot be left to happenstance. A static economic order in the future seems as unlikely as the perfection of human ability to manipulate nature at will. These conditions being so, it then becomes vital—in the precise meaning of that word— to work out a practical (if less than ideal) legal, economic, and social system of regulation that will encourage a healthily operating life cycle.

9

The prospect for resource control

DEMAND THAT GOVERNMENT SUPPLY RENEWABLE RESOURCES

The United States has had a long-standing public policy on renewable resources, both for their development and their exploitation. Development, which includes simply making them available, has taken place on the governmental level through non-market processes, insofar as the renewable resources have not been left purely to nature. Their exploitation, on the other hand, has been carried on through market mechanisms generally in private hands. The most prevalent form, of course, has been simply the private economic unit, capturing the resource it wants. This exploitation may involve drawing in the resource to the manufacturing mechanism or employing it as the receiver of wastes. In both events, the conventional service market is by-passed. Because of the impact common to both these kinds of exploitation, demands for further government services have arisen continuously.

Individual demands have affected both the quality and quantity of flow resources at such a rate that governmental intervention has become increasingly necessary to help nature make up the deficiencies. Users of these resources are much less enthusiastic about having government critically examine the need for many of these demands or recognize the costs that government will have to absorb if public funds replace nature as the supplier of the wherewithal for resource renewal. The poet Richard Moore has applied his talents to stating the problem:

> . . . into our channeled valley drips the spillage
> Where junkyards cover fields once used for tillage.
> Our means are modest, but our needs are great
> Which softly sung commercials can create.
> Some call it enterprise; I call it pillage.[1]

But that is a poet expressing himself. The government cannot permit itself such stark attitudes, although it seems quite obvious that what the poet would call "pillage" is an inextricable part of all economic activity. The pencil factory on which H. D. Thoreau sustained his Walden experience required some taking from nature, and it is a commonplace of philosophy that death makes life possible. Government eschews this sort of contemplation and prefers a more tangible fact analysis with less emotional content.

TECHNICAL METHODS OF JUDGING CONSEQUENCES OF SUCH DEMAND

According to government administrators, political and social demands that the government supply the economic base for sustaining renewable resources can be judged best in the simulated and mathematical models of systems analysis. Underlying these models is the notion that there is a need to take into orderly account the important relationships among the individual economic, institutional, or technical elements of processes, structures, and problems. The various elements and their relationships compose systems, and the organized methodical study of these holds out promise for more completely based governmental decisions. The tools developed since 1940 in the field of electronic computers provide the means, public officials have concluded, for controlling the use and the regeneration of the flow resources. Systems analysis is neither poetry nor humanist philosophy, but many students of the problem are convinced that it offers a way of consciously planning the kind of unification of public philosophy that previously was not possible.

As applied to river control, the concept for this kind of planning was first put forward in 1853 by Charles Ellett, Jr., in his proposals for governing all the uses of the Mississippi and Ohio rivers. But these schemes could not be implemented before the electronic computer: the important relationships were so numerous that pre-electronic computational techniques were unable either to identify and trace the relationships or to evaluate the consequences offered by alternative proposals for changing these relationships. Step by step, the process is simple, but in setting up the models called for in systems analysis, the overall effect poses extremely complicated tasks.

Of the two kinds of models used, mathematical and simulated, the former gives the most exact analytical solutions, but it does this through a drastic simplification which sacrifices realism to exactitude. Simulation models can handle a version somewhat closer to reality, but they give only an estimate of a system's behavior as it occurred at one particular point. To get the larger picture of how the whole system would perform in response to changes in differing variables, many simulations must be made within the computer. The simulation technique is aided by sampling theory, which makes the final picture a good deal more complete than it would otherwise have been.

But it is the mathematical model that has the advantage of giving results which appear to be exact. If dollar values are attached to resource changes that require investment (dams, water-carrying processes, and power stations), and if at the same time the dollar values of the ensuing benefits are calculated (the resulting water supply or hydroelectric power, for example), the answer will produce in easy-to-grasp dollar form the gross benefits less costs. But to make the mathematical model manipulable, a simplicity has to be imposed that provides an answer something less than ideal in terms of the total realism of the problem.

The random character of renewable resource flow makes it impossible to abstract from it future assumptions possessing certainty. A close study of records, with samples taken at intervals, gives the likely limits of the problem, but this process is conjectural. If resource flows are presumed as known and predetermined, the problem is simplified but, in most situations, at the cost of realism. The study limits as set up by investigation have a way of flattening out which is mathematically disheartening. Until the drought in the Pocono-Catskill Mountains began in 1961, the previous limit for droughts in that area had been calculated at two years, and all water use calculations had been made within that premise. But all such calculations lost some validity when the drought continued, spread, and intensified itself in an area from southern New England to northern Virginia. This gave graphic reinforcement to the random character inherent in predictions concerning the renewable resources.

Computational facilities have increased greatly since the end of World War II, but the basic data upon which they feed has not kept pace. This should scarcely be surprising. Even if there *had* been general interest in flow resources, there was in the past no point in collecting information for which no means of handling had been devised. Now that there is both a growing interest and a mechanical means of assimilating data, the collections of information have begun to grow. The very requirement of feeding the computers has set up a bureaucratic logic that has accelerated the gathering of data to be stored in the machines.

Yet it would be misleading to imply that the difficulty is purely one of a shortage of data. The mathematical model used in 1965 for analyzing river systems had to operate within rigid fact assumptions, and in the mid-1960's experts claimed that no great breakthroughs were in sight. When a simulation model is designed to produce an effect of verisimilitude, severe programming difficulties may be posed. Records for resource flows are usually very brief. When fed into the model, these short runs have produced a result that, like the mathematical model, failed to take into account the changing nature of the flow of the renewable resources. For studies of streamflow, this deficiency is avoided by a programming method which generates synthetic sequences of streamflow for as many years as desired.

Year by year, informational, technical, and mathematical improvements are being made that may make a total, realistic analysis possible for the total flow of the renewable resources. In the period prior to 1975, however, during which decisions must be made that will affect the quality of life for a long while after that date, the decisions will have to be made without the optimal assistance of the electronic computers.[2]

DIFFICULTIES INHERENT IN THESE TECHNICAL METHODS

The difficulty is inherent in the decision-making process, and many authorities fear the "drastic simplifications" of systems analysis. They fear that the consequences will be a futile complaint to a machine which has botched the operation entrusted to it, followed by a statement that nothing can be done about it. Academics, whose experience with computers has included encountering this situation in matriculation processes, have been particularly fearful. In the past, the standard of efficiency has too often meant the very least dollar cost on a narrow engineering sense of building facilities meant to enhance the value of some renewable resource. This narrow meaning would be very easy to translate into computer language.

Since Jeremy Bentham made his great impact on American thought in the mid-nineteenth century, all statements of public policy could be said to stand for the proposition, "The greatest good for the greatest number," or, as the modern welfare economists express the divine calculus, "Maximizing net benefits optimally." Some economists believe modern complexities are so great that this context is no longer adequate. Measuring values may be so difficult that they have to be excluded from any model in systems analysis and that, for the models to function, it is necessary to accept restrictions imposed by political decision-making.

In the real world, and hence necessarily in the world of models representing aspects of it, there are three levels of constraint functioning upon any change: the physical, the economic, and the political. They are interrelated, especially in the political tradition which tends to preserve previously valid solutions to physical and economic problems after their viability has been lost for anything other than politics. This is the purely negative relationship. Yet every physical, economic, or political activity has an effect upon the others that makes simplicity an ideal rather than a goal in practical decision-making concerning the renewable resources, whether one talks of models or of the real world.

Some years ago, the sociologist Helen Merrell Lynd expressed her anxiety over the breakup of problems of a social and economic nature into what appeared to be their constituent elements. She agreed that this did simplify the job of studying nature, that the technique made comprehension of the smaller parts possible, and that abstracted reassemblies of a model kind could be carried out once the larger problems were fragmented. What worried her was the fear that the process was not only inadequate for a complete understanding but might even lead to outright maladjustments due to a misreading of the information supplied by such detailed investigations.[3]

From her point of view, the whole may be greater than its identifiable parts; and, because of that discrepancy, an exact knowledge of those parts may still produce a completely erroneous description. Hope for solution is to be found in the total problem. Only after a purpose has been found that would give direction to analysis should programs be set up employing mathematical and simulation models. This raises the old argument concerning the derivation of values. But beyond this are the issues of present sufficiency of data, present ability to manipulate models, and present computer technology through which simulations of reality are programmed. These exist at a level which makes modest restraint the language most appropriate for systems analysis. The enthusiasts, who say that values can be derived from empiric data through computer analysis, ultimately may be right. But at the present time, and for at least this generation, even the enthusiasts concede that values will continue to have the appearance of external impositions upon the operation of computers, systems analysis, and upon the decisions relating to the physical, economic, and political conditions of the renewable resources.

An example of external impositions has been the federal irrigation policy for western American land. Economists and specialists in many physical sciences have often lamented the decision to shift so much agriculture from humid to arid country. This shift has made possible a factory-type agricultural corporation, enormously profitable to the entrepreneur or corporation engaged in it. Up to the mid-1960's, costs for water in the arid areas have been met by agencies of the state and federal governments. And the threat of impending underground drought is producing the demand that the government supply needed water from remote sources with little contribution from the beneficiaries other than what their general tax dollar provides. To the criticism which economists and scientists have made over this past and prospective history, the *Reader's Digest* has replied dramatically:

> There is something magnificent about large scale re-making of the country, the way we have made paradises [and] . . . more good comes . . . than can be shown in 'cost-benefit' calculations. . . . You can see how out of an irrigation ditch— like Venus from the waves—there rises that shining piece of civilization, California.[4]

People with this outlook claim that the resource conservationists favor a static economy. They argue that the economists, who wish to internalize costs otherwise producing only benefits for the renewable resource users, are opposed to a progressively expanding economy. Their position is strengthened by arguments that growth in gross national product in Europe and North America has been due to an exploitation of resources made in defiance of the conservationists and through a process of investment which ignores the warnings of cost-conscious economists. However, unless the current economy is at a take-off point from which renewable resource utilization can in the future proceed without regard to the natural physical condition of the resources or the economic costs of using them, a more thoughtful course will have to be adopted. At the present time, contrary to the optimists, very few observers think such a take-off point has been reached.

ECONOMIC TECHNIQUES FOR COPING WITH POLLUTION

There are three possible ways of handling pollution costs for renewable resources.

First, the polluter can pay a charge to the recipient of the polluted resource. Under this approach, the payment can either be compulsory or made by mutual agreement between the emitter and receptor of the pollution as to the charge and the level of pollution which will be tolerated.

The second method has several forms: costs can be internalized, either by merging the polluter and the recipient of the pollution into one firm, or by merging such public agencies as water and sewage treatment plants, or by imposing a charge to be spent reducing the effect of the emission. The last currently seems most effective to economists. This charge may cause polluters to adjust their emissions so as to reduce the adverse effect in terms of which the charge would be calculated. In conjunction with this, the public control agencies would have to set the limits above which emissions would not be permitted. Without these publicly imposed constraints, economic units might decide to adjust the emission charges as just part of their accounting for costs and benefits. Emission charges should not be allowed to become a fine whose payment could be calculated into costs, thereafter ceasing to have any public purpose apart from a revenue characteristic. Emission charges are not taxes. Rather they are efforts at a public level to help internalize the full costs of using some renewable resource.

Certainly emission charges represent a more modest constraint upon the operation of private or other economic units than the third possibility of handling pollution costs. Under it, the government, through its pollution control agencies, would take over and operate the activity that produces the external effect.

Effluent charges, effluent standards, and effluent zoning are all efforts at producing a more socially meaningful, efficiency-inducing distribution of the whole costs related to renewable resource use. Individual units making decisions within a resource problem shed are not able to adopt methods governing their relations to resources that would be economic in terms of the entire resource shed. Planning by some collective entity, whether a public agency or a trade association, may help to set up general criteria for a balance between private and public costs throughout the resource shed.

In a comprehensive plan to counteract pollution, there are several factors to be considered. These include: the physical quantities of the waste and of the receiving resource; the physical relationship one pollutant bears to another in affecting the receiving resources;

the avoidance of double-counting of either costs or benefits; the task of allocating the pollution sources and costs among the different economic sectors in the resource shed; and the job of setting up the cost of pollution attributable to any one sector, including the total cost of pollution imposed upon that sector by the operations both of pollution itself and the efforts made at controlling it. Currently, an accurate estimate of all these factors is not possible. Indeed, it is possible that, when accumulated, the knowledge necessary for such an estimate will reveal that certain factors are too intangible to be given any value other than zero in the technical manipulations of the planning system set up over a resource shed.

In planning, modern system analysis can do little more than gather information, direct attention to difficulties, and assist the making and implementation of decisions. It is not for planning to provide the network of aesthetic values that make many public efforts possible. The five-day work week, which has produced the greatest pressure for resource improvement in the United States, rests on a social change entirely divorced from the technical planning function. Maybe a programmer could presently give this pressure a value other than zero in the planning system, but such a condition could scarcely have been predicted, and the future importance of even a known social condition like this is not easy to forecast.

Yet the inability to cope with all the larger problems of society and the economy within the design system for a single resource shed ought not to prevent effort at coping with the problems. After all, what is the objective in economic terms of efforts to regulate the effect of pollution? The optimum, as economists see it, has been reached when the investment needed to secure control equals the value of the resources saved which would have been destroyed if pollution had gone on unchecked. Therefore, in this view, the law should cause effluent charges to equal the value of any resources saved.

If adopted, effluent charges should have a sliding scale capable of rising or falling with the level of pollution. With an adjustable scale, the polluter has an incentive to cut down on the harmful content of his effluent, either to prevent a rise in the effluent charge or to produce a reduction in it. If the charge is levied simply as a flat tax without regard to the possible changing condition of the resource which receives the effluent, the polluter's incentives will run the other way. If the charge is too low, he will treat it simply as a nuisance cost to be paid and forgotten. If the charge is too high, but not high enough to halt the production process which causes pollution, the polluter will work his process all the harder—and perhaps more carelessly in control of emissions—in order to cover the cost of the high effluent charge.

The control agency which administers the emission charges must have the power to set constraints and to vary them if there is to be a testing of the response of polluters to the control measures. This is particularly true where little can be known about the entire gamut of costs and benefits. Setting constraints simply determines the least value that society attaches to those ideals it is attempting to attain. Because cost-benefit analysis for a long while yet, perhaps a generation, will be no more than a guideline to policy, these constraints will play a large role, perhaps even the major part, in protecting the renewable resources. Economic techniques may oust constraints from this importance, but at the present—for better or worse—legal limitations imposed by public agencies are more significant.

DIFFICULTIES INHERENT IN REGULATION THROUGH CONSTRAINT

Just as economists have worried that too much reliance will be put upon cost-benefit figures that are only cash-oriented or that conceal behind pseudo-certainty ignorance and misinformation, the physical and biological scientists have had a dubious view of such constraints as quality standards. For years they insisted that the knowledge to set standards simply did not exist, because to get it would require a merging of expertise from engineering, meteorology, geology, zoology, bacteriology, chemistry, soils, and a much longer list of disciplines and technologies. Aldo Leopold, one of the leaders in ecology, furthered this view by insisting that the outstanding achievement of the twentieth century was neither radio nor television but the complexity of the land organism.[5] The job of setting standards in the quality of renewable resources has proven sufficiently difficult, at any rate, to have caused many chemists and biologists to oppose the legal institution of quality standards in effluent discharge and resource condition.

Precisely this sort of scientific opposition led Congress in the Water Quality Act of 1965 to mute the distinction between "standards," which lawyers urged, and "criteria," which many scientists argued were all the present state of knowledge could justify. The act does provide for standards of quality designed "to protect the public health or welfare, enhance the quality of water, and serve the purposes of this act," taking into consideration "their use and value for public water supplies, propagation of fish and wildlife, recreational purposes, and agricultural, industrial, and other legitimate uses." In passing on any standards adopted under these provisions, the act instructs the courts to give "due considera- to the practicability and to the physical and economic feasibility of complying with such standards . . . as the public interest and the equities of the case may require." However, in the final formula- tion the standards are confused with criteria. If the Secretary "determines that . . . State *criteria* and plans are consistent with [requirements of the act], such State *criteria* and plans shall there- after be the water quality *standards* applicable to . . . interstate water." [6]

In the statement of the managers of the act when it was before the House of Representatives, the word "criteria" was never men- tioned. The whole emphasis of the managers was upon quality *standards* as minimum requirements for all polluters to meet and as legally tangible mandates in the conduct of and performance by persons emitting waste into interstate rivers.[7] As a teacher of re- gional planning, Fred Clarenbach, said about the act, "We are apparently only at the beginning of a new phase of political- administrative bargainings and legal struggles which will test whether this kind of standards approach to the pollution problem is governmentally viable."[8] Muted or not by a Congress anxious to please both those concerned with immediately strict enforcement and those perturbed over a present lack of exact scientific knowl- edge, the concept of minimum standards has been incorporated into the federal legislation and in the future this idea can be expected to grow.

A very important pragmatic reason to doubt the efficacy of standards lies in the acute shortage of trained people in a wide variety of scientific and professional disciplines required by water pollution management. The Taft Sanitary Science Center, whose founding goes back to 1912, was for many years the only federal research installation in this field, and its staff was quite small, whereas the states did little or nothing compared to the size and growth of the problem. By 1965, the Taft Center had 150 staff members; there were 17 ancillary laboratories and 130 federal river sampling stations; 35 states had water quality agencies responsible for the development of comprehensive programs to deal with water pollution; and between 1956 and 1966, the states greatly increased their expenditures for water pollution control, although half of them still had only trifling programs. The shortage of trained personnel for the available jobs can only be compounded by the 1965 federal legislation: nine new laboratories, 170 new sampling stations, establishment of a research information retrieval service, and numerous requirements imposed on the states which have been left with the main burdens of water pollution control. Unless extensive training programs are set up, many of them of an on-the-job type, even an undignified scrambling for personnel will not unearth the needed people.

For many years, hostility to the constraints of quality standards has caused water pollution control administrators to oppose stream classification systems and licenses for polluters. Like standards for effluent discharge and for the quality of the receiving resource, the apparent simplicity of these latter devices has had a strong appeal to lawyers.[9] They have had considerably less vogue among men actually working in the field. The stream classification system, as it has worked in Massachusetts, sets up permissible conditions ranging from clean to waste-carrying waters either for a part or for an entire stream. Right away, such an approach thrusts the classifying agency into difficulties: a valley whose stream has been classified as clean may have trouble thereafter in attracting industry, while classifying a stream as one for waste-carriage may set back overall efforts at valley improvement. The survey required is an extensive one, and even a state as small as Massachusetts has been working on it over a decade.

Stream classification is a never-ending job, since it is always hoped that the economy will be dynamic. And of course the physical condition of any stream not utterly destroyed by waste *will* be an ever-changing one. There is a passive element in the process since so much energy must go into description. Furthermore, a classification may cause a political response in the affected area which may disrupt the agency's work, or perhaps worse, may evoke a smug or apathetic reaction. An irate regional association formed to change the conditions of a low classification might attract a disproportionate amount of attention from a small overworked agency. But in the long run a far worse response would be "Yes, the state boys are right! Stink Creek was always bad, and now the state says nothing can change it."

The same danger of passivity is present in the concept of a licensure of pollution. This assumes that it would be best to establish maximum tolerable limits for reception of waste by a given body, and then to grant licenses to individual emitters up to that amount. This attitude has perhaps been reinforced by the static nature of improvements in waste treatment and disposal which between 1900 and 1965 made so little theoretical advance. Certainly, licenses would be more meaningful if treatment facilities were not able through improvement to render previously written licenses anachronistic. If the licenses were to have more than nuisance value to the licensees, there would have to be the certainty in conditions that marks most property values. But the changes in waste emission and treatment which technology can produce over the coming decade would make the fixing of present conditions through a system of licensure a grave mistake.

Industry and government alike, in the area of waste treatment, need to be encouraged to seek technological improvement rather than to turn to methods which might hold back technical progress. In addition, and probably more pertinent to the attitude of pollution control administrators, there is the widespread opinion that licensing is a complex and time-consuming business requiring lengthy hearings, taking of testimony, and proceedings on appeal which would prevent the agency from doing other work or developing a more rational and efficient method of dealing with the problem.

Standards, classifications, and licenses have each been charged with being difficult to administer. This is in part due to a current lack of useful criteria which possess broad applicability and because of the shortcomings of measurement devices. But beyond these technical problems lies the larger one of insufficient public commitment to preserving the renewable resources. It is fear of this that makes so many administrators in this area doubtful of the burdensome use of legal constraints to protect the renewable resources.

THE COSTS OF INADEQUATE KNOWLEDGE

Doubt concerning the adequacy of legal restraints has led many scientists working in the renewable resources to push for research-study programs that would establish the physical, chemical, and biological limits within which the presence of contaminants must and can be permitted. No one has yet discovered the quantitative relationship between the pollutant and its environment which causes the changes in quality that are regarded as undesirable. Only recently, for example, air pollution control experts have concluded that their problem is not any one of the components discharged into the air, but rather the chain of reactions and transformations that are caused by interacting pollutants and such physical conditions as radiant energy and humidity. The drastic and frightening incidents of mass suffocations do not really demand extensive investigations. Chronic exposure to low pollution levels over a lifetime should cause the greatest concern.

Pollution control has been uncoordinated in the past, growing on a case-by-case basis in a context of lenient public attitudes toward polluters. Up to the mid-1960's, despite intellectual stagnation in the development of technical control devices, and despite the grievous lack of much-needed knowledge, a quantity of technology that had never been applied to the existing problems still persisted. The situation showed no sign of improving automatically in the presence of changing economic activities and the more subtle insults caused by newer kinds of pollutants. A charge has been made that this history of casual leniency accounts for the hostility which pollution control authorities express toward forms of control like classification, standards, and licensure. Their prejudice, it has been said, gave them an unwillingness to move in any direction until total knowledge had been accumulated and perfect certainty attained. In short, the accusation has been made that administrators have used the need for research as a means of fending off demands for closer enforcement.

Legislative efforts at breaking up the alleged effects of this attitude can be illustrated by two British statutes: the Clean Air Act of 1956 and the Water Pollution Act of 1963. Each makes a sharp division of responsibility between theory and enforcement. The Clean Air Act puts local authorities in charge of monitoring air conditions, issuing local regulations, and enforcing the law against polluters (alkaline wastes excepted). In this aspect of the operation, the emphasis is entirely upon a description of the situation, an application of the general law to local conditions, and the enforcement of the law upon local offenders. Air pollution research is divorced from all this activity. The research is conducted by three central ministries and is administered under the Departments of Scientific and Industrial Research and the Medical Research Council in the Privy Council. A similar division of enforcement and research marks the British water pollution legislation.[10]

If a conservative weight against more strict control does come from research-minded personnel, their isolation from enforcement should raise the restraint and allow the development of better regulation of renewable resources. It will also confer a neutrality upon the research personnel, so that their statements will not be regarded as colored by the enforcer's attitudes or by the ambitions of an administrator to build a good enforcement record. The risk is the isolation of the enforcement personnel from recent advances, from the change in attitude that contact with research people can produce in even the most pragmatic warden, and from the awareness of the tentative nature of so much scientific knowledge as it is now and will continue to be. In addition, as an examination of the British statutes shows, much of the separation occurs for administrative convenience anyway. Once an agency grows past a certain point, research tends to become isolated from the law enforcement branches. Indeed, the greater risk probably is that research people have too little influence rather than too much.

The pragmatic law enforcer and construction engineer tends to repeat what experience and his early education have taught him, only somewhat enlarged in scale. He lacks the knowledge which the researcher may have and which would permit a different approach. In the 1960's, the United States is at the point of accumulating huge quantities of water to be used largely for waste carriage and dilution purposes. This will require expenditures at which the mind reels, especially when the present gross *underloading* of water facilities for these purposes is recalled. Streams have become polluted because of a refusal to reduce the dilution factor and not because of a shortage of water. The same refusal to practice an economy of scale has produced demands for more water accumulation and transferral systems instead of the application or development of other water conservation techniques.

What this continuing application of traditional water distribution ideas requires is the redistribution of water over the earth's surface in a different time sequence and to different places than the natural allocation of water provides. The dam builders, the proponents of water transfer projects like NAWAPA and Feather River, and the great canal builders for irrigation uses ultimately are proposing nothing less than this. Massive movements of water over great distances are prominent features of modern water resources development projects. As demands for water mount with population growth and industrial expansion, such transfers involve larger volumes of water to be transported over longer distances by bolder engineering works.[11]

There is no question here of the economic bases of the demands having been analyzed and found valid in terms of comparative costs of water use, or of possible need for water in places from which it is taken. Cost-benefit ratio analyses are run, of course, before any transbasin diversion project can be begun. But these analyses have been repeatedly challenged by economists as inadequate even in the factors considered. A RAND Corporation study argued that an interest rate on these public water projects ought to include the costs to equity capital, and that this would have provided an interest rate since 1950 of at least 10 percent in lieu of the 2.5 to 4.5 percent rates which have been calculated for government resource projects between 1950 and 1965. The basis for these calculations, whatever figure is arrived at, is the rate at which the benefits expected to occur over a future period are discounted in order to obtain a present value that can be used for purposes of comparison with the present value of the costs incurred during the period. There is general agreement that the rates used by governmental agencies have been too low, even if the RAND estimate is regarded as too high, and that, under contemporary conditions, a rate of at least 6 percent is thought by the majority of economists to be the better of the two extremes.[12]

Perhaps more important, however, is the persistent belief among many scientists that these projects do not encompass enough factors in their calculations. If the proposed Rampart Dam is built in Alaska, the major duck-breeding marsh grounds for the North American continent will be destroyed. If the proposed coastal water transfer canal is built in the Texas Gulf area, breeding grounds for huge quantities of commercially exploited marine life will be eliminated. Although there is some dispute whether either destruction would be total, and considerable dispute as to whether the wildlife breeding in these areas would also be destroyed, there is no doubt that breeding would be reduced.

There can be little doubt at all about the attitudes of the water planners behind these projects: they have looked with contempt and impatience at all such objections. Somehow the persons who fear for the Gulf of Mexico fishing industry and for much of the migratory bird population that wings across and out of the North American continent have been lumped with the ladies' club president in her flowered hat who is perturbed by vivisection as practiced on lap dogs.

Yet, even if these physical qualities represent values hard to express in cash terms, there is also the charge that it is economically unwise to deprive a presently underdeveloped area of water in order to transfer its contents to another zone. This, it is argued, is the equivalent of transferring the region's economic future as well. The argument on these lines runs on the premise that it is not possible to quantify a decision of this sort so that it can be expressed in the terms of a cost-benefit analysis, not even if the interest rate should be set far higher than the RAND study's recommendation. Inquiry in these matters should include more than the hydrologic and technical aspects of the problem. The growing uses for renewable resources in recreation, in the protection of wildlife habitat, and as a means of determining the quality of both urban and rural life, must not be overlooked if the appraisal is to be truly realistic.

POSSIBLE COSTS OF ERROR IN RESOURCE CONTROL

Stewart Udall has said that "Helter-skelter is a pretty good description [of federal planning] . . . Somebody decides a project should be built and that single project is studied, rather than the entire river basin." [13] But with water demands for every use growing and with costs increasing, competition among overlapping water resource management systems has been compelling a more general approach. Regional organizations for water resources have been set up in all parts of the United States.

Since the mid-1920's, many short-term efforts have studied, made plans and recommendations, and then departed the scene, leaving nothing behind them to carry on a coordinated program of work among the renewable resources. Some results have been valuable, but a permanent organization had to be created to ensure the feedback of ideas which would keep planning from being a disembodied enterprise. Too often, the engineer with his mind on the "bold" public works approach has had an insufficient knowledge and appreciation of less spectacular devices such as taxes, special benefit assessments, pricing policies, shoreline and flood plain zoning, subsidies, and other measures that a comprehensive plan could produce without requiring massive construction.

Yet the work goes on in classifying water resources as if the bold promise of such public works projects as large-scale water transfers were presently known to be the proper physical and economic solutions to impending water problems. The prospect of these transfers has prompted pressure groups to push for statutes limiting the use of water to its originating watershed in order to protect that area's general population, economy, and developmental future. Part of this pressure also comes from the fact that legal compensation would go only to the holders of water rights and that nothing would go to the other economic activities adversely affected. When Los Angeles in the 1920's wanted the water from the Owens

Valley, these "peripheral" interests caused the difficulty. Only the outright purchase of the valley at what were then considered peak prices settled a veritable guerrilla war which Owens Valley residents launched against the Angelenos' water project.

Some of these protection statutes, like the 1965 Texas Act, have limitations of time within which the water "surplus" areas will be protected. This has beeen called derisively the "fifty-year lockup"; and pathetic hypotheses have been posed in which thirsty cities perish, having been statutorily denied salvation "for the purpose of preserving, for the benefit of sportsmen, marshes inhabited by game birds." [14] The federal government has avoided taking a stand, although the implication in congressional enactments is against transfers.[15]

But such legislation is very inadequate protection, quite aside from the fact it can be repealed any time. Except as forbidden by Congress, the federal government has power to ignore such state restrictions in its own purchase and use of water rights. River basin development has been the result of federal action; most of the money spent has had a federal origin; the federal government traditionally takes a view transcending local ambitions; and federal action can be expected to resort to large-scale water transfers unless diverted to alternatives. Even the general recognition that the states have a prior claim on unused water can mean very little if the federal government decides to move toward the concept of a nationally operated "strategic water bank." [16]

Another of the uncertainties is the fact that no watershed is a complete hydrological entity because there is a certain amount of both surface and subsurface interchange. The drawing of the basin lines is for most areas a very difficult task. The state of Texas has over 7,500 named streams but, depending on how the physical data have been appraised, only eleven or fifteen "major" river basins. Flat lands lying in the middle and upper reaches of rivers are extremely ambiguous in their hydrologic location; and for purposes of securing the legal protection that is offered by statutes forbidding water transfers, their location is hard to determine.

The problem of large-scale water transfers is a vexing one. To prohibit them may deprive a growing area of water, and the prohibition may only benefit a few businessmen in the valley of origin.

The prohibition may also sacrifice present use for future needs which may never develop in the area protected from water transfer. In lieu of these statutory prohibitions, some observers would vest permit power in an administrative agency which would grant the permits only if the benefits to the whole area prospectively exceeded the harm to the basin of origin—an indication, certainly, that few permits would be denied.

Absolute limitations upon the allocation of water, whether in the form of statutes, compacts, or treaties, are, after all, suspect. Some water specialists, at any rate, feel that flexibility should be maintained in adapting water allocations to developing future requirements. Some of these men even go so far as to say that the public should have the power under eminent domain to force the exchange of private water rights.

The amorphous rights of local and state governments in water are exemplars of such "flexible" property interests. Counties, municipalities, special districts, and the like are regarded as creatures of the state. The state therefore has claimed the power to take their real property or contract rights without compensation, although some recent case law implies that such a power extends not to "proprietary" but only to the "governmental" interests of these local entities. To which of these categories water interests will be assigned remains an unsettled question, but, so far as the state is concerned, water rights developed by the local entities will be held "proprietary," for the most part. The regulatory power of Congress over navigable rivers permits a similar extinction without compensation of rights held by or from the states. And here there is no "proprietarial" protection or any limited definition of the federal government's navigable easement.[17] But it is doubtful if the rules will remain so "flexible" in the presence of ever heavier local and state water investments. The same reasons for protecting investments hold for private water interests.

For the same reasons that they dislike rigid limitations on resource use, renewable resource specialists regret the relinquishment to the states of former inherent federal powers over water. Congress has been reluctant to assert its powers against the states; the approach it has preferred to take has been subsidization. This policy has rarely failed to get the states' ultimate cooperation.

Pressure is growing to transfer water for agricultural, municipal, wildlife, recreational, and environmental purposes. The costs of transporting water show every sign of increasing, yet the attitude toward water as a free or subsidized good remains very strong. Water rates in New York City were raised in 1870 and then not increased again until 1934. In the United States as of 1965, only 3 percent of irrigation water, 3 percent of water for industrial use, and 13 percent of domestic water were supplied by profit-seeking firms. The bulk of water used is either self-supplied or comes from politically controlled organizations which have non-economic reasons for holding down water charges, as is shown by the higher rates that companies owned by municipalities levy on non-residents.[18] Agricultural, industrial, and municipal water users have no wish to pay the reasonable facsimile of the "full economic cost" of making water supplies available to them. Under such conditions, a turning toward the federal government could be expected; and if there should be a response, then, unless alternatives truly do not exist, the costs of such a mistake would be incalculably huge.

CREATION OF ALTERNATIVE CONTROL METHODS
FOR RENEWABLE RESOURCES

The total redistribution of water on the North American continent or the transport of desalinated ocean water into the continent's interior may prove necessary if no change occurs in the growing demands for water, particularly if government continues to respond to these demands by attempting to supply water free or at less than cost. Yet before that drastic course is resorted to, obviously, efforts should be made to cut back on the use of the environment, water included, for the carriage and retention of waste, and attempts at more inclusive cost-benefit analyses might be tried. To accomplish these ends requires creation of a government control body that knows how the total environment can be employed productively by the country's economic activity, that can set up a cost-benefit analysis program more inclusive of physical factors than analyses used elsewhere, and that can use techniques for organizing data and criteria so that decisions can flow directly from the information gathered, if political circumstances make that possible.

The effectiveness of any reaction to the problem raised by the impact of modern economic activity upon the quality of the environment depends upon the public policies and institutional arrangements made. Private activity and the actions of individual public agencies must take place within the scope provided by law and public policy. Single economic units or associations representing special interests can scarcely be expected to concern themselves with the general social welfare, even if possessed of a high degree of altruism and public spirit. Under an encompassing design for renewable resource use, public institutions must balance returns from differing economic practices in the general community so that society will enjoy maximum returns in cash and in forms not expressible in cash.

The institutional organization most often recommended for these ends is one that follows the problem shed contours of any particular renewable resource. For water, the shed is usually a river basin, including the precipitation and the underground waters moving toward the lowest levels in the basin. For air, the shed would be a region having meteorological similarities, containing closely related economic activities and concentrations of population, and including less developed areas upwind. Other renewable resource sheds are more difficult to define in a general way. Soil pollution can be something as narrow as the difficulties of solid waste disposal or as broad as biocide dispersal, while problem sheds for game, forests, and fish in the open seas will have widely differing sizes.

All of these problem sheds overlap and interlock in a way that makes even the problem-shed approach to administration a difficult one. Because of this overlap, creation of a National Commission for Environmental Protection and a cabinet-level Department of Natural Resources has been urged. Still, the emphasis remains upon the regional problem-shed approach to each of the renewable resources, and the agencies most emphasized for utility have been the river basin commissions. The only river basin commission which had been fully organized by the mid-1960's for objects other than study, high-level planning, or a few specialized purposes was the Delaware River Basin Commission.[19] Other river basins, however, will base their organizations on the Delaware pattern, and the exist-

ing commissions will probably be reformed along its more operational lines. This kind of permanent interstate-federal compact
agency offers the most promise for long-run improvement in planning and implementing the planning of water resources for a region.

The Delaware Basin Commission's powers are quite broad. It
can sell bonds to raise capital funds, and it prepares a cost-sharing
plan for member states and the federal government. The commission can accept from its members grants, appropriations, and both
reimbursable and non-reimbursable fund advances for either capital or operating expenses. Its other possible sources of revenues
include special benefit assessments and sales of products and
services.

Like other commissions created under interstate compacts, the
Delaware Basin's is heavily dependent upon federal funds; for
practical reasons, this subordinates the commission's basin program to overall federal requirements. Thus, although the commission is directed to establish "uniform standards and procedures for
project evaluation, cost allocations, and determination of project
priorities, and also the establishment of formulas for cost sharing,
reimbursement, and payments in lieu of taxes," most knowledgeable
persons have concluded that the commission will make no efforts
to improve on any standards and procedures set up by federal
agencies or cost-benefit analyses used at the federal level. James
Wright, the executive director of the commission, has put it this
way: "We have gone slow because we have taken a couple of pressure groups to our bosom; we now want to see how well we can
dance before we invite anybody else to the party. . . . What we
have tried to do is to avoid their coming to an either/or position,
a complete black-or-white, take-it-or-leave-it proposition, because
if you do that, particularly in the early years of an agency, you are
liable to be a hero or dead—but the hell with insurance policies,
you know." [20]

The commission's hardest job, which it has been reluctant to
tackle, is the equitable reapportionment of the water. An Industry
Committee has been appointed, and its first discovery was learning that quality control could be had at a minimum cost if differential standards were imposed on the various discharges coming
into the river. This difference has seemed inequitable to many ob-

servers. "If anybody is going to suffer, let's all suffer together," seems a preferable motto. Nevertheless, the economically sensible thing to do is to draw up standards on the basis of regional and seasonal differences and to make them responsive to technical change, despite legal and political difficulties. Such standards would represent a crude balancing of benefits and costs. But unless the commission could accomplish the same result through an effluent charge system alone, the effort at setting minima for stream quality should not be given up. The commission certainly cannot ever give assurances concerning the stability of standards beyond what "the art would permit" and the promise that changes would not be capricious.

In fact, these problems are so difficult that some experts believe they cannot be solved either with a state or a problem-shed approach. The fiscal load, these critics charge, will become so great that local communities will not submit themselves to the burden; and the renewable resources are not a sufficiently powerful dimension around which to unite people for multi-purpose objectives on a problem-shed regional basis. These problem-shed units will constitute governments of considerable magnitude and joint political cost. The energy and commitment called for transcend the amounts of money that many authorities believe are available in relation to such specialized functions or to the states themselves. In this view, only the transcendant wealth and power of the federal government as nationally applied would be sufficient.

DIFFICULTIES IN FEDERAL CONTROL OF RENEWABLE RESOURCES

Even those who have the greatest faith in the problem-shed approach expect a great deal from the federal government. The federal government should, they think, help finance and stimulate the establishment of problem-shed agencies; set up minimum requirements for the competence of personnel, program composition, and the financial support coming from non-federal sources as a prerequisite for receiving federal funds; act wherever problem-shed agencies do not exist at the state or regional level; and help to develop model state legislation and interstate compacts. Given this sort of requirement for federal action, it is not difficult to explain the optimism of men who see as inevitable complete federal operation of the programs for managing the renewable resources.

Beginning with Lord Shaftesbury in the mid-nineteenth century and continuing through Gifford Pinchot in the twentieth, persons concerned with the problems of life-cycle resources have turned to the prospect of strong control by a central government. There is a kind of touching faith in the call for the appointment by the President of a federal board "composed of a relatively small number of public-spirited men," "statesmanlike individuals," who would give a "dynamic" quality to "the total national effort." [21] It is certainly true that this kind of service seems to be missing at the local, state, and regional levels, but there is some reason to wonder if any better service will come from federal sources. The federal government may look good because it has so sharply confined its control over renewable resources to something far less than the full authority it could have exercised. Its greater involvement is surely occurring, but all the problems of resource specificity, value choices, and cost allocations have not yet beset the federal administrators. The very fact that these problems have truly become too much for local, state and regional governmental units to handle suggests that the federal government may also be hard-pressed for answers. There need be no euphoric joy expressed at the arrival of federal control; a nod of recognition at the grim necessity will do.

FORMATION OF A PUBLIC POLICY TOWARD RENEWABLE RESOURCES

The working out of a political policy at any level is difficult. Public policy must settle upon the objectives to be sought and the constraints to be imposed. The imposition of constraints—standards, charges, and prohibitions—enables society to reach objectives that cannot be obtained through subsidization or through the chance of allowing the renewable resources to be exploited as free goods.[22] This last recourse has been made possible by the copious renewable resources which the North American continent has for so long made available to the entrepreneurs within the economy. And American public policy has traditionally favored the approach of subsidies. The subsidies might be federal money for irrigation, or state money for drainage, or local money supporting low water rates, but the use of the general fund at every level of government continues.

Subsidy programs will grow larger than ever before, but public policy, as formed at every level of government, must take increasing note of other ways to reach objectives and to impose constraints. In the long run, of course, government cannot replace the natural conditions which persisted for centuries until man began to make significant inroads. Not even the scope of the contemporary American economy can provide the wherewithal to perform that task if the view persists that the renewable resources are free goods.

Costs to the renewable resources that may be external to the economic activities that impose them are called spill-over or spattered effects. But they occur within the larger economy, and they are not external to it. Even if the harm done is not entirely destructive in either an economic or a physical way but is singled out as the result of an aesthetic demand for a higher-quality environment, these costs must still be borne within the larger economy. For these "external" costs there is no cornucopia external to the general economy which will make them up.

It may be that the welfare economists are right in claiming that government can develop some sort of analog to the market which, through bargaining among representatives of contending interests, would allow an outcome which satisfies all interests. Even if the analog gave no more than a rough notion of the priorities attached to values and of the variety in the values to be structured into decision-making, the help from welfare economics would be great. Unfortunately, the better argument may lie with those economists who say that such analogs are not possible. And, however this is resolved for purposes of prediction, there are always the dismal prophecies of the neo-Malthusians.

Yet, whatever the accuracy of the various economic schools of analysis, the fact remains that the day of the free good in renewable resources has drawn to an end. Efforts to substitute government subsidy for natural process must be more expensive than bringing costs within a scheme of resource specificity and of internalizing all costs to the economic or social process imposing them. Even if the subsidy approach is kept, there should be at the very least precise knowledge of what a program is costing. Once the costs of such subsidies have been appraised, however, the beneficiaries should not be surprised if they are asked either to share the bulk of them or to forgo the proposed benefits. And if government must replace nature as the free supplier of the renewable resources, then there should be no repining at the costs, whether they are economic, social, or physical.

10

The choices in controlling the environment

VARIABLE IMPORTANCE OF PARTICULAR RESOURCE USES

When the use of the water wheel for flour milling and similar operations spread throughout the Roman Empire in the fourth century A.D., it produced a severe economic crisis. Huge investments in slaves were reduced to a fraction of their previous value because the water wheel could provide more energy, more work, and more output at a small initial cost and with practically no upkeep. Samsons were no longer needed to turn the millstones. The effect was so severe even upon the free labor market that the widespread use of the water wheel probably did more harm than good to contemporary society.

Yet in terms of ultimate social progress the water wheel was worth the price the Roman imperial economy had to pay. Similar advances in the quality of life have been made at no less cost. Indeed, some economic dislocation is to be expected with every change in economic activity, however generally beneficial its ultimate effect upon society may be. As the ancient Romans knew only too well, these threatening changes come from the most unexpected sources. Their very unexpectedness, as a matter of fact, makes them extremely difficult for the social structure to absorb.

In 1963, the dollar value of tourism in Kentucky was nearly three times that of coal mined by strip and auger methods. Suddenly, an industry which had previously contributed importantly to the state's economy was a serious threat in a changed situation: mining was damaging Kentucky's parks and tourist industry, ruining rivers for fishing and water supply, destroying the land's agricultural productivity, and threatening the property tax base. In some counties, the strip-mining operations are expected to cut out 50 to 70 percent of the land which, after mining, is assessed at 75 cents an acre.

Under these conditions, the local tax base disappears, and the basis for any revival of the local economy becomes very hard to find. Certain rivers are so silted up and made so acid by mining that they support neither the fish in them nor the game upon their banks, and their water cannot be used either industrially or municipally. The strip-mining companies employ relatively few workmen, in comparison with either the old closed-shaft mines or the current recreation industry. And strip-mining benefits only a few miners, the coal operators, and the purchasers of lower-priced coal and low-cost electricity—this at the cost of permanent damage imposed upon the water, forest cover, wildlife, and soil of Kentucky, together with the industries dependent upon them. But more important, strip-mining takes away all chance of an economically viable future for the affected areas.

Some observers claim it is possible for the strip-miners to restore the landscape by back-filling, grading back to the approximate original contours, and replanting vegetation. But at legislative hearings the loudest applause is most often for those members who are against being too "severe" on the industry. It is certain that anyone trying to enforce land restoration requirements on the miners of eastern Kentucky will have his chance to be a hero, if the industry ever concludes that some particular rule is too harsh.

Although the profit rate is highest for strip-mining, the profit margin in the coal industry has been historically narrow. In what other enterprise did the Mellons and Rockefellers once go bankrupt? But the poet Wendell Berry raises the hardest question of all when, in a comparison of profits and losses, he asks if there is any hope at all for a region with mineral extraction in an era of strip- and auger-mining, or if it has become plain that strip- and auger-mining will have to be stopped in order to save the natural environment.[1]

It is not at all certain, even if the strip-mining industry were to cooperate, that restoration would be always possible after strip methods had been used. Soils are very badly turned over, so that sterile earths may have been brought uppermost. Or the topsoil of the region, even if re-laid by the graders, may be too poor to permit a sufficiently rapid recovery by vegetation before it is eroded away. In such shattered areas, the game population of wild rodents increases and, if any grass cover is left, the deer numbers also grow. Tender young shoots or saplings are often eaten away before any growth is possible. There is also the presence in many worked-out seams of acids which seep through the soil to kill every plant at its roots. Even where the acid fails to reach the roots of growing plants, it seeps into nearby waterways to kill every living thing.

There are no places more eerie than some of the restored areas in southern Indiana. The coarse hillocks are covered with fir trees, and the acid waters of the mines lie still at the base of the hillocks undisturbed by any motion. The restoration has been a success, but the seeping of acid will go on into the indefinite future.

And where restorative efforts are avoided by means of bankruptcies, bribery of enforcement officers, or deceitful plantings of dead seedlings, the results are no different than if the statute books were silent. Few states have strip-mining restoration acts; those that do exist are mostly post-World War II provisions. They are not retroactive, so no more has been done about the abandoned strip mines than about the slag heaps, gob piles, culm banks, and tailings of the abandoned shaft mines, except in the one or two instances such as Pennsylvania's clearing the Schuylkill of culm.

Most conservationists believe that the language of the land restoration statutes is far too lenient to the strip-mining industry. And even this permissive language can scarcely be said to have been severely enforced in any state. Though the public has general support for the land restoration statutes, persons who are concerned more specifically seem always most to admire owners who are successful in avoiding law enforcement. The aesthetic and economic losses pass unnoticed, because the sportsman is pleased at what he bags in the eroded scrub growing over the old workings. The tourist is pleased with the parks he visits and of course pays no attention to the blasted areas he will never see. The coal buyer is pleased at a price lower than it would be either if shaft mining were still in vogue or if the strip-miners had to effectively restore the land. Finally, the regions exploited are pleased by the very reduction in usable land which strip mining imposes, since after stripping of the land the natives can satisfactorily claim that they are powerless to change things.

Under these conditions, the laments occasioned by strip mining convey about as much grief as fourth-century Romans did when they saw the economic effects of the water wheel. The principal difference between Rome then and America now is that enough capital is available to the United States for a variety of choices that were utterly impossible in the Rome of Diocletian.

HOPE FOR AUTOMATIC SALVATION FROM RESOURCE USE

Unfortunately, this plentiful capital has meant less than it should in the United States. Seymour Melman has claimed for several years that there has been a gross misallocation of capital away from improvements in the quality of environment and in the industrial base of the economy. The fixed investment ratio in the United States has had a persistent overall decline since 1945.[2] Despite the upturn in water treatment investments since 1958, the general decline has had to mean a serious lack of sufficient capital allocations to the protection of renewable resources. In 1951, commenting on the problem, the Commission on Conservation Education in American Schools said, "The cost of our industrial supremacy, of wars, and of our efforts to establish peace, has been stupendous in terms of resource use. . . . The basic natural resources which are essential to the vigor and security of our nation—soil, water, plants, animals, and a lengthy list of minerals . . . to some extent through necessity, but more often through exploitation, sheer indifference, or thoughtlessness, we have wasted."[3] The intervening years have changed the situation in no way, except to complicate it through the sharp rise in interest rates. There is the same demand upon the renewable resources and the same slight investment in their protection.

The hope remains that resource exploitation will somehow produce resource salvation. In the Southwest, because of the shortage of water to support the carefully created economic activities at an ever-accelerating pace, concern has been expressed over the wastage of water by phreatophytes. It is true that the removal of the Indian to his reservations, and the ensuing stoppage of grass burnings, has permitted tree invasion in areas previously bare of anything except grass cover. But many biologists seriously question how great a loss of water this growth has produced in the Southwest, since the evaporation rate runs so high, and the plants, including trees, draw water from levels above the aquifers.

Although nearly all run-off and stream flow is appropriated for irrigation, the bulk of the water used in the Southwest is pumped from layers deep within the ground. If every phreatophyte were removed, the easing of demand upon the water supply would be scarcely perceivable. Measures such as lining the irrigation canals with impermeable sides or covering artificial storage reservoirs with non-absorptive membranes will make far more water available for commercial exploitation.

Yet a federally financed program for the destruction of phreatophytes is being carried on with the same enthusiasm as the old federally financed programs of predator extermination or pest eradication. The idea of the "tin-roof watershed," with its bare mountains, or simply grass, to increase the run-off, is the underlying objective. The trees can be seen from the air, lying on the mountainsides like giant hay. They are set to burning in the winter, and the phreatophytes stand especially high on the list for eradication.

Despite the enthusiasm, the water saved in such a way as to be economically significant will be insignificant. The number of problems raised in this campaign will probably be as great as those brought forward by the predator and pest eradication programs. Selective cutting of trees to permit snow retention is one thing; but cutting the new black cedar growth off the mountains, without tight grazing controls, may cause serious erosion in regions where the demands for grass are high.

Yet if a chemical can be spread to kill a species of insect, or if poisoned bait can be flung out for coyotes, or if tractors can tear out trees with chains, there must always be strong sentiment in the background. Destruction promises the quick permanent answer in lieu of the slower promises held out by other methods. The effects of destruction often betray easy optimism by proving far wider than usually anticipated when the programs are initiated. If eradication finally occurs, the reasons frequently have little to do with the program.

It has been predicted that after 1980, the United States will suffer a severe shortage of lumber, as well as a land deficit for recreational purposes and grazing. Certainly the sparing of the scant scrubby phreatophytes in the Southwest could do nothing to offset this shortage. Yet, unless major investments are made in research, development, and conservation of resources, the problems will become very severe indeed.

In 1965, the Surgeon General of the United States claimed that the country was at least a decade late in "controlling the pollution of our environment. . . . We are either going to do something about the pollution . . . or we literally are going to drown in [waste]. . . . Industry [has been] almost oblivious to any responsibility in this direction. . . . We are now getting some response. But it is awfully late, and we are going to need a lot more cooperation from industry than they have put into it thus far." [4]

The Surgeon General was not exaggerating. In 1966, 43 percent of the waste entering the Hudson River received no treatment of any kind, and fishing in the river had ceased as a commercial enterprise because several stretches could support only eels and one ten-mile section at Troy-Albany was dead to aerobic water life.[5] The Southeast, which for years lured industry by promising freedom from water pollution control, had found by 1965 that its over fifty inches of annual rainfall and its swiftly flowing rivers were hopelessly insufficient to meet the demands of modern industry. The Georgia State Water Quality Board reported that the Chattahoochee, the Coosa, and the Savannah rivers had reached "critical" conditions under a prevailing situation in which wastes entering them received either very sketchy treatment or none at all. Georgia, which had been luring twentieth-century industry with the promise of maintaining a nineteenth-century climate of resource protection, found that the very success which this inducement produced has itself been the source of a catastrophic decline in the quality, availability, and utility of the state's water resource.[6]

Although at one time the quantity and quality of such entities in nature as water, air, and soil could be relied upon by human activity, the situation has changed. America's surface water has been so used and reused as an economic asset that it is misleading to consider it a purely "natural" resource. The same is so true for air and soil that, simply to preserve their economic utility, what has been called "this wild scheme of the elimination of all pollution at its sources" ultimately must be instituted.[7]

Sewage waste in the future will be recycled, and at each cycling about 75 percent will be recovered as usable water. In 1965, cities were spending an average of 17 cents per thousand gallons to get fresh water to the point where it was ready for distribution. (The cost of salvaging water from sewage fell into that category of expense.) Since it can be proven statistically that the main course of American rivers is through the human alimentary canal, it would seem to be economically more sensible to salvage potable water from sewage at this cost than to turn to the far more expensive water transfer and desalinating techniques so commonly regarded as tomorrow's solution to water problems. Even the mechanical aeration of putrid rivers by pumping may offer more of a solution than the more elaborate water proposals, since if badly polluted streams could be salvaged where water was needed, hauling water long distances at greater comparative expense would not be necessary.[8]

GAP BETWEEN RESOURCE CONDITIONS AND PUBLIC AWARENESS

Ever since the Crown in the seventeenth century appointed "the Water Poet," John Taylor, "to co-operate with the water-baily in clearing the river [Thames] of dead hogs, cats, and carrion horses," the pollution of streams has worsened steadily, with government showing little originality in counteracting it. In the 1640's, Taylor secured his appointment by recommending to Charles I and the Lords Commissioners that the rivers could be cleaned and dredged by putting the unemployed and beggarly poor to work.[9]

Such schemes have always had appeal, and governments have often responded. But protecting the renewable resources rarely seems to have an importance equal to other contemporary difficulties, whatever the age. After all, in 1649, Charles I lost his crown and his head together. Beside such problems, water purity must have seemed of slight importance indeed. Presidents of the United States in our own century must view water with about the same perspective. It always has been as Sir Edwin Chadwick, the father of the English public health movement, put it, that "Public men know nothing, want to know nothing, [and] hate to be told anything, which does not openly and directly affect their political position and safety." Even when they express a sincere interest, their concern in the protection of the renewable resources remains "the minor measure of a minor department."

The change in living patterns, both in Europe and in North America, has helped to extend a similar kind of buffer between the consciousness of the public and the condition of the natural resources employed in the modern economy. The drought in the American Northeast in the 1960's had been severe for three years before the city populations became aware of it. Shallow-rooted trees, like the dogwood and poplar, had been dying in large numbers; trees with deeper roots, unable to draw enough water for their whole system, had dead crowns by the thousands; the use of irrigation had been sharply curtailed; and the dairy industry had been seriously embarrassed. But the urban populations knew nothing of this until the announcements of public officials informed them that the reservoirs in the New York metropolitan area were perilously low and the water in the Delaware was threatened with salt water invasion.

Of course, part of the reason for this unawareness lay in the fact that only modern demands for water and modern methods of supplying municipal water made the drought a problem. Enough rain had fallen along the seaboard to maintain dry farming, the traditional method of agricultural operations. Only irrigation farmers and those with the poorest soil were adversely affected. The system of trapping water in the mountains for New York City's water supply deprived the Delaware of the water needed to hold back the salt water front, so that salts could push far upriver. Although the low rainfall was unprecedented and prolonged, its consequences came largely from the type of demands made upon water under modern requirements for quantity, modern systems of gathering and storage, and modern need for waterways as receiving bodies to dilute and carry waste. The Northeast's drought of the 1960's proved to be peculiarly a twentieth-century phenomenon.

Under non-drought conditions, in New York City the use of water averages 150 gallons a day per person—water so pure and soft that the greatest problem with it is the corrosive effect on the pipes. At the same time the use of water in London averages fifty gallons a day per person—probably more an indication of the lag between English and American economic practices than any show of superiority in English techniques. The character of the American economy is such that very little foreign experience can be copied. When polled, three out of four Americans thought the government at every level—federal, state, and local—should take steps to provide more water for industry and municipalities.[10] Plainly, in any choice between restricting water use and expanding the supply at the expense of the general fund, Americans would overwhelmingly choose the latter, and the ratio would probably be highest among business and political leaders.

Regard for the quality of the environment has traditionally been low within the economic and political leadership. In 1834, Sir James Scarlett, later Lord Abinger, appeared in court to defend the London gas works for polluting the Thames. His argument was as simple as a cartoon: "If it can be shown that the comfort and security are much promoted by particular works, it would be absurd to say that the poisoning of a few fish was a thing not to be tolerated. . . . It is a matter of sound reason and good policy to have these things which are advantageous to the public." [11]

The possibility of the loss of present economic advantages is not the only thing that mobilizes support against measures to protect the renewable resources. Anything which might discourage the continued growth of the economy will bring out the opposition of chambers of commerce and labor unions alike. Some reason can always be found to get political support to suppress resource protection, as when Henry Schricker, then governor of Indiana, said in 1942, ". . . it would be irrational to attempt punitive action against industries . . . exerting themselves on war production."

With such attitudes in the wind, it should be no surprise, therefore, that the major sources for the pollution of Lake Michigan have come out of the Calumet District along the Indiana-Illinois border and have included United States Steel, Youngstown Sheet and Tube, Inland Steel, Republic Steel, Cities Service, Sinclair and Mobil Oil Companies, International Harvester, Union Carbide, and Lever Brothers. Public protection and public favor has made it possible. In 1965, United States Steel alone daily poured into the Calumet, Grand Calumet, and Little Calumet rivers over 13,750 pounds of ammonia nitrogen, 1,500 pounds of phenol, 1,700 pounds of cyanide, 54,000 pounds of oil, and a total waste emission of 230 million gallons.[12] The only surprise in this situation was that so few state and local politicians came forward to argue that industry was doing the best it could do.

A sense of crisis can, of course, produce attitudes much more amenable to improved resource use. The bickering and litigious proceedings which had marked New York City's use of mountain water from shortly after World War I to the mid-1950's were suppressed in the mid-1960's in the presence of the drought. This peace was made possible because of the machinery of the Delaware River Basin Commission and the substantial federal presence of the Water Resources Council. Instead of the sort of argument that had marked the past, the Commission was able to issue an order allocating water resources within the basin, and a situation that could have meant a decade of court contests was brought within a unanimous agreement.

The Delaware River Basin Commission machinery was important because it provided a means of settlement and enforcement which had not existed previously. Of considerable, though less tangible, significance was the existence of the falling levels in New York's reservoirs and the rising salt line in the Delaware. These were no less powerful persuaders for some speedy allocation of existing water resources, since the traditional patterns of special pleading and diversionary court processes would have produced a prompt economic crisis.

When the physical quantity or quality of a resource falls below the needs of the local economy, that economy will perish unless society takes steps to improve or alter the resource base. The disappearance of a stock resource like ore or a flow resource like timber produces ghost towns and perhaps great regional suffering. But to destroy the renewable resources of water, air, and soil is to work a real destruction that, at the last moment, is bound to produce strong and popular counter-measures. Whatever the permanent reality of water shortage in the Northeast, the sense of urgency in the mid-1960's elicited some attention, though not nearly enough. Even real crisis in the renewable resources can only put Americans at the beginning of the beginning.

SIMILAR REACTIONS TO THREATS OF RENEWABLE
RESOURCE SHORTAGE

In most of the eastern United States, water shortage is not a matter of an overall physical absence of water. Rather, the shortage is the result of institutional failures and the peculiarities of local demand on every level from the most bucolic to the most urban communities. New York lets the Hudson River roll by her and uses it for nothing except a waste receptacle. Instead of pushing for the improvement of this potential water supply, New York City adds to the pollution and uses this condition to justify not drawing the Hudson water into the city system.

Ultimately, New York, for the sake of its future economic growth, will have to do what water experts as far back as 1950 told the city administration it would have to do: draw water from the Hudson. Only the threat to economic growth and sustenance will call forth public measures relating to the better use, improvement, and protection of the renewable resources. As long as high-quality mountain water could be supplied to New York industry in sufficient quantity, no one objected to the abandonment of the newly-built Chelsea pumping station on the Hudson in 1953, since the water at Chelsea would have required extensive treatment and even after treatment would have lowered the traditional quality in New York City mains. However, in the absence of enough purer water to meet the growing demand in New York, there must be an ultimate resort to the Hudson and an unprecedented resort to anti-pollution measures for the whole Hudson river basin.

In 1938, $10 million was regarded as too high a price to clean up the Hudson. In 1965, the voters of New York State voted for a $1 billion bond issue to do the job. Requirements for economic growth carry the greatest weight, even if much of the talk is about improving the quality of the environment. Public men may speak about the need for conservation, but a *New York Times* reporter summed up the importance of any renewable resource when he said the way it was used "will affect future land values, factory location decisions, the growth of cities and entire regions. It will help determine where people live, work and play, and what they pay for a host of things they eat and use." [13] Aesthetics, amenity, and the quality of life were not prominently emphasized in the list.

This superordinate importance of the place held by economic growth in relation to the renewable resources is general throughout American society, no matter how small or large the community. Lansdale, Pennsylvania, a small city dependent on wells, developed during the Korean War an industrial growth program that by 1957 had produced a water "famine." The aquifers upon which the city's wells depended could not recharge at a rate equal to the withdrawals, and a program of merely enlarging existing wells or sinking new ones could not be the answer to the community's self-created problem.

Of course, the city of Lansdale could have accepted the limitation of its aquifers' recharge rate as constituting the limit of the local economy. Instead, a group of businessmen and public officials organized and appealed to the Montgomery County Commissioners. The result was a long-term plan to be partly fulfilled between 1962 and 1987, payable through water rates and out of the general county funds, for enough water for unstinted economic growth during the next half-century. The president of the newly formed local water association said the plan would "save" the community from "water famine," and a county commissioner replied that it was "a cooperative effort between the citizens of the area and all levels of government."

Unfortunately, the ambitious scope of the plan kept it from being immediately useful, and temporary contracts had to be made with surrounding towns. This arrangement irked interests in these neighboring towns a bit, to think that Lansdale was growing at their expense. But Lansdale's problem was too acute for niceties. As the superintendent of the Lansdale Water Authority said, "Our situation is worsening daily and our future is bleak, municipally, economically, and industrially, unless we can get the water we will need in the years ahead." Lansdale hopes by 1971 to be out of the critical phase of its water shortage. If it *is,* however, the solution will have been the result of economic pressure because, until the wells began going dry, Lansdale took the renewable resource base of its economic growth for granted.[14]

After all, the same condition produced a not dissimilar result in the very different community of Nashville in Brown County, Indiana. Because of a traditional shortage of water, Nashville had early given up hopes of attracting industry and had even accepted a low level of agricultural activity in the county because of poor soil and scant water. The primitive level of life, recounted in the droll books of Abe Martin, the humorist, is best evidenced by the county's place names: Gnawbone, Needmore, Scarce o'Fat Ridge, Bearwallow, Possom Trot, and Stony Lonesome. Shortly before World War I, an artists' and writers' colony was established in this quaint place, and from this early beginning, a recreational industry has developed based upon the proximity of the city of Indianapolis. But even for a recreation-based economy, water is in severely short supply.

A new reservoir does extend its shallower end into the county, but that end is expected to be silted up by 1975. The Bloomington, Indiana, reservoir also projects into the county but, as the local paper says, "our end consists of cattails and mud-flats." The source of water supply for Nashville and Beanblossom, the only two towns in the county having piped water, has been the lake in the state park. But in 1961 the state department of conservation, which operated the lake, announced that there was insufficient water in it to permit the least expansion in water service.

The level of much water service in Brown County is indicated by an announcement in the local paper that ". . . users . . . at the faucet in the alley back of Jimmie Davis's where the public has had the privilege of buying water . . . have carelessly left the water running. The Board voted to remove this outlet within 60 days in which time it was felt the present users could find another source." The Brown County Water Resources Study Commission stated the problem very clearly when it reported, "Due to the county's shortage of water and consequent inability to provide for wealth-producing industry, the resort development is imperative, if the county is to compete with its neighboring counties for the tourist trade and residential building so important to its wealth." [15]

The reaction of this remote community has been no different from those of the bustling little industrial city of Lansdale, Pennsylvania, or of New York itself. From Brown County, Indiana, to New York City, the consensus has been that where economic growth is threatened by the inadequacy of the renewable resource base, the money should be found to enlarge that base in some manner. With water, this enlarging may mean gathering it locally, as Brown County would like to do along Salt, Beanblossom, or Greasy Creeks; or gathering it in remote reservoirs, as New York City has done in the Neversink and Pepacton; or transferring it from one basin to another over vast distances, as California is doing under the Feather River project; or converting salt to fresh water with atomic power, as Riverhead, New York, has been doing; or going eight and a half miles away to pipe it from a large river, as Lansdale, Pennsylvania, has decided to do.

Vast alterations in natural disposition of renewable resources will always be undertaken if the expenditures can be justified by the preservation of an established economic activity or a pattern of economic growth. The only difficulty is getting the money. In Nashville, Indiana, local capital has not been available, and the local tax base has proven too narrow to support the kind of heavy expenditures that resource readjustment requires. But local aspirations remain; and, like so many other small communities in the United States, this one has hopes of federal assistance under the wide range of available federal programs. Here, too, there is a close similarity between the village and the metropolis. If New York does use Hudson River water, the use will have been made possible because the State of New York will be funding a $1 billion debt incurred in order to clean up the river.

From the smallest county seats like Nashville, Indiana, up through the largest city in the United States, there is a need to turn to larger units of political wealth and power for resource improvement funds, since the programs always seem to exceed the local financing base. Yet the discussion hinges on the problem of raising the capital to pay for the costs of making more of some particular renewable resource available for exploitation by the local economy. If the capital can be raised, there is rarely any issue over spending it for purposes of expanding the use of renewable resources.

AGENCY FORM FOR CONTROLLING THE RENEWABLE RESOURCES

In the raising of this money and in the spending of it to expand the renewable resource base of the economy, the administrative agency is the most favored instrument. When Jeremy Bentham was asked by the Portuguese Cortes to prepare an all-comprehensive code of laws, he retired to his study to "sit down like Napoleon in council to redraw the administrative map." In his reforming plan, he conceived of central administrative agencies having complete custodial, planning, and operational control over the "quantity, quality, and proportionality" of what a later generation would call the renewable resources.

Under Bentham's plan, there was no room for civil suits by injured parties against those perpetrating the harm. Instead, he had his central agencies use as their operative arms a military civil service.[16] This was very much upon the order followed in the United States in relation to the Army Corps of Engineers. Beginning with the Mississippi River Commission Act in 1879, the federal Rivers and Harbors programs, and the California Debris Commission in 1893, the Army Corps of Engineers has been delegated many of the operative powers of federal agencies in charge of improving land and water conditions.

On the Continent, Bentham's contemporary, reformer Johann Peter Frank, had announced as early as 1766 that a country's general health and welfare could be properly protected only while they were in the control of police who would exercise the public executive authority through administrative control. Whereas the philosopher John Locke, when asked by the Duke of Albemarle to draft a frame of government for the Carolinas in the 1670's, could only turn back to the feudal forms of regulating use of resources, Frank could tell the Viceroy of Lombardy in the 1780's what Bentham told the Portuguese Cortes in the 1820's: that control over the renewable resources would lie neither under feudal lords nor judicial process but would devolve upon the administrative agency as a means to total, rational, routine control over the renewable resources.[17]

Although the administrative agency has not reached the degree of control urged by Frank and Bentham, there has been some qualification of the enthusiasm for administrative process as the only means of controlling the renewable resources. As early as 1887, Gabriel Bugnottet announced that *"chinoiseries constituent le système de la centralisation"* and that the administrative method required the simultaneous existence of judicial suits as correctives which would define and encourage the operations of law enforcement by the administrators.[18] Jacob Beuscher, a teacher of American property law, followed this line of argument when he said, "It seems that increasingly the orders that come out of administrative agencies receive less and less attention. As a 'symbol' of our society, a court order receives more respect than an administrative one."

The courts have evolved over the years a property interest in the renewable resources that limits any user's employment of those resources, like water and air, which have a common use. Although the states, through a wide variety of forms, can regulate the private use of these common resources by devices like zoning or prohibitions, a state cannot disturb these partly conceptualized property "rights" that have been so slowly developed since the nineteenth-century decisions of Justice Story, Chancellor Kent, or Chief Justices Gibson and Shaw. Riparians along streams and persons actively using air for economic activity have been made co-sharers of a use-interest in the stream or atmosphere. The eighteenth-century milldam acts, the nineteenth-century drainage and cranberry acts, and the twentieth-century irrigation acts are all predicated upon a right to share mutually the use of these commonly utilizable resources. So nearly do these interests resemble the traditional property rights that Professor Beuscher says, "It is really amazing that we do not find more of our [common resource-using] citizens, who have failed to get satisfactions from various kinds of administrative agencies, . . . go[ing] to court to sue for an injunction and damages." [19]

LIMITS OF THE JUDICIAL REMEDY IN PROTECTING RESOURCES

The reason for this reluctance to use the courts probably lies in the general inadequacies of the judicial process in handling the problems of renewable resources. For one thing, both the state and private resource users prefer the regulatory processes of public administration, because under them it is easier to exercise a basic power rarely talked about in government: "the power to make a deal." Once a case comes into open court the flexibility in handling the problems of the individual situation is often lost. The judicial process must consider the broad general purposes it serves which are quite unrelated to the situation of the renewable resources.

For this reason, it has been urged that all cases involving renewable resources should be referred to a single court in each state which would build up an expertise and special procedures. But with only a few exceptions, the Anglo-American judicial tradition has been against the creation of courts of special jurisdiction on the grounds that persons are entitled to a judicial proceeding that is free of the prejudice that comes from expertise and that permits an independent examination of the dispute under rules that are generally valid for settling all contested situations.

Unfortunately, generally valid rules can be barriers to justice in specific situations. For example, a generally useful rule confines an expert to answering the hypotheticals put to him rather than allowing him to speak as an expert about facts personally known to him in a case. If he testifies as to the latter, his testimony is not that of an expert but of a material witness. It is a commendable rule, generally, but in specific cases, if the expert has become a witness too early in the assembling of evidence, his expertise is a hindrance and not a help in the law suit.[20]

So difficult is the burden of proof for plaintiffs that the Committee on Pollution of the National Academy of Science–National Research Council has urged that the rules of procedure be changed in the following particulars: that the court be empowered to join all parties in the problem shed, so that a disposition of all related rights might be had in one action in which all possible proof could be offered; that in nuisance actions brought by private persons, the plaintiff need prove only that he was damaged rather than that his damage was peculiar to him because different in kind; that the courts have the power to appoint within pollution control agencies a so-called master in chancery to take technical advice on behalf of the court; that injunctions against joint polluters should be possible under which the polluters themselves would have to work out the way of meeting judicially declared standards; and that the plaintiff has met his burden of proof when he has shown that reasonable resource standards are not being met, without having to go on to show the specific contribution of the defendant to the claimed harm.[21] These changes were considered necessary to make the judicial process more amenable in renewable resource litigation for encouraging more resort to the courts by aggrieved complainants.

Yet, despite opposition to these changes from counsel for industrial polluters, it is doubtful if these modifications would be enough to make the judicial a serious rival in popularity to the administrative process where the renewable resources are concerned. It is the function of courts to settle individual disputes and not to serve as the regulators of problems requiring a constant, flexible, routine, and, above all, *general* approach. If the courts tried to operate differently, the judicial process could not help the individual get relief for his specific problem.

The courts are for the individual claiming specific help for his hurt, whereas the administrators exist to regulate the overall problem. Indeed, the administrators have more than the negative duty of trying to minimize adverse effects. They have the positive obligation to take those creative steps which would enhance the quality of human life. But even if their goals should prove far more modest, the administrative agencies exist for purposes quite different from those of the courts.

If they are to dramatize their efforts, the administrative agencies themselves must resort to the courts. The publicity attendant upon court proceedings is often more effective in securing compliance than the fine or forfeiture imposed. These trials are courses in the education of the public, if the administrative agency prepares its case properly.

In the Eastern European socialist systems, it was found, administrative orders that factories cease pollution lacked meaning until the factory managers were individually brought into court and personally fined. Convictions have not been easy to get, because of the plea that production quotas made a different course of action impossible, because of the fear that a heavy fine might compel the manager to take steps that would harm the local economy, and because of what has been called "clubbiness" shared by the local magistrate and factory manager which excludes the humbler bureaucrats of the resource protection administration.

This last complaint, which administrators level against judges, is universal. Administrators frequently are urged by judges and local leaders not to be "over-strict" or to "hurt the cause of pollution abatement by impractically high forfeitures." It is an attitude that implies a need to moderate the proper zeal with a caution that is the result of the courts' being too much influenced by local opinion or not sufficiently sympathetic to the requirements of protecting the renewable resources.

Yet the most sympathetic trial judge can find himself in a dilemma from which it is almost impossible to emerge with a decision satisfactory to both the resource administrators and those who are engaged in utilizing the resource for economic purposes. As a Wisconsin trial judge explained it, "To permit the continuation of the nuisance would be violative of the rights of riparian owners to enjoy the pure, clean waters adjoining the property. On the other hand, to require that the defendant . . . desist from utilizing the present method of disposing of [its] effluent . . . would result in depriving the whole community . . . and would result in a major catastrophe." [22]

Sympathy for the renewable resource administrators is, unfortunately, of little more help in solving their difficulties than a similar general sympathy is for the economic activity that produces those difficulties. Courts throughout the world probably are "sympathetic" to both purposes, just as it can be assumed that public administrators working in the protection of renewable resources are rarely hostile to economic growth. In fact, these agencies themselves, along with units of local government, are often the chief merchandisers of the various resources used in the economy. The work of public officers frequently is what makes it possible for these resources to be assembled, developed, and made available for economic exploitation. Distinguishing between improvement of a resource to protect it and improvement of a resource to ease its exploitation can involve making a hard distinction.

But in either situation, it is largely the administrative agency that does most of the work, the judicial process being subordinate. Although the courts serve a valid independent function in determining property rights to renewable resources—by individual decisions in single cases litigated before them—the main burden of regulation has gradually been delegated, through the twentieth century, upon public administrators. Any insistence that this regulation could be carried on better by the courts has simply been rejected. For equally valid reasons, the simultaneously reached conclusion, implicit in twentieth-century regulation, has been reached: that the fate of the renewable resources cannot be left to the invisible operations of the market.

NEED TO ENLARGE INSTITUTIONAL DEVICES
WHICH PROTECT RESOURCES

The gradual easing out of the judicial process and the *laissez-faire* market has not bothered economist-specialists very much. Some experts hold, for instance, that the court and the market are the *last* places in which one would rationally try to plan anything. What *does* concern these observers is that so little has been done to use devices other than regulation to control the situation.

Taxes could be imposd on undesirable practices or upon the initial sale of merchandise which contaminates the environment after use, with the latter tax being based on the cost of eventual disposal. Effluent charges or assessments levied on those benefiting from protected or reconditioned purer renewable resources could also be considered. At a time when a spokesman for the American chemical industry could claim that at least 15 percent "of the capital investment is now going into clean-up devices for air, water, and land," without coming anywhere near the minimum quality needed in any of these, it is plain that new institutional control devices need to be tried.

Allen Kneese, an economist interested in the way physical controls can be effectively imposed upon renewable resources, has commented, "I feel if we are to cope with the . . . problems both effectively and economically, we must look beyond direct regulatory practices to new, and what some may consider revolutionary, approaches. A most promising possibility in this regard is a tax or levy on waste discharge . . . [to] utilize the incentive for private gain to achieve the social purpose of reducing waste discharge in an economical manner." [23]

There is something to be said, too, for other proposed tax inducement programs, which are designed to give specificity in economic terms to the renewable resources and to internalize the costs of their use, so that the economic activities which use them must also account for the overall charge. As the economy continues to make ever-increasing demands on the renewable resources, the fiscal load will become greater and therefore harder for the community to bear, even if that community is the entire United States. The statement German Arciniegas made when he was the Colombian Minister of Education, that "man belongs to an organic cycle, which includes the species and the cosmos, man and the earth," [24] may be the sort of poetry that inspires effort to protect the quality of the environment, but the far less exalted language of economics,

law, and the sciences better expresses the detailed changes in conduct necessary to accomplish that end.

The ecumene—the areas of the world into which the effects of
human culture reach—is not limited to those places where men
reside or confined to functioning in the service of man. It encom-
passes all the changes that human culture has exerted on the
physical universe, from the innumerable pieces of junk left floating
in space by astronautical exploration to the changes in fauna and
flora on the earth. It is nearly impossible to find anywhere in the
world either virgin soil or primeval forest, since human economic
activity in some form has penetrated either intentionally or otherwise into quite remote places.

There is probably no sadder evidence of this than the probable
extinction of the whale in the northern Pacific Ocean. These migratory mammals traditionally have been regarded as a free good to be
uncontrollably exploited. To that end, a heavy investment has been
made by Japanese businessmen and a Russian state trust since
1955. Between them in 1965, these instruments of private and state
capital took eighteen thousand whales from the northern Pacific and
converted them into highly saleable margarine, hand lotion, and pet
food. It has been a very profitable business, but as an employee of
the United States Fish and Wildlife Service said, "They are killing
the goose that laid the golden egg"—or, in economic parlance, the
heavy capital investment is threatened with loss because of heavy
exploitation of the resource to which the investment has been
directed.[25]

It is very similar to the situation prevailing in the Alaskan
salmon fisheries, except that in Alaskan waters even regulations designed to keep the salmon-taking equipment obsolete have failed to
halt exploitation of the resource beyond its powers of replenishment. It is predicted that the chinook salmon in the Pacific Northwest will be extirpated no later than 1980; but if the 1965 run of
only 15 percent of what was needed for species preservation continues, extinction will come much sooner.[26] Whenever a resource
is no one's property until reduced to some single exploiter's physical possession, pleas that consumers exercise voluntary self-restraint
are economic folly.

In fact, merely to regulate in physical terms, whether to hold exploitation to a maximum sustained yield or to a minimum level of waste invasion, is not likely to succeed if economic conditions are not given primary consideration. The physical and biological environment constitutes no more than a major constraint on economic activity. From a human viewpoint in a competitive economy, where the marketing outlook determines the intensity of efforts made at any given time, a resource has value as it can be measured in cash or as the quality of life in the economy is affected by resource use. Economists claim that it is impossible to make sense of conservation except in economic terms. Why produce or conserve at all, unless the end products are worth more than the cost of producing them? If they are not, there is neither a resource use nor a conservation problem. Physical condition becomes important only if the economic value of the resource is assumed.

What gives a sense of ambiguity to the problem is the difficulty of bringing resource-condition and environmental quality problems into the language of economics. Strangely enough, under modern conditions it is not water, soil, or air which are real and tangible. In their physical state, renewable resources are extremely hard for contemporary institutional structures to comprehend or to deal with in such a way as to protect them from destruction. Normally, it is first necessary for the resources to be described in the "real" and "tangible" language of cash. In the past, economists were prepared either to exclude many of these problems from economics or to adopt the view of theorists like S. V. Ciriacy-Wantrup and Erich Zimmerman that society had to establish strict, government-enforced physical constraints within which the cash equations of economics could be permitted to work. But in recent years, economists have tried to extend the conscious manipulation of the economy to an area as wide as the impact which economic activity itself has had upon the human environment.

SIGNIFICANCE OF ATTITUDES IN USE OF RESOURCES

The renewable resources are so significantly interrelated that changes in the physical world also affect the biotic or living resources. The unifying factor resides in the economic activity which is the source of the change. When chemical pollutants permit an increase in algal growth, the physical condition of the water and the biological functioning of fish life are both drastically changed. When biocides persist in the soil, the chemical constituency of the soil is altered; lethal damage can be suffered by plants drawing on that soil and by game feeding off of those plants. Other incidents could be adduced, but the point of all of them is the inextricable oneness of the physical and biotic environments insofar as the economic activity of human culture is concerned.

Man's increasing dominance over nature has created this unity of its organic and inorganic elements. It is a unity of common peril resulting from the demands which modern urban industrial economic and social forms make upon man's surroundings. Commentators as different in their attitudes as Lewis Mumford, the historian of city life, and Eugen Diesel, the German folk-theorist, have observed that nature is no longer permitted the freedom of transmuting itself from form to form by processes lying outside human activity. Instead, it is human enterprise, largely for economic ends, that works to transmute nature into some seral form which, from its artificial quality, is inevitably unstable and transient.

This enterprise of course makes possible the full scope of economic activities previously either unknown or narrowly confined to small sectors of the renewable resources. Although an ascending spiral of material prosperity has been the result, it has been purchased at a record high cost of instability in the human environment and in the relations between that environment and economic activity. There may have been isolated examples of this in the past, such as the unstable agriculture base that underlay Mayan civilization, but everywhere in the world today this instability is either prevalent or in the process of being instituted.

During World War II, the Chinese savant Wou Saofong declared that this rising dominance over nature was the result of the "Westerners' erroneous view of life," compounded for them by capitalism, Greek ideas, and Christianity; and that in this regard, "China's behavior in the society of nations, throughout its long history, is above criticism . . . because China knows how to face the ever changing world with immutable moral precepts." Prejudices similar to these, though in different contexts, can be matched from Western authors. As Oswald Spengler put it, "All economic life is the expression of soul life." A whole "organic" school of thought exists in Western economic history that would find no cause for quarrel when Spengler says, ". . . the economic foundation of the great Culture is always a mankind that adheres fast to the soil, and nourishes and supports the higher economic forms." [27]

Such ideas have always had considerable popularity; but their authors, like Henry Adams with his thirteenth-century Virgin overcome by his twentieth-century Dynamo, continuously have to hearken back to some distant past or to a reorganization of society so basic that the discussion has to be cast in Utopian terms. Certainly Asia can no longer assume an attitude of timeless superiority on the subject of the economic exploitation of the renewable resource base, if indeed Asia ever could. Quite apart from deforestation in China and soil exhaustion in India, which have an ancient history, the twentieth century has seen a major effort at industrialization from the Suez to the Bering Straits and from the Urals to Oceania. Neither the entrepôt economies of Formosa and Hong Kong nor the industrializing economy of continental China seem to meet Wou Saofong's test any better than Western Europe or North America seem to have met Oswald Spengler's prediction of a "new" economics that would be beyond art and philosophy. Past "immutable precepts" and recurring demands to be "practical" have not been of much assistance in coping with modern man's relations with his environment.

Far from moving beyond art and philosophy, the modern theorist on renewable resource matters has been thrust back to the fundamental questions of what constitutes property, economic value, or the quality of life. More basic questions, other than those of a purely spiritual and moral character, cannot be asked. Speaking not of the twentieth-century weapons of war, which so often terrify in prospect, but considering only present economic practices, the savants have thundered: "Never in history have the destructive forces of man worked with more deadly efficacy. . . . Ignorance of the delicate balance of ecological relations in nature, failure to realize the repercussions . . . of seemingly innocent actions, . . . emphasis on immediate market values at the expense of irreplaceable basic costs . . . [have made] the same tools that proved their effectiveness in producing a vast output of immediate values . . . equally effective in damaging the permanent assets which alone can assure the sustained flow of current production for the future." [28]

The issues raised suggest the questions which must be asked concerning the purpose of economic and social activity in modern urban industrial society. Among the questioners are economists such as John Kenneth Galbraith, biologists like René Dubos, and lawyers of the type of Willard Hurst. The questions can be made to penetrate the various levels of society; there are no easy answers.

The *New York Times* and *Barron's Weekly* can legitimately differ over the decision of the Federal Power Commission to permit the building of "the world's largest pumped storage hydroelectric project" upon Storm King Mountain. *Barron's* may be right in claiming that the project will permit closure of obsolete power plants that pollute the air; that it will give New York City a local power source which the November 1965 blackout showed was badly needed, if only as an emergency alternative to the national power grid; and that "in economic terms its benefits would ripple far and wide." The *Times* may be equally right to say it will "irreparably damage one of the nation's greatest historic and scenic treasures." It is indeed, the probability that both are right which makes this choice, like most relating to the use of the renewable resources, such a vexing one.[29]

Private persons, of course, can take personal steps toward the conservation of some natural resources by gifts and dedications to organizations like the Natural Lands Trust. Organizations such as this have been established "to acquire, maintain, and preserve

natural woods, fields, streams, marshes, seashore, and other areas
. . . [in order] to preserve natural areas in their unspoiled state for
public enjoyment, for their environmental value, and for the protection of wildlife." [30] This is a commendable effort and it will add
some acreage to the "social forests" which will be so badly needed
if Senator Ernest Gruening is right in predicting a population of one
billion in the United States by the time the children of the 1960's
reach retirement age under the social security program. It is a plan
which deserves the encouragement it has received through tax de-
ductions and exemptions.

But even if the dedication of open lands by private philanthropy
should prove substantial, the solution of the problems of conservation and the quality of the environment will not be solved by any
such eleemosynary approach. Only if the major economic activities
can be brought into line with the totality of the human environment which they require can any balance possibly be struck which
would have both generality and comparative stability.

ROLE OF BALANCE IN HUMAN ENVIRONMENTAL CONDITIONS

Any stability in the environment bought through economic and
legal institutional devices would be such only in comparison with
the current relationship between urban industrial economic activity
and the environment. The sort of balance which nature reaches in
the seral climax of any area is not possible once human activity has
been introduced on anything beyond a berry-gathering economic
level. The Arcadian shepherd was a profoundly disturbing ecological element. The potato in Ireland, cacao in Africa, rubber in
Malaya, quinine in Indonesia, and cotton in the American South
may now seem quite natural where they are found. But this twentieth-century locale represents a profound wrenching disturbance of
the natural order in which each of these plants was moved from a
native habitat to its present economically significant location.

Every equilibrium in the state of nature most divorced from
human action is dynamic, which means that it is subject to counter-
vailing pressures that could produce change. The human presence
introduces new pressures or intensifies existing ones. With some

areas like the Appalachians excepted, it is not possible to protect renewable resources by simply withdrawing the human element. The very growth of the world's populations and the accelerating material demands of an urbanizing, industrializing world make the removal of the human population on any large scale impossible.

Some say a nuclear holocaust could change this, although at great cost to the physical and biological world. Furthermore, the importance that renewable resources have is one that has been largely determined by the rates of population and economic activity which have been steadily accelerating since the seventeenth century throughout the world. Whether nuclear warfare reduced the world population by 90 per cent, as some experts predict, or by the relatively low figure of 20 percent which others have forecast, the effect on the renewable resources would hardly be beneficial.

At best, nuclear war would reproduce the situation that prevailed in much of North America in the nineteenth century, when the indigenous populations of Indians, Eskimos, and Aleuts were so reduced that there was a seral resurgence which produced an abundance of fish in the streams, an addition of game on the land, and a movement of the forest out onto the plain. When, for example, deaths from tuberculosis at the Saskatchewan Qu'Appelle Valley Indian reservation ran at a yearly rate of nine out of every hundred in the population, it might be expected that the removal of the native peoples at this speed would permit a re-establishment of any former ecological balance which their cultural activity had upset.

Barring the total extinction of humanity, or something very near it, nuclear warfare could accomplish very little more benefit for the renewable resources than did this near extinction of the indigenous North Americans. Any physical benefit would ensue, one should note, only if blast and genetic effects on the landscape and the biota were quite minimal. As it might bear upon the fate of our renewable resources, a vast nuclear disturbance would be a clear example of "the remedy worse than the disease."

The solution of any problem man has in his relation to environment cannot be solved by catastrophic events such as nuclear war, or by a nostalgic effort to return to a simple past in the manner of the Amish, or by appeals to altruism in the style of the early American Conservationist movement, or by an unrestrained exploitation. The only answer lies in working the whole mass of renewable resources out of the category of free goods and into a cost-benefit analysis reflective of the total price paid for their development. So long as water, or air, or wildlife have economic value to the individual only insofar as they are his possessions, then for so long will these resources be exploited to the point of destruction.

Naturally, only a stable society and economy that can establish a present value for the future good condition of some resource can allow the establishment of these values. A substantially feudal land tenure system in Sweden protected the country's long-term forest capital, and a conservative peasantry has maintained the excellent natural soil conditions of northwestern Europe. Where society and the economy are highly unstable, however, with a demand for immediate cash return, the renewable resources are sacrificed for short-term gains.

The United States has traditionally been in precisely such an unstable situation. The popularity of large-scale farming under lease in the 1960's is predicated on the continuance of the conventional American sacrifice of soil values for current income. And in the mid-1960's lumbering continues to exceed replacement of growing trees, even in the face of a prediction of a severe timber shortage by 1980. In economic terms, it is essential to make the renewable resources specifically controlled economic units and to establish constraints within which the total cost of their exploitation can be internalized, if balance between man and his environment is ever to be established.

INCREASED RESOURCE DEMAND AS THE SOURCE FOR INCREASED RESOURCE REGULATION

The problem of the renewable resources is not one of imminent exhaustion, although, unlike the stock resources, these renewable resources have probably had a rising cost in production per unit. Science and technology have reduced perils of the kind predicted by Thomas Malthus and Stanley Jevons. The progress made in genetics under Gregor Mendel's law may be the largest single factor accounting for the fantastic increase recently in agricultural output, an advance which is all the more important as the gains have been achieved without much increase in the direct cost of production.

The terrible threats which Malthus and Jevons saw hanging over future society have been largely dissipated because of an expansion in science and technology. Insofar as this knowledge is supplied by the efforts of government, it constitutes a free good replacing the "free goods" role which the renewable resources have played for so long in the economy. A great deal of technical advancement in protecting such common renewable resources as water and air has been held back because no economic incentive existed to conserve these resources. Needed technology has been held back for economic reasons and not because of technical difficulties. Once the economic significance of a better technical apparatus has been established by the users of air and water, the technological improvements have followed or will do so shortly.

It is upon the economic and legal level that much of the difficulty is generated. Permit systems, effluent charges, receptor levies, and assessments for the actual cost to the public treasury of supplying some renewable resource to a beneficiary have all been suggested. In addition, a system of standards, classifications, and regulations is urged in order to establish the constraints upon the physical environment within which economic employment of that environment would have to operate.

A system of permits and charges would lead to property interests which arise in some part or aspect of the resource on behalf of those using it. Experts who advocate such a system presume that, at best, it would cause each owner to behave as economically toward his property in a renewable resource as he behaves toward other personal economic assets and, at the least, that he would be compelled to calculate as part of his operational costs the deleterious effect he has had upon the renewable resource used in his activity.

Many observers are convinced that such a system of exclusive and alienable permits represents a signing away of the public domain and an invasion of the individual's rights in what have been the common resources. Yet at its worst, such a system would be no more than an enclosure under title-deeds of resources which industrial activity has already largely engrossed. Here the spectre of a poll tax to be paid by every citizen for the air he breathes looms up. As a spectre, it might not loom so large if the public realized to what an extent the public domain has been privately engrossed and to what extent the public is already paying a tax in personal health and comfort because of the toxic, allergenic, latent-disease-activating, and sublethal-cumulative substances discharged into the air.

Because of this present and accelerating demand upon the total environment made by the economic activity of modern, urban, industrial society, pressure has built up for constraints, for the establishment of "thresholds" of abuse below which quality cannot fall, and for the overall public regulation of the use made of the human environment. It is this kind of pressure which in the mid-1960's Secretary of the Interior Stewart Udall interpreted as "a nationwide mandate . . . [for] the greatest expansion in conservation activity since Theodore Roosevelt's day." [31]

Biologists, ecologists, most conservationists, many lawyers, and some economists have always favored the regulatory approach which sets the conditions under which the economy may use the renewable resources. The only problem has been that there has never been enough investment in the process of regulation to make it able to claim more than that "things would be a lot worse if it weren't for the regulations." The majority of economists claim that this will always be true if the major burden of protecting the renewable resources is not borne by economic devices specifying the quantity of the resource used and internalizing the cost of using it.

There are few voices to claim that regulation is not needed, that constraints should not be imposed, and that some changes in the property law are all that are required to do the job of controlling the demands made by the economy on the quality of the environment. Regulation by itself would continue to be inadequate, if past experience is any guide. But the past experience in exploitation of American forests also indicates that the establishment of units of private property in such resources as water, air, and fish in open waters would be insufficient as a single device to protect them from a destructive exploitation.

An improved establishment of constraints in the use of the renewable resources and development of legal and economic devices which permit a better internalizing of the costs of utilizing the renewable resources are changes around which an increasing body of agreement is congregating. It is increasingly clear that the time has come "to atone for the mischief of generations." This realization, along with pressure from the White House, has put through Congress between 1964 and 1966 more legislation designed to improve the water, soil, air, and other renewable resources of the United States than has been passed in many previous decades. Yet these federal statutes, despite their size and number, represent only the beginning of a program which might ultimately establish an effective system of constraints upon the way in which economic and social demands can be made upon the environment.

THE TASK AHEAD IN COPING WITH ENVIRONMENT
UNDER GROWING DEMANDS

Up to the mid-1960's, all federal legislation, all state administrative law enforcement, and much of the thought in social science concerned with the relationship between the renewable resources and the economy constituted only a very modest start at coping with the problems of man's relationship to his environment. The biggest test for the efficacy of a mandatory national system of effluent charges has been just getting started in England under 1963 legislation. If it proves as successful there as it has on the much smaller scale of Germany's Ruhr, it will be widely copied. Otherwise, many nations will continue to do what Warsaw recently did when its Vistula water-intake filters became too clogged with silt and scum for further use: switch to other water sources.

Despite the persuasive arguments of the cost-internalizing economists, the United States has not taken to them. However this mistrust could change rather quickly either if the English effluent charge system proved effective or if enforcement actions on stream standards were to become sufficiently severe, as to fines and forfeitures, that industry would find it more economical to switch over to the predictable cost burden of the effluent charge system. But an enforcement program of such scope and power would require a commitment of effort at the state and federal level that is not possible even with the spate of federal legislation that came after 1963.

The likely course of action at the public level will be an eclectic effort to compromise the various views and to produce a system that will try to accommodate all reasonable demands. The property rights in certain flow resources like water, which the courts have been evolving, will be more firmly established. Paradoxically, this is most likely to happen under statutes, such as Iowa's 1945 water act, which have declared these resources to be part of the public domain, usable only by permit. These permits ultimately will prove permanent, despite time limit provisions in the enabling acts, because the investments made under them will make their retraction by the state politically, if not legally, difficult. The permits will give a degree of certainty not known before under the riparian system and will erode away the vested rights of non-user riparians in stream water.

Accompanying these permits and any charge system on the emission into or the reception of a flow resource, there will be more extensive enforcement of resource criteria, standards, classifications, and other quality control devices. In this way, the law will try to compromise the views of those, on the one hand, who believe the prime solution is to specify and internalize the costs of the renewable resources used, and those, on the other, who urge as the best course the imposition only of rigid constraints within whose limits the economy could utilize the renewable resources.

This difference of opinion is not much harder to resolve than the dispute between the users of persistent biocides and those who argue that the steady accumulation of individually sublethal doses of these agents is highly deleterious to birds, fish, animals, plants, and people. Commercially, the biocides have been successful, just as the massively applied chemical fertilizers have increased agricultural production enormously, though at the price of much stream and some ground water nutrient pollution. Biologists may claim an eventual ineffectiveness for the biocides, and soil specialists may argue that no soil can be permanently kept above its natural fertility quotient. But the short-run economic benefits are so great that agricultural experts throughout the world want more, not fewer, of the persistent biocides and chemical fertilizers.

The highly toxic biocides, which disperse quickly, are not popular because of their risk to ignorant agricultural laborers, whereas the persistent biocides can be used without a chance of killing the users in the act of applying them. The chemical fertilizers have made possible a soil improvement program that exceeds anything which the use of natural fertilizers, even including a wider use of human excrement in North America, might have accomplished. The choices here are ones government could not prevent economic activity from making, and the dangers will have to be very positively proven before government regulations can intervene. In the United States, however, there will be an effort in government to impose regulations moderating the quantities and frequency of applications of the biocides and the chemical fertilizers.

It is the function of government to adjust conflicting views. Government's greatest peril arises when the views ought not to be compromised because one view is in error. This possibility exists very strongly in the renewable resources and their relation to economic activity. The opponents of the persistent biocides and those who call for strict constraints on water and air pollution claim that a different course will be disastrous to the quality of the environment. The economists, who oppose government subsidy of renewable resources because it keeps them free goods and who call for the specific ownership of these renewable resources by their beneficiaries, argue that in no other way can the costs be internalized into the exploitative process; and that, without this specification and internalization, there will be a disastrous lowering in the quality of the environment.

To avoid the consequences of both prognostications would require basic economic, legal, and social changes which government wants either to avoid or to keep to a pace of slow and moderate alteration. The public authorities at both the legislative and administrative levels will act to accommodate these disparate views and will adhere to neither one nor the other. It is the traditional way of government; and, at a very slow rate, it even permits an ultimate, tacit, unconscious swinging around to one view when that one proves to have a monopoly of right. No government today is trying to disperse miasmic vapors, although in the nineteenth century the pythogenic theory fought a strong rear-guard action against the germ theory and forced the governments to take a compromising position between the two contending views—the one wrong, the other right. Such a solution could recur once more if the current views on what to do about renewable resources should have a similar reason for being uncompromisable.

Deputations of this sort have been waiting on the sovereign to do something for several centuries. The sixteenth-century English women who went to Westminster to see Elizabeth I about "the filthy dangerous poisonous use of coal" were simply part of a procession that stretches down to the present. The reformer W. H. Churchman called his remarks "truisms" when he told the 1870 meeting of the Western Social Science Association, "Purity in the air we breathe is one of the prime necessities of life, and, therefore, an essential condition of physical and mental health." He might have said the same thing about the importance of soil, water, and the biota of which man is a part.[32]

Despite fears to the contrary, the problem is not that the renewable resources will disappear or even that technology will be unable to switch to a poorer or damaged resource level. The exhaustion of the richer stock resources can be offset by technical improvements in those of lesser quality. Technology can also repair or compensate for damage to renewable resources, but probably without the reduction in cost which seems to have attended substitution in the stock resources. But man's fate is so bound up with the life-cycle resources he cannot allow them to deteriorate beyond a certain point.

Economic activity has been a threat to renewable resources since 1800. But the general effect which urban industrial society has had upon the quality of the environment is even more crucial. How the relationship between this society and its natural milieu develops before the year 2000, and the way in which necessary economic, social, and legal institutions are ascertained and established, constitute one of the major problems in the late twentieth century.

The wrong institutional response to the problem of the life-cycle resources could make man's future quite unpleasant. Depending on other events which are not part of the economy's relationship to the renewable resources, a suitable institutional adjustment could produce a future ranging from just tolerable all the way to a human superiority beyond all expectations. It is man's peculiarity that the choice is so largely his to make.

Man converts resources to purposes which are both destructive to human effort and highly useful to human enterprise. The path often depends upon the position of the person making the judgment. Yet, though intent frequently determines whether a man regards his acts as destructive or beneficial or both, the consequences of such actions upon nature are always disturbing and the changes often permanent.

It is not possible for humanity to continue its existence and not continue its profound disturbances of nature. But a certain carelessness, somewhat akin to the outlook of soldiers under siege, can be discarded and a greater concern for the power man has upon nature could be adopted. In *Paradise Lost,* John Milton described the preparations of the Fallen Angels to battle God; what he ascribed to the Infernal Powers on a day of great effort is about par for any eight-hour shift in any urban industrial state in the late twentieth century.

> . . . Sulphurous and nitrous foam
> They found, they mingled, and with subtle art,
> Concocted and adjusted, they reduc'd
> To blackest grain, and into store convey'd;
> Part hidden veins digged up . . . of mineral and stone,
> Whereof to found their engines and their balls
> Of massive ruin; part incentive reed
> Provide, pernicious with one touch to fire.

Even when not beset by war or national defense, the ordinary practices of industrial civilization have much the same effect on nature as if wide-ranging destruction were the prime intent. Sometimes it is unavoidable. Ever since his Fall in the Garden, man has occasionally had to practice on pretty much the same level as the Infernal Powers after their casting out of Heaven. Wars, the exploitation of nature for survival and amenity, and the mere existence of people in the elements make a certain degree of harm to nature inevitable. To admit this is to be neither Satanic nor vicious. But to be careless beyond this necessity is certainly vicious and may result in something not very different from the self-destruction of Milton's Satan. Poisoning, or processing, or burning up the world around us may produce profit, pleasure, and even grandeur satisfactory to the sick and carelessly selfish. Aside from them, however, human creatures who have at least as much intelligence as Milton's Satan ought to be able to give a little more thought to the available alternatives and to choose those with some promise of permanence, safety, and comfort.

In the presence of an awesome power capable of consuming the universe—and perhaps even the worlds beyond this world—it may sound very humdrum to speak of health, or economics, or the long-term possibilities available to mankind. Any apocalypse or routine battle of angels has a greater appeal, and several millennia of poetry testify to it. But disregard of consequences and a love of death and destruction do not comprise the whole of the human spectrum of desires; and if something else can be offered in a favorable light, then it is man's wisest duty to at least examine the choices. Lacking the immortality of angels, this more modest course seems the best.

Notes

CHAPTER 1. THE ORIGINS OF ENVIRONMENTAL CONTROL

1. *Indianapolis News,* June 13, 1966. Estimates are based on a study by research economists of the United States Department of Agriculture.
2. Jean de Lipkowski, French Deputy and specialist in military-economic affairs, has made this point forcefully in *Atlas,* XI, No. 6 (June 1966), 330–331.
3. Ben H. Bagdikian, "The Rape of the Land," *Saturday Evening Post,* June 18, 1966, p. 94.
4. I am indebted to Professor William L. Griffin for this comparison.

CHAPTER 2. DETERMINING RESOURCE SUFFICIENCY

1. Harold J. Barnett and Chandler Morse, *Scarcity and Growth: The Economics of Natural Resource Availability* (Baltimore, 1963). The Duke of Argyll's own highly abstract opinion is in *The Reign of Law* (New York, 5th ed., 1884), pp. 154–155.
2. Pierre Laffitte, "Mineral Ores: A Challenge to Europe," in Nigel Calder, ed., *The World in 1984* (Baltimore, 1965), I, 47.
3. Karl Brandt, "Moral Presuppositions of the Free Enterprise Economy, *The Intercollegiate Review,* II (October 1965), 111–112.
4. President Lyndon B. Johnson, "Conservation Message," H. Doc. 387, February 23, 1966, 89th Cong., 2nd Sess., *Cong. Record,* CXII, 3519.
5. François Bourlière, "A New Balance Between Man and Nature," in Calder, *op. cit.,* I, 53–54.

6. Constantinos Doxiadis, "Plans for Future Cities," *Milwaukee Journal,* November 7, 1965.

7. Charles Richard Van Hise, *The Conservation of Natural Resources in the United States* (New York, 1926), pp. 373–374.

8. Allen V. Kneese, *Water Pollution: Economic Aspects and Research Needs* (Washington, 1962), p. 2. Citations are from a report by Nathaniel Wolman and others.

9. Stanley A. Cain, "Foreword" to Richard A. Cooley, *Politics and Conservation: The Decline of the Alaska Salmon* (New York, 1963), p. xii.

10. Willard F. Libby, "Man's Place in the Physical Universe," *Bulletin of the Atomic Scientists,* XXII, No. 7 (September 1965), 16, reprinted in J. R. Platt, ed., *New View of the Nature of Man* (Chicago, 1965), pp. 1–15.

11. Orris C. Herfindahl and Allen V. Kneese, *Quality of the Environment* (Baltimore, 1965), p. vi.

12. Maynard Hufschmidt, "Minutes of Legal-Public Administration Panel," National Academy of Sciences–National Research Council, Committee on Pollution, Division of Physical Sciences, April 5–6, 1965, p. 123.

13. Anne McLaren, "Optimists versus Pessimists," in Calder, *op. cit.,* II, 182.

14. Committee on Terminology, Urban Planning and Development Division, American Society of Civil Engineers, *Journal of the Hydraulics Division, ASCE,* XCI, HY3, Pt. 2, May 1965, p. 14.

15. Hufschmidt, *loc cit.* The italics are his.

16. "Weather Information Services of the Environmental Science Services Administration," Memorandum of the Secretary of Commerce to the President, September 13, 1965, *Presidential Documents,* I (1965), 261.

17. John Kenneth Galbraith, as quoted in the *Milwaukee Sentinel,* November 5, 1965.

18. S. T. Lowry, "The Classical Greek Theory of Natural Resource Economics," *Land Economics,* XLI (1965), 204–208.

19. Citations are from remarks made by Philip Lambert, Director, Instructional Research Laboratory at the University of Wisconsin, Madison, *Capital Times,* November 10, 1965, p. 21.

20. "Report of the Cabinet Committee on Natural Beauty, October 2, 1965," *Presidential Documents,* I (1965), 363–364; "Presidential Remarks at the Signing Ceremony of the Assateague Island Seashore National Park Bill," September 21, 1965, *op. cit.,* 291–292.

21. *Time,* November 19, 1965, pp. 47–48.

22. Herfindahl and Kneese, *op. cit.,* p. 63, quoting Gordon Fair; Abel Wolman, "The Metabolism of Cities," *Scientific American,* CCXIII, No. 3 (September 1965), 185.

23. Earl Finbar Murphy, *Water Purity* (Madison, 1961), p. 92 and note.

24. John Bird, "Farewell to Farmer Tuttle," *Saturday Evening Post,* December 4, 1965, pp. 34–46; "Statement of President Johnson on Sign-

ing the Food and Agriculture Act of 1965," *Presidential Documents,* I (1965), 454.

25. Lord Keynes, "William Stanley Jevons," in *Essays in Biography,* ed. Geoffrey Keynes (New York, 1951), pp. 265–267, 295, 304.
26. Barnett and Morse, *op. cit.,* p. 262.
27. *Presidential Documents,* I (1965), 361.

CHAPTER 3. THE COSTS OF WORKING AGAINST NATURE

1. John Kenneth Galbraith, as quoted in Michael Harrington, "The Politics of Poverty," *Dissent,* XII, No. 4 (Autumn 1965), 423.
2. The ideas mentioned are those of the economic geographers Kenneth Boulding and Gilbert White, and of the economist John Krutilla. The Flood Control Act of 1936 is an Act of June 22, 1936, Ch. 688; 49 Stat. 1570.
3. Wesley Marx, "Can Thousand Palms Survive the Sand?" *National Observer,* November 8, 1965, p. 11. For beach sand problems, see Krueger, "Governmental Control of Beaches and Tidelands," Address to the American Beach and Shore Preservation Association, San Diego, California, October 31, 1966.
4. Anthony Scott, *National Resources: The Economics of Conservation,* Canadian Economic Studies No. 3 (Toronto, 1955), pp. 6, 18–19, 22. The charge scheme derives from the work of Allen V. Kneese, John Krutilla, and Orris Herfindahl at Resources for the Future, Inc., Washington, D.C. The Task Force on Federal Flood Control Policy recommended a charge scheme and zoning to prevent flood plain settlement. U.S. 89th Cong., 2nd Sess. (1966), House Doc. No. 465; and see Exec. Order 11296, August 10, 1966, 31 F.R. (1966) 10663.
5. John Kenneth Galbraith, cited in Harrington, *op. cit.,* pp. 425–426.
6. E. N. Munns, "Sedimentation Problems of the Land," Proceedings of the Federal Inter-Agency Sedimentation Conference, May 6–8, 1947, pp. 29 ff.; John R. Sheppard, "Total Sediment Transport in the Lower Colorado River," paper presented at the Convention of the American Society of Civil Engineers, Phoenix, Arizona, April 10–14, 1961; "Sedimentation Resurvey of Guernsey Reservoir, 1957," Sedimentation Section, Hydrology Branch, Division of Project Investigation, Bureau of Reclamation, U.S. Department of the Interior, August 1958, pp. 27–31; "The Foundations of Conservation Education," Committee on Conservation Education Pamphlet No. 3, Washington, W. W. Horner and Richard W. Horner, "The Role of Applied Science in Conservation," National Wildlife Federation, 1941, pp. 73 ff.
7. Sheppard, *op. cit.;* "Determination of Total Sediment Load on a Stream by the Modified Einstein Procedure," Program No. HY–100, Electronic Data Processing Section, General Engineering Branch, Bu-

reau of Reclamation, U.S. Department of Interior, Denver, September 1957, p. 8. In 1950, Hans Albert Einstein worked out the presently employed method of measuring sediment content in stream flow. The Einstein procedure is used conjointly with the equal transit rate method of sampling which B. C. Colby developed in 1946.

8. NANA dispatch, *Indianapolis News,* October 21, 1965. Otto Thope attributes the basic principle of his scheme to the coal pipeline operated in this country by the Consolidated Coal Company. The coal is diluted with water to form a mixture called "slurry" for pumping through the line in order to cut transportation costs and make coal economically competitive with oil and natural gas. Eric H. Reichl developed the slurry patent: U.S. Patent No. 3,073,652, January 15, 1963.

9. J. W. Wark, F. J. Keller, and H. R. Felty, "Reconnaissance of Sedimentation and Chemical Quality of Surface Water on the Potomac River Basin" (July 1961), in *Potomac River Basin Report,* VII, Appendix H, North Atlantic Division, Baltimore District, U.S. Army Corps of Engineers, Washington, February 1963, p. 1.

10. Wyman Harrison, W. C. Krumbein, and W. S. Wilson, "Sedimentation at an Inlet Entrance," U.S. Army Coastal Engineering Research Center Technical Memorandum No. 8 (December 1964); *Quest for Quality,* U.S. Department of Interior Yearbook (1965), p. 18.

11. Bill Werley, "Phoenix: Drought Underground," *Saturday Review,* October 23, 1965, p. 76. The federal statutes mentioned are the Mississippi River Commission Act of June 28, 1879, Ch. 43, 21 Stat. 37, and the Rivers and Harbors Appropriation Act of August 11, 1888, Ch. 860, 25 Stat. 424.

12. Michel Batisse, "Learning the Value of Water," in Nigel Calder, *The World in 1984* (Baltimore, 1965), I, 48–49. The prediction was made by the Natural Resources Research Division.

13. Ira N. Gabrielson, "Making Conservation Effective by Government Action," *Proceedings of the Inter-American Conference on Conservation of Renewable Natural Resources,* Denver, September 7–20, 1948, Department of State Publication 3382, p. 730.

14. Scott, *op. cit.,* p. 96.

15. Fred A. Clarenbach, "Water Pollution Policies and Politics," paper presented at the Seminar on Pollution Control and Abatement, Iowa State University, Ames, November 7, 1965.

16. Peter Bart, "Commuters' Community in Catalina's Future," *New York Times,* November 21, 1965.

CHAPTER 4. URBAN INDUSTRIAL CULTURE AND ITS
LIVING ENVIRONMENT

1. Appendices I–III (March 1, 1965) to Pt. I, *Hearings on S. Res. 27,* Subcommittee on Reorganization and International Organizations, Committee on Government Operations, U.S. Sen., 88th Cong., 1st and 2nd Sess's., Agency Coordination Study, S. Res. 288 (Interagency Coordination in Environmental Hazards [Pesticides]), p. 43.
2. 7 U..C.A., Sec. 135 (1); 7 C.F.R. 362.25 (a) of the Pesticides Regulation Division, U.S. Agricultural Research Service.
3. *Congressional Record,* CVIII, No. 146, August 17, 1962, pp. 15891–15892.
4. Frank A. Vorhes, Jr., Chief, Division of Food, Bureau of Biological and Physical Sciences, FDA, "Letter," in *Hearings on S. Res. 27,* p. 681.
5. *Ibid.,* pp. 565, 568.
6. Act of June 25, 1947, c. 125; 61 Stat. 168, 7 U.S.C.A. 135–135R as amended August 7, 1959, P.L. 86–139, 73 Stat. 286; May 12, 1964, P.L. 88–305, 78 Stat. 190 and 24 F.R. 10835 (December 28, 1959) and 7 C.F.R. 362.116 (c), effective October 1, 1965. The language of 362.116 (c) (2), which might have a wider purpose, was the same in 1959 and in 1965; it is clearly not of primary importance.
7. U.S. v. Bodine Produce Co. (D.C., Ariz., 1962) 206 F. Supp. 201, interpreting the Food, Drug, and Cosmetic Act of June 25, 1938, Ch. 675, Sec. 408, as added to by the Pesticide Chemicals Amendment Act of July 22, 1954, Ch. 559, Sec. 3, 68 Stat. 511, as amended by the Food Additives Amendment Act of August 28, 1958, P.L. 85–791, Sec. 20, 72 Stat. 948, 21 U.S.C.A. 346.
8. *Hearings on S. Res. 27,* pp. 18–19 on Department of Agriculture, pp. 642–643 on activities leading up to creation of Toxicology Study Section of NIH on February 16, 1959; Act of August 1, 1958, 72 Stat. 479, as amended by the Act of September 16, 1959, 73 Stat. 563 and the Act of October 1, 1965, P.L. 89–232, 79 Stat. 902.
9. The Board, endorsed by the Secretaries of Defense, Interior, and Health, Education, and Welfare, was established by a letter of the Secretary of Agriculture, June 22, 1961. It held its organizational meeting August 30, 1961.
10. Statement of Dr. Robert J. Anderson, in *Hearings on S. Res. 27,* pp. 783, 795.
11. "Memorandum of Agreement" among Secretaries of Agriculture, Interior, and Health, Education, and Welfare, April 27, 1964, 29 F.R. 5808; "Federal Committee on Pest Control—Functions and Pro-

cedures," 29 F.R. 12945; "Fact Sheet," Executive Secretary, Federal Committee on Pest Control, n.d.

12. Stanley Cain, quoted in House Report No. 1002, September 14, 1965, U.S. Code Congressional and Administrative News, 89th Cong., 1st Sess., II, p. 3303, from his testimony of June 22, 1965, *ibid.*, pp. 3305–3306. Robert M. Paul, Cain's deputy assistant secretary, was chairman of the Federal Committee on Pest Control.

13. *Hearings on S. Res. 27*, pp. 5–7, 19. The problems listed are from a statement of August 28, 1962, to the Pesticide Panel of the Federal Council of Science and Technology.

14. John Bird, "Our Dying Waters," *Saturday Evening Post*, April 23, 1966, p. 31; 7 C.F.R., Ch. 3, 1965 Supp., pp. 147, 153.

15. *Cong. Record*, CVIII, pp. 15891–15892; speaking of the Insect Identification and Parasite Introduction Research Branch of the U.S. Agricultural Research Service, *Hearings*, p. 778; *Quest for Quality*, p. 65; Subpanel on Improved Pest Control Practices, Environmental Pollution Panel, President's Science Advisory Committee, *Restoring the Quality of Our Environment* (November 1965), pp. 286–287, 290–291.

16. *Restoring . . . Environment*, p. 93.

17. Hermann J. Muller, "Genetic Effects of Chemicals," paper presented at Food and Drug Scientific Seminar, October, 1963, *FDA Interbureau By-Lines*, September, 1964.

18. J. J. Hickey and L. B. Hunt, "Initial Songbird Mortality Following a Dutch Elm Disease Program," *Journal of Wildlife Management*, XXIV, No. 3, 259–265. The article is listed in *Hearings*, p. 978. See also Bird, *op. cit.;* and a speech given by Robert M. Paul to the National Audubon Society, November 10, 1962, F.F. 18028–62.

19. "Report to President Johnson of the Cabinet Committee on Natural Beauty," October 2, 1965, *Presidential Documents*, I (1965), 359.

20. *Ibid.*, p. 358; David G. Hall, Chairman, Committee for Public Information, Entomological Society of America, *Hearings*, Table 1, p. 983—the report is undated, but internal evidence suggests that the data were gathered in 1961; *Hearings*, pp. 23, 47, 48–51; *Restoring . . . Environment*, p. 76.

21. Gladwin Hill, "Are We Running Out of Water?" *Look*, December 14, 1965, p. 31; John Lear, "The Water Crisis: What Brought It On?" *Saturday Review*, October 23, 1965, p. 24; *Time*, December 3, 1965, p. 82; "Means of Causing Artificial Ice Age Described in Climate Study," *Indianapolis Star*, March 15, 1966, p. 42.

22. Erich Zimmermann, *World Resources and Industries: A Functional Appraisal of the Availability of Agricultural and Industrial Materials* (New York, 1951), pp. 404–405.

23. Robert L. Rudd, *Pesticides and the Living Landscape* (Madison, 1964), pp. 142–143, 173–176, 183, 187–188, 191–192.

24. Muller, *op. cit.*

25. "Peru's Fishermen Defeat Guano Birds, But Farms Suffer," *New York Times,* March 13, 1966.

26. Ted Trueblood, "Let's Kill Off the Ladies," *True,* November, 1964, p. 100. Trueblood says that Northern Pacific Railroad shipments of buffalo hides fell from two hundred thousand in 1882 to three hundred in 1884. In the latter year, a buckskin sold for a quarter.

27. Durward L. Allen, *Our Wildlife Legacy* (New York, 1962), pp. 5–10. That a Plains Indian might eat from ten to twenty pounds of buffalo meat each day seems almost incredible. But Allen believes that it is the greasy quality of the meat which permits such large quantities to be eaten at a sitting.

28. Richard A. Cooley, *Politics and Conservation: The Decline of the Alaska Salmon* (New York, 1963), pp. 17–19, 24, 72.

29. "Announcement of Establishment of Experiment Station . . . in Laurel, Maryland," September 6, 1965, *Presidential Documents,* I (1965), 221.

30. Gustav Swanson, "Wildlife and Its Conservation in the United States," in *Proceedings* of the Inter-American Conference on Conservation of Renewable Natural Resources, September 7–20, 1949, pp. 578–579; E. I. Kotok, "The Ecological Approach to Conservation Programs," *ibid.,* pp. 473–474, 476–477; F. G. Renner, "Range Conditions: A New Approach to the Management of Natural Grazing Lands," *ibid.,* pp. 528–529.

31. Paul G. Hayes, "State Prairie Sought," *Milwaukee Journal,* October 31, 1965, quoting James H. Zimmerman, Arboretum Naturalist, University of Wisconsin; Raymond F. Dasmann, *The Destruction of California* (New York, 1965), pp. 61, 65–68.

32. Philip O. Foss, *Politics and Grass: The Administration of Grazing on the Public Domain* (Seattle, 1960).

33. "Presidential Remarks . . . Assateague Island," *Presidential Documents,* I (1965), 292.

34. "The Problem," National Academy of Sciences–National Research Council, Committee on Pollution, August 20, 1965, pp. 8–10. A final version was published as *Waste Management and Control,* A Report to the Federal Council on Science and Technology, NAS–NRC Publication No. 1400, Washington, D.C., 1966.

35. President Lyndon B. Johnson, "Preservation and Improvement of the Natural Beauty of America," October 2, 1965, *Presidential Documents,* I (1965), 356.

36. Advisory Board on Wildlife Management of the U.S. Department of the Interior, March 1964, in *Quest for Quality,* p. 65.

37. "The Problem," *op. cit.,* pp. 18–19, 21–22.

38. *Ibid.,* p. 33. One should also bear in mind that as of June 30, 1962, there were registered under the Insecticide, Fungicide and Rodenticide

Act alone 54,316 formulations, which included 494 active ingredients. *Hearings on S. Res. 27*, p. 59.

39. *Indianapolis News*, April 20, 1966, quoting Dr. Carroll M. Williams, former chairman of the biology department, Harvard University.

CHAPTER 5. THE RISKS OF POLLUTION

1. Erich Zimmermann, *World Resources and Industry* (New York, 1951), p. 8.
2. *Milwaukee Journal*, November 7, 1965. As a material, this mastic is only ten years old. No one knows how long it will last.
3. Dato Sir Alexander Oppenheim, "Asia," in Calder, ed., *The World in 1984*, II, 173.
4. Abel Wolman, "The Metabolism of Cities," *Scientific American*, September 1965, pp. 186–187.
5. Bob Rose, "L.A. Cries for Help," *Chicago Daily News Service*, April 1, 1966; Igor Stravinsky, *New York Review of Books*, May 12, 1966, p. 10. The basic California Air Pollution Control Act is Stats. 1947, Ch. 632, *Cal. Health and Safety*, Sec. 24198 *et seq.* (West 1955). The motor exhaust legislation is in *Cal. Health and Safety*, Sec. 24378 *et seq.* (West Supp. 1965) and *Cal. Vehicle*, Sec. 27150 *et seq.* (West 1960).
6. Martin Gansberg, "Some Dirty Air Comes from Sea," *New York Times*, July 8, 1965, citing Mr. Donald Pack, deputy director, laboratory, New York City Weather Bureau. On May 3, 1966, the New York City Council passed an Air Pollution Control Ordinance described as "the toughest in the nation." This act would prohibit the burning of soft coal, outlaw incinerators in new buildings, set rigid restrictions on the burning of fuels, and provide for heavy fines.
7. M. Mason Gaffney, "Applying Economic Sanctions," *Bulletin of the Atomic Scientists*, XXII, No. 4 (June 1965), 24.
8. Charles G. Bennett, "12 of 18 Planned Sewage Plants Are in Use Here," *New York Times*, November 9, 1965; Homer Bigert, "Water Use Curbs Held Temporary," *loc. cit.*, quoting Herbert Howlett, Chief Engineer, Delaware River Basin Commission.
9. Dean Frank J. Trelease, "Legal Aspects," a paper presented at the session on Water Quality Management, 36th Annual Meeting of the Water Pollution Control Federation, October 6–10, 1963, in *Journal of the Water Pollution Control Federation*, XXXVI (1964), p. 1088. President Johnson's Ten Year Water Research Program, prepared by the Committee on Water Resources Research of the Federal Council for Science and Technology, says the United States has no crucial water shortage and has adequate water for the foreseeable future. "Report" (GPO, February 1966) and *Presidential Documents*, II (1966), 420.

10. A. K. Meetham, *Atmospheric Pollution* (New York, 1964), pp. 260–261; Admiral Hyman Rickover as quoted in the *New York Times,* October 28, 1965.

11. Report of the Garbage Committee, City of Houston, November 30, 1964, in *Compost Science,* VI (1965), p. 9, with a list of the different companies having differing, competing, proprietary methods of composting.

12. "Clean Air and Water in a Complex Society," *Du Pont,* No. 28 (1965), p. 1; "The Problem," National Academy of Sciences–National Research Council, Committee on Pollution, August 20, 1965, pp. 9–16, 33–36, 43–46, 81.

13. Interview with Mr. Harold Jacobs, principal consultant, Engineering Department, E. I. Du Pont de Nemours and Co., in *Du Pont,* No. 28, p. 11; "The Problem," pp. 7, 36, 41, 98–99.

14. Preliminary Report, Subcommittee on Land Use Plans, Law, and Finance, to the Chairman, Technical Committee of the Lake Mendota Problems Committee, Madison, Wisconsin, September 7, 1965, pp. 4–6, quoting from the research of W. T. Edmondson; "The Problem," pp. 3, 7–8, 31–32, 84–86. The introduction of "German" carp, following their display at the Philadelphia Centennial Exposition of 1876, has been a sad American story, but the English ignored the American experience. The Deeping Fen Drainage Board at Crowland, England, imported four hundred "Chinese" carp from Hong Kong with "hopes that the fish will eat away weeds, saving an estimated $11,400 a year in clearing costs." *Milwaukee Journal,* November 14, 1965.

15. On the calculations of Professor Gordon Fair, Chicago compares favorably to the national average of 5 percent annual average of waste carried in combined sewer systems by-passing treatment plants, with this by-passing waste accounting for 10 percent of the actual bio-oxygen demand. National Academy of Sciences–National Research Council, Committee on Pollution, Legal-Public Administration Panel, Minutes of April 5–6, 1965, p. 16. Professor Fair thinks the cost of dual sewers would be $20 billion, not counting the tearing up or replacing of streets, but this disparity simply indicates that no expert can calculate the cost.

16. Bennett, *loc. cit.* The other facilities include "extensive storm sewer work in South Queens, storm sewers in the Rockaways, complete sewer systems on Broad Channel, four plants and diversion sewers on the Eastchester Bay and Hutchinson River areas, and chlorinating facilities in Queens and the Bronx along the shores of the Upper East River," which indicate how ambitious these programs have to be.

17. "The Problem," p. 58; Wolman, *op. cit.,* pp. 184–185; Bennett, *loc. cit.*

18. Zimmermann, *op. cit.,* p. 73.

19. Paul Goodman, "Open Letter of November 20, 1965 to John Lind-

say," *The New York Review of Books,* December 23, 1965, p. 9; Peter d'Alroy Jones, *The Consumer Society: A History of American Capitalism* (Baltimore, 1965), pp. 18–19, 321, 356.

20. Morris Neiburger, "Smog Today and Smog Tomorrow," *The Nation,* December 6, 1965, pp. 432–435.

21. *Delaware Basin Bulletin,* V, No. 3 (October 1964), 1–2.

22. Roderick Nash, "Review," *Forest History,* IX, No. 2 (July 1965), 31, in which he discusses the ideas of Leo Marx, an American cultural historian; "Public Policies and Institutional Arrangements," *Du Pont,* No. 28, p. 18.

CHAPTER 6. NATURE AS A FREE GOOD

1. Henry Hallam, *History of Europe During the Middle Ages* (New York, 1900), II, 230. There was some colonial legislation for the Broad Arrow, so it was not strictly a prerogatival act. Lawrence S. Hamilton, "The Federal Forest Regulations Issue," *Forest History,* IX, No. 1 (1965), 2.

2. Emma Lou Thornbrough, *Indiana in the Civil War Era, 1850–1880, The History of Indiana,* III (Indianapolis, 1965), pp. 364–365, 405. Steve A. Wilson, "Bidding Fierce at Auction," *Indianapolis Star,* December 12, 1965. From the same woodlot, forty-two trees sold for $11,600; the remainder on the ninety acres of timber brought $6,755.

3. Martin and Margy Meyerson, "Multiple Choices," Calder, ed., II, p. 83, develop the idea of neighborhood rotation.

4. "Records Set in Federal Forests," *Milwaukee Journal,* October 3, 1965.

5. Joseph A. Miller, "The Changing Forest," *Forest History,* IX, No. 1 (April 1965), 21–23; Hamilton, *op. cit.,* p. 2; Clifford E. Ahlgren, "Review," *Forest History,* IX, No. 1, 26.

6. Robert E. Bedingfield, "Automatic Billing System Is Stressed," *New York Times,* September 12, 1965, quoting William H. Cochrane, President, Neptune Meter Company.

7. Edward T. O'Toole, "Vast Diversion Plan Is Pressed to Tap Canadian Rivers," *New York Times,* September 12, 1965, relies heavily on information supplied by George S. Moore, President, First National City Bank of New York. The plan, prepared by Ralph M. Parsons Company, a Los Angeles–New York engineering construction firm, has been submitted to the United States Senate Special Subcommittee on Western Water Development. The Canadian Northern Affairs Minister told the American Bar Association that sale of Canadian water on this scale "is not now negotiable, and I am not certain that it ever will be," *Indianapolis News,* August 15, 1966, p. 27.

8. Bill McCormick, "Find Practical Way to Desalt Water," *Madison*

Capital Times, September 16, 1965; *Time,* October 1, 1965, p. 79B; Moshe Brilliant, "Plants in Elath Desalting Water," *New York Times,* September 12, 1965; Letter from John W. Simpson, Group Vice President, Westinghouse Electric Corp., in *Time,* October 15, 1965, pp. 17–18; Letter of F. A. Loebel, President, Aqua-Chem, Inc., *op. cit.,* p. 18.

9. Abel Wolman, "Metabolism," pp. 182, 184; Elizabeth M. Fowler, "Most Private Water Concerns Are Small and Closely Held," *New York Times,* September 12, 1965.

10. Interim Report to the President, Water Resources Council, September 10, 1965, *Presidential Documents,* I (1965), 240. This report limits itself to suggestions for co-ordination of reservoirs in the Delaware River basin, but the implications are clear.

11. 43 U.S.C., Sec. 616b (a) (1964); 76 Stat. 391 (1962), which accepts for federal projects the limits of the Colorado "watershed-of-origin" legislation.

12. Statements of President Johnson to the First International Symposium on Desalination, October 4 and 7, 1965, *Presidential Documents,* I (1965), 367, 368, 381–382.

13. Report, Committee on Urban Development, National Citizens Commission on International Cooperation, White House Conference on International Cooperation, November 28–December 1, 1965, Document 18, p. 3.

14. Edward Counselman Higbee, *Farms and Farmers in an Urban Age,* (New York, 1963). Statement of President Johnson upon signing the Food and Agriculture Act of 1965, November 18, 1965, *Presidential Documents,* I (1965), 455.

15. Chris Lecos, "New Soil Maps Completed for Building Plan Guidance," *Milwaukee Journal,* October 3, 1965. The survey for the Southeastern Wisconsin Regional Planning Commission took two and a half years, cost $260,000, and covered 1.6 million acres of undeveloped land contiguous to urban areas in seven southeastern Wisconsin counties.

16. Marvin Beatty, Department of Soils, College of Agriculture, University of Wisconsin, and William Kochelman, chief land use planner, Southeastern Wisconsin Regional Planning Commission, address, "The Interpretive Use of Soil Surveys," to the Planning Club, University of Wisconsin, October 28, 1965.

17. Report on the First Indiana Governor's Conference on Natural Resources and Natural Beauty, in Don Fermoyle, "The Goal for Miss Indiana," *Indianapolis Observer and Courier,* December 17, 1965.

18. M. Mason Gaffney, "Soil Depletion and Land Rent," *Natural Resources J.* IV (1965), pp. 541–542.

19. Claude Parsons, "Forest Chief Leaves Job," *Indianapolis Star,* December 18, 1965.

20. Barnett and Morse, *op. cit.,* p. 67. John Stuart Mill thought that

Carey's "exception" to Ricardo's view was not very important, because the phase of using the poorer resources first is relatively so brief, *ibid.,* pp. 67–68. For the views of Karl Marx, see Hans Blumenfeld, "The Modern Metropolis," *Scientific American,* CCXIII, No. 3, (September 1965), 68. For Tolstoy's use of the name "Malthus," see *Anna Karenina,* tr. Constance Garnett (New York, Heritage Press, 1952), pp. 675–678. On the efforts to revive Appalachia at public cost, see Appalachian Regional Development Act of 1965, P.L. 89–4, 79 Stat. 5; Executive Order 11209, March 26, 1965, 30 F.R. 3929.

CHAPTER 7. CALCULATING RESOURCE SUFFICIENCY

1. Barnett and Morse, *op. cit.,* pp. 170–172, on forestry; Fig. 31, p. 210, on fishing (though the authors prefer Fig. 14, p. 172, which is clearly *contra* to the scarcity hypothesis); and pp. 255–256, on water, where it is the cost of extractive output that is considered. See also James A. Crutchfield, "Address to the Alaska Science Conference," August 1957, quoted in Richard A. Cooley, *op. cit.,* p. 67.
2. The Illinois Central Railroad began its suburban commuter service in Chicago in 1856. *Life,* December 24, 1965, p. 60.
3. Leland M. Corliss, "A Review of the Evidence of Glue-Sniffing—A Persistent Problem," *The Journal of School Health,* XXXV, No. 10 (December 1965), 442–449. Dr. Corliss discounts more severe descriptions as being by people who "really get carried away with themselves when talking about glue-sniffers."
4. René Dubos, *Man Adapting* (New Haven, 1965), p. 211, citing a comparative study in Seward and New Florence, Pennsylvania; *ibid.,* p. 379. The figures of greatest growth seem to be from California, p. 217, and New York, p. 378; *ibid.,* pp. 218–219.
5. *Indianapolis Star,* December 19, 1962, quoting Nicola Zurlo of the Milan Clinic of Medicine and Labor, and "the director of the Genoa University Health Institute," for the connection between lung cancer and air pollution.
6. Thomas D. Crocker, "Air Pollution Control in Polk and Hillsborough Counties, Florida," *Bulletin of the Atomic Scientists,* XXII, No. 4 (June 1965), 17–19; *Florida Administration Code,* Rules of the Florida Air Pollution Control Commission (1966), Ch. 28–3.03.
7. Dubos, *op. cit.,* p. 385. The company argued that "no *recent* complaints had been made by *residents.*" As Dubos observed, most residents are economically dependent on the phosphate industry for employment so that any complaining might be muted.
8. Thomas D. Crocker, "The Structuring of Atmospheric Pollution Control Systems," Seminar on the Economics of Air Pollution, United States Public Health Service and American University, Washington,

D.C., April 21, 1965; reprinted in Harold Wolozin, ed., *The Economics of Air Pollution* (New York, 1966), pp. 61 ff.

9. M. Mason Gaffney, *op. cit.,* p. 20.
10. Gordon Fair, *op. cit.,* p. 44.
11. Anthony Scott, *op. cit.,* p. 4.
12. Crocker, *op. cit.,* pp. 17, 19.
13. Adam Smith, *The Wealth of Nations,* ed. Edwin Cannan (New York, 1937), p. 691.
14. S. V. Ciriacy-Wantrup, "Water Resources and Economic Development," Agricultural Policy Institute, North Carolina State University Series 16 (August 1965), p. 5. A cost-and-benefit flow "comparison need not always be in quantitatively precise, pecuniary terms. Frequently, information about the order of magnitudes and the direction, relative speed, and sequence of projected changes in benefits and costs is sufficient," pp. 10, 7, 4, his italics. In this article, Ciriacy-Wantrup is discussing the water resource, but his views can be extrapolated to all renewable resources. On Liberman and Sun Yeh-fang, see Meng Kuei and Hsiao Lin, "On Reactionary Economic Programmes," *Peking Review,* IX, Nos. 43–44 (October 21–28, 1966).
15. Ciriacy-Wantrup, *op. cit.,* p. 8.
16. Crocker, *op. cit.,* p. 10.
17. "The Problem," pp. 8–9. Though this list is said to exclude "legal, social, institutional and political techniques" from consideration, it does set the physical limitations within which these must work. For further analysis of the items in this list, see pp. 11–18.
18. Kneese, *op. cit.,* p. 12.
19. Herfindahl and Kneese, *op. cit.,* p. v.
20. Jerome W. Milliman, quoted in F. J. Trelease, H. S. Bloomenthal, and J. R. Geraud, *Cases and Materials on Natural Resources* (St. Paul, Minn., 1965), p. 55.
21. Edgar M. Hoover, *The Location of Economic Activity* (New York, 1948), pp. 196 ff.
22. Recommendation B1 in *Report of the Environmental Pollution Panel,* President's Science Advisory Committee, November 1965, pp. 17–18.
23. Dubos, *op. cit.,* p. 415.

CHAPTER 8. LEGAL CONCEPTS AND RENEWABLE RESOURCES

1. J. Willard Hurst, "The Use of Law in Four 'Colonial' States of the American Union," *Wisconsin Law Review* (1945), pp. 580–581.
2. Panel discussion, "What Can We Do to Make Our Cities More Habitable?" in *The Air We Breathe: A Study of Man and His Environment,* ed. Seymour Farber and R. H. L. Wilson, with J. R. Goldsmith

and Nello Pace (Springfield, Ill., 1961), pp. 224 ff.; Earl Finbar Murphy, "English Water Law Doctrines Before 1400," *American Journal of Legal History* (1957), p. 104; G. Graham Waite, "Public Rights in Maine Waters," *Maine Law Review,* XVII (1965), 198–200.

3. Walter Firey, *Man, Mind and Land: A Theory of Resource Use* (Glencoe, Ill., 1960).

4. Morrill Homestead Act of May 20, 1862, c. 75, 12 Stat. 392.

5. Pre-emption Act of September 4, 1841, c. 16, Secs. 10–15, 5 Stat. 453; Swamp Land Act of September 28, 1850, c. 84, 9 Stat. 519; Mining Act of June 26, 1866, c. 262, 14 Stat. 251; Desert Land Act of March 3, 1877, c, 107, 19 Stat. 377.

6. An attempt to correct the harm of hydraulic mining is the California Debris Commission Act of March 1, 1893, c. 183, 27 Stat. 507.

7. Larry K. Harvey, "A Mandatory Permit System for the Acquisition of Water Rights in Idaho," *Idaho Law Review,* II (1965), 42.

8. Harold H. Ellis, "Water Rights and Legislation in the Eastern States," Conference on Water Resources and Economic Development in the South, March 22–23, 1965, in "Water Resources and Economic Development in the South," Agricultural Policy Institute, North Carolina State University, Series 16 (August 1965), pp. 109–133.

9. *Ground Water Legislation in Europe,* United Nations Food and Agriculture Organization Legislative Series No. 5 (Rome, 1964), pp. 1–6. The statements concerning European groundwater law are as of July 1, 1963.

10. Jack Hirschleifer, James De Haven, Jerome Milliman, *Water Supply* (Chicago, 1960).

11. Fla. Ann. Stats. (Supp. 1965) Sec. 373. 011 *et seq.,* and Act of May 30, 1962, *Dziennik Ustaw* 1962, "Water Law," have striking similarity for statutes that were written independently of each other. The idea of administering underground waters through controlling hydrologic shed-aquifers goes back at least as far as the Uniform Underground Water Law for Western States, proposed by the Association of Western Engineers and recommended by the National Resources Planning Board, NRPB *Bulletin* (1934), pp. 135–136, which is criticized in Woodruff and Williams, "The Texas Groundwater District Act of 1949," *Texas Law Review,* XXX (1952), 862. See also Harnsberger, "Nebraska Ground Water Problems," *Nebraska Law Review,* XLII (1963), 721.

12. President Lyndon B. Johnson, "State of the Union Message," January 12, 1966, *U.S. Code Congressional Service and Administrative News,* 89th Cong., 2nd Sess., 19.

CHAPTER 9. THE PROSPECT FOR RESOURCE CONTROL

1. Richard Moore, quoted in Dan Wakefield, "Waiting for Reality: Death of a Small Town," *The Nation,* September 20, 1965, p. 97.
2. This discussion is particularly indebted to the writings of Maynard Hufschmidt and Hans Albert Einstein.
3. Helen Merrell Lynd, *On Shame and the Search for Identity* (New York, 1958).
4. Wolfgang Langewiesche, *"What* Water Shortage?" *Reader's Digest,* January 1966, p. 210.
5. Quoted in Gerard A. Rohlich, "Federal Legislation Impact on Wisconsin," Governor's Conference on Water Resources Management in Wisconsin, October 14–15, 1965, University of Wisconsin Water Resources Center, March 1966, p. 12.
6. Water Quality Act of October 2, 1965, P.L. 89–234, 79 Stat. 903, Sec. 5 (c) (3), (5), (1), my italics. Reorganization Plan No. 2 of 1966, February 28, 1966, *U.S. Code Congressional and Administrative News,* 89th Cong. 2nd Sess., pp. 456 ff., transfers many of these functions from the Secretary of Health, Education, and Welfare to the Secretary of the Interior, who also serves as chairman of the Water Resources Council, effective May 10, 1966.
7. "Statement of the Managers on the Part of the House," Conference Report to the Water Quality Act of 1965, September 17, 1965, 89th Cong., 1st Sess., United States House of Representatives Report No. 1022, pp. 9–13.
8. Fred A. Clarenbach, "Western Regional Planning of Water Resources," Water Resources Center, University of California at Los Angeles, August 1, 1964, *op. cit.,* p. 14.
9. "Water Pollution-State Control Committee," *Vanderbilt Law Review,* XVII (1964), pp. 1369–1370.
10. A. R. Meetham, *Atmospheric Pollution,* ed. D. W. Bottom and S. Cayton (New York, 1964) Chart 1, p. 262; Chart 2, p. 263; Clean Air Act of 1956, 4 and 5 Eliz. 2, c. 52; Water Resources Act of 1963, 11 and 12 Eliz. 2, c. 38, and Federation of British Industries Circulars No. 1 (January 1965) and 2 (March 1965), "Control of Water in England and Wales."
11. Corwin W. Johnson and Larry D. Knippa, "Transbasin Diversion of Water," *Texas Law Rev.,* XLVI (1965), p. 1035.
12. Hirschleifer, De Haven, and Milliman, *op. cit.,* pp. 144–145, citing R. Giguet and G. Morlat on the "universal phenomenon of the perennial overoptimism" of public agencies in calculating benefits and costs in their prospective analyses. Fred A. Clarenbach, *op. cit.,* p. 20.

13. Clarenbach, *op. cit.,* pp. 38–39, quoting a statement made March 24, 1964.

14. Johnson and Knippa, *op. cit.,* p. 1052, commenting on Texas *Laws* (1965), c. 297, Sec. 3(b), p. 588.

15. Water Resources Planning Act of July 22, 1965, P.L. 89–90, 79 Stat. 244, Sec. 3 (d); Fryingpan-Arkansas Project Act of August 16, 1962, P.L. 87–590, 76 Stat. 392, Sec. 5; City of Fresno v. California, 372 U.S. 627 (1963); Statement of President Johnson in signing the Nevada Water Project Act, October 22, 1965, P.L. 89–292, 79 Stat. 1068, *Presidential Documents,* I (1965), 431, commenting on Sec. 6, proviso.

16. Report to the President of the Water Resources Council, September 10, 1965, *Presidential Documents,* I (1965), 240.

17. Sho Sato, "Legal Considerations Incident to Regional Planning and Allocation of Water Resources," Conference of the Water Resources Center, University of California, June 4–6, 1964, reproduced as Chap. 3 of Clarenbach, *op. cit.,* p. 27. See also Morreale, "Federal Power in Western Waters," *Natural Resources Journal,* III (1963), 1.

18. Joseph L. Sax, "Municipal Water Supply for Nonresidents," *Natural Resources Journal,* V (1965), p. 54.

19. On the way most interstate river commissions have functioned in the past, *Medicine at Work,* I, No. 9 (September 1961), 4.

20. James Wright, in National Academy of Sciences–National Research Council, Division of Physical Sciences, Committee on Pollution, Legal-Public Administration Panel, Minutes of April 5–6, 1965, pp. 65–66.

21. "Public Policies and Institutional Arrangements," National Academy of Sciences–National Research Council, Division of Physical Sciences, Committee on Pollution, Conference of August 20, 1965, Woods Hole, Mass., p. 13, p. 31.

22. Allen V. Kneese, *Water Pollution,* p. 33 n, "Hence the great importance of not considering constraints immutable and of testing the sensitivity of costs to them."

CHAPTER 10. THE CHOICES IN CONTROLLING THE ENVIRONMENT

1. Livingston Taylor, "Strip Mining Is Called Ruinous," *Louisville Courier-Journal,* January 19, 1966; Wendell Berry, "Strip Mine Morality: The Landscaping of Hell," *The Nation,* January 24, 1966, p. 99; Harry M. Caudill, "Paradise Is Stripped." *New York Times Magazine,* March 13, 1966, p. 26.

2. Stephen Rousseas, "Review" of Seymour Melman, *Our Depleted Society* (1965), in *Dissent,* XIII, No. 1 (January–February 1966), pp. 105–107.

3. *Conservation Education in American Schools,* 29th Yearbook of the American Association of School Administrators (Washington, 1951), pp. 11–12.

4. *New York Times,* March 1, 1965, quoting remarks of Dr. Luther Terry on WGN-TV, Chicago, February 28, 1965.

5. E. J. Kahn, Jr., "The Majestic Polluted Hudson," CBS News: The 20th Century, January 23, 1966.

6. Gladwin Hill, "Atlanta Loses Ground in Fight on Pollution," *New York Times,* March 2, 1965.

7. Gary Brooten, "Natural Water Vanishing," *Philadelphia Inquirer,* May 13, 1965, quoting T. E. Larson, chief of the chemical section, Illinois State Water Survey, "Address to Symposium on Water Quality," American Society for Testing and Materials, May 12, 1965, and Leon W. Weinberger, chief of the basic and applied sciences branch, Division of Water Supply and Pollution Control, Public Health Service, United States Department of Health, Education, and Welfare.

8. Karl Abraham, "Usable Water Can Be Reclaimed from Sewage Cheaply," *Philadelphia Bulletin,* April 6, 1965, p. 18, quoting an address of R. B. Dean, Taft Sanitary Engineering Center, to the American Chemical Society; "Scientists Seek to Perfect Separation of Sewage from Water"; *New York Times,* March 1, 1965; *Health Bulletin,* June 5, 1965, p. 5.

9. Wallace Notestein, *Four Worthies* (New Haven, 1957), pp. 198–199.

10. Gallup Pole, *Friday Release,* July 30, 1965.

11. Rex vs. Medley *et al.,* 6 Car. and P. 292, 172 Eng. Rep. 1246 (1842), pp. 297–298.

12. Gladwin Hill, "Pollution Curbs Urged by Chicago," *New York Times,* March 3, 1965, quoting a federal study read at an interstate conference on water pollution called in Chicago by the U.S. Department of Health, Education, and Welfare; and "Pollution Case Opens in Chicago," *New York Times,* March 2, 1965, quoting Maurice LeBosquet of the United States Public Health Service, who also gave statistics for many other industrial polluters.

13. Albert L. Kraus, "Water Supplies: Nation's Riddle," *New York Times,* March 25, 1962.

14. *Norristown* (Pennsylvania) *Times Herald,* November 13, 1962, and *ibid.,* November 12, 1962.

15. *Brown County* (Indiana) *Democrat,* August 31, 1961, "Water Study Commission Meets with Landowners"; "Water Resources Study Commission Holds First Meeting," *ibid.,* August 24, 1961, p. 1, at p. 4; "Water Supply Survives Hot, Dry Weekend," *ibid.,* September 7, 1961, p. 1. In the next five years, conditions did not change, *ibid.,* July 14, 1966, p. 1.

16. Jeremy Bentham, *Collected Works,* ed. Bowring (London, 1843), Constitutional Code, c. XI, Sec. x, Art. 15. The pertinent agencies in

his proposed cabinet were the Ministries of the Domain, of Preventive Services, and of Health. *Ibid.,* Constitutional Code, c. XI, Sec. v, Art. 9, Subarts. 1, 2. To prevent conflict, Bentham had all orders to the military engaged in such work issue out of the Prime Minister's office rather than from the Ministries concerned, *ibid.,* Constitutional Code, c. XI, Sec. x, Art. 15.

17. Henry E. Sigerest, *The Great Doctors: A Biographical History of Medicine,* trans. Eden and Cedar Paul (New York, 1938), p. 227.

18. G. Bugnottet, *Etudes Administratives et Judiciares* (Paris, 1887), p. 100; G. Bugnottet and A. Noirpoudre de Sauvigny, *Etudes Administratives et Judiciares,* 2 vols. (Besançon, 1888–1890), I, 56.

19. Jacob H. Beuscher, in National Academy of Sciences–National Research Council, Division of Physical Sciences, Committee on Pollution, Legal–Public Administration Panel, Minutes of April 5–6, 1965, pp. 114, 89–94, 90.

20. Compare the results in Green, Adm'x. v. Ashland Water Co., 101 Wis. 258, 77 N.W. 722, 43 L.R.A. 117, 70 A.S.R. 911 (1898) with the praise for its principles by Fred L. Luehring, "Testimony in Terms of Opinion," *Wisconsin Law Review* (1945), p. 613.

21. Recommendation in "Public Policies and Institutional Arrangements," National Academy of Sciences–National Research Council, Committee on Pollution, Woods Hole, Mass., Conference, August 20, 1965, pp. 21–26.

22. Schildhauer v. Woodruff Utility District, Vilas, Wisconsin, Circuit Court, April 15, 1956, Gerald J. Boileau, circuit judge, manuscript decision. A file of such manuscript decisions is kept by the director of the Wisconsin State Committee on Water Pollution. Similar expressions of difficulty are in Haft, *et al.,* v. Western Condensing Company, Sheboygan, Wisconsin, Circuit Court, January 10, 1949, Henry A. Detling, circuit judge, from the same file.

23. *Delaware Basin Bulletin,* IV, No. 3 (July 1963).

24. Hugo Fernando Artucio, "Future Citizens of Latin America," in *Treasury for the Free World,* ed. Ben Raeburn (New York, 1946), p. 99.

25. NANA dispatch, *Indianapolis News,* January 26, 1966, p. 16, quoting Captain Don Gamble, a whaler currently working for the United States Fish and Wildlife Service.

26. Richard A. Cooley, *Politics and Conservation* (New York, 1963), pp. 200–201; and *Newsweek,* February 7, 1966, p. 22.

27. Compare Wou Saofong, "Chinese View of a World Order," ed. Raeburn, *op. cit.,* p. 242 and p. 244, with Oswald Spengler, *The Decline of the West,* trans. Charles Francis Atkinson (New York, 1927), II, pp. 470 and 474 n.

28. Erich Zimmermann, *World Resources and Industries* (New York, 1951), p. 150, citing Carl Sauer.

29. Compare the "Editorial," *New York Times,* March 10, 1965, with the "Editorial," *Barron's,* March 1, 1965, p. 1.
30. "Announcing a Natural Lands Trust," Girard Trust Corn Exchange Bank, Philadelphia, n.d.
31. *Time,* January 28, 1966, p. 18, which is superior to *Time's* claim that the creation in late 1965 of the United States Water Pollution Administration was due to a 1963 series of articles in the *New Republic* by James Ridgeway on the pollution of Raritan Bay. *Ibid.,* p. 74.
32. W. H. Churchman, *The Air We Breathe,* read before the Western Social Science Association, June 7–8, 1870 (Indianapolis, 1871), p. 2. He recounts appalling conditions among factory workers due to industrial waste emissions into the air. Pp. 23 *et seq.*

Bibliographical note

A complete description of the literature concerning regulation of the renewable resources is an impossibility. A solitary scholar could not prepare even a comprehensive bibliography of the field. And if one hopes to develop a familiarity with specific items, the list must be limited still further. The depth and scope of the problem derives from the complexity of modern economic activity and the extent to which such activity has a symbiotic relationship with the "chemical wheel of life," the life-cycle or renewable resources. To make too generous a sweep over disciplines affected by the broad character of the problem is to acquire a superficiality of little use. To probe deeply at any one spot is to produce another of the monographs and special studies that crowd library shelves and microcards. Decades of the most intense reading and study would scarcely be enough to create a scholar with a real grasp of the topic.

One of the hardest problems revolves about the amount of apparently unrelated knowledge which a student must bring to any aspect of the exploitation, regulation, or protection of the renewable resources. In a fairly complete sense, late twentieth-century renewable resource law is a cross between a property law that goes back to the Middle Ages and the public administrative law that developed after the middle of the nineteenth century. Yet a lawyer practicing this kind of law would need to know far more than the doctrines relating to the renewable resources in these two specific legal areas. There is no way that the need to know the whole of law might be moderated in this field, because at every turn some rule of evidence or of the fisc is brought forward to have a powerful influence upon the life-cycle resources. To say that all books on law are pertinent may not be helpful, but it is almost true. The same comprehensive background is required of other disciplines—the economists, political scientists, and sociologists who have come to the study of problems inherent in the renewable resources—and of the physical and biological scientists as well who have applied themselves especially to the point at which economic and social activity touches their general disciplines. It is not possible to know at what place to draw the line that defines an economist or a biologist as being particularly involved in renewable resource exploitation rather than working in his overall field. Consequently, there is no way to comment upon the pertinent literature in any way that is not skewed to the interests and reading of the person or persons doing the commenting. This means that omissions must appear which can be legitimately criticized; but aside from an apology, little can be done about the fault.

This is a selective list of sources which have been particularly valuable to one student of the problem of man's using and regulating the use of the renewable resources. Basic books in the various disciplines have not been included, even though they are pertinent. Elementary sources must be consulted in order to understand the location of the problem; but they are not part of the literature which is specific to the subject contained under the title of regulating the renewable resources.

Instead, this bibliography includes only those works that are significant within what is commonly called renewable resource regulation. The selection may appear rather narrow, but unless the reader is to be thrown into a mass of unassimilated data, there has to be the application of a selective principle. Here, specific sources have been listed because they emphasize ways of coming to grips with the problems that arise from the use which the economy makes of the renewable resources and the task of regulating that use over the future.

Anyone who investigates the condition and the regulation of the renewable resources finds that government documents are indispensable. In the future, this importance will vastly increase. The list of government documents has been prepared simply to suggest the types available. In the same way, examples of business publications have been chosen in order to indicate the rich sources of information available there. Thereafter in the bibliography, items are listed in the standard manner.

A. GOVERNMENT DOCUMENTS

1. UNITED NATIONS

a. General Assembly

United Nations Commission on Permanent Sovereignty over Natural Resources, 3rd Sess., "The Status of Permanent Sovereignty over Natural Wealth and Resources," 2 vols., A/AC.97/5 Rev. 1, December 27, 1960.

b. Specialized Agencies

Dante Caponera, *Water Laws in Moslem Countries,* FAO Development Paper No. 43, Rome, 1954.

Ground Water Legislation in Europe, FAO Legislative Series No. 5, Rome, 1964.

2. *UNITED STATES*

a. Federal Government

EXECUTIVE OFFICES FOR THE PRESIDENT

"Restoring the Quality of Our Environment," Report of Environmental Pollution Panel, President's Science Advisory Committee, November, 1965.

"Ten Year Water Research Program," Report of Committee on Water Resources Research, Federal Council for Science and Technology, February 1966, with President Johnson's Cover Letter of Transmittal to Congress, *Presidential Documents,* II (1966), 420.

Report to the President, Water Resources Council, September 10, 1965.

FEDERAL DEPARTMENTS

Yearbook, United States Department of Agriculture.

Quest for Quality, United States Department of Interior Conservation Yearbook (1965).

FEDERAL AGENCIES

"Sedimentation Resurvey of Guernsey Reservoir, 1957," Sedimentation Section, Hydrology Branch, Division of Project Investigations, Bureau of Reclamation, United States Department of the Interior, Denver, August 1958.

J. W. Wark, F. J. Keller, and H. R. Felty, "Reconnaissance of Sedimentation and Chemical Quality of Surface Water on the Potomac River Basin," in *Potomac River Basin Report,* VII, Appendix H, February 1963, North Atlantic Division, Baltimore District, United States Army Corps of Engineers.

Wyman Harrison, W. C. Krumbein, W. S. Wilson, "Sedimentation at an Inlet Entrance," United States Army Coastal Engineering Research Center Technical Memorandum No. 8, December 1964.

GOVERNMENTAL RESEARCH: FEDERAL FINANCING

F. L. Mann, H. H. Ellis, N. G. P. Krausz, *Water-Use Law in Illinois,* University of Illinois Agricultural Experiment Station Bulletin No. 703, Urbana, 1964.

SEMI-GOVERNMENTAL

"Natural Resources, a Summary Report to the President of the United States," National Academy of Sciences–National Research Council, Washington, D.C., Publication No. 1000, 1962.

"Minutes, April 5–6, 1965," Legal-Public Administration Panel, National Academy of Sciences–National Research Council, Washington, D.C.

"Tentative Report," Committee on Pollution, Woods Hole, Massachusetts, Conference of August 20, 1965, National Academy of Sciences–National Research Council, Washington, D.C. Published in final form as *Waste Management and Control,* A Report to the Federal Council for Science and Technology, NAS-NRC Publication No. 1400, 1966. Citations throughout this book refer to the "Tentative Report."

UNITED STATES CONGRESS

Appendices I–IV (March 1, 1965) to Part I, Hearings on S. Res. 27, Subcommittee on Reorganization and International Organizations of the Committee on Governmental Operations, United States Senate, 88th Cong., 1st and 2nd Sess. (1963), Agency Coordination Study, S. Res. 288 (Interagency Coordination in Environmental Hazards: Pesticides).

b. *State Government*

STATE AGENCY

State of California, The Resources Agency of California, Department of Water Resources.

Indiana Water Quality 1964, Monitor Station Records–Rivers and Streams, Indiana State Board of Health and Stream Pollution Control Board (1965).

GOVERNMENTAL RESEARCH BY STATES

"Pesticide Residues in Wisconsin Fish," Survey Report, February 14, 1966, Wisconsin Conservation Department, Research and Planning Division.

c. Local Government

Report of the Garbage Committee, City of Houston, Texas, November 30, 1964, in *Compost Science,* VI, (1965), 9.

Preliminary Report, September 7, 1965, Subcommittee on Land Use Plans, Law and Finance to the Chairman, Technical Committee, of the [Madison, Wisconsin] Mayor's Lake Mendota Problems Committee.

B. GOVERNMENT–SPONSORED CONFERENCES

1. UNITED STATES

a. White House Conferences

"Beauty for America," Proceedings of the White House Conference on Natural Beauty, May 24–25, 1965.

b. Federal Agency-Sponsored Conferences

Food and Drug Scientific Seminar, October 1963.

2. INTERNATIONAL

Proceedings of the Inter-American Conference on Conservation of Renewable Natural Resources, Denver, September 7–20, 1948, International and Conference Series II, American Republics 4, No. 8, Department of State Publication 3382.

3. STATES

Wisconsin's Governor's Conference on Water Resources, October 14–15, 1965, Water Resources Center, University of Wisconsin, March 1966.

C. BUSINESS DOCUMENTS

1. INDUSTRY PUBLICATIONS

"Clean Air and Water in a Complex Society," *Du Pont,* No. 28 (1965).

"A Report to the Nation," National Technical Task Committee on Industrial Waste, August 1961.

"The Colorado," *P-G and E-Progress*, XXXVIII, No. 1, Pacific Gas and Electric Co., January 1961.

2. TRADE ASSOCIATIONS

Federation of British Industries, "Disposal of Trade Effluents in England and Wales 1962," FBI Handbook, May 1962.

3. PROFESSIONAL ASSOCIATIONS

The Committee on Terminology, Urban Planning and Development Division, American Society of Civil Engineers, prepared a list of recommended definitions, *Journal of the Hydraulics Division,* ASCE, XCI, HY3, Pat. II, May 1965, p. 14.

Session on Water Quality Management, 36th Annual Meeting of the Water Pollution Control Federation, October 6–10, 1963, in the *Journal of the Water Pollution Control Federation,* XXXVI, (1964).

4. FINANCIAL INSTITUTIONS

"Water," *California Savings and Loan Investor,* Quality Group of Insured California Savings and Loan Associations, I, No. 1, Fall 1965.

"Announcing a Natural Lands Trust," Girard Trust Corn Exchange Bank, Philadelphia, n.d.

D. PRIVATE ASSOCIATION PUBLICATIONS

"The Foundations of Conservation Education," Committee on Conservation Education Pamphlet No. 3, Washington, D.C., National Wildlife Federation, 1941.

Conservation Education in American Schools, 29th Yearbook of the American Association of School Administrators, Washington, D.C., National Education Association, 1951.

High Dams and Upstream Storage, Proceedings of the Second Annual Water Resources Conference, Montana State University, June 28–29, 1957, Albert W. Stone, ed. (Missoula, Montana, 1958).

The Law of Water Allocation in the Eastern United States, Proceedings of a Symposium Held in Washington, D.C., October 1956, by the Conservation Foundation, David Haber and Stephen Bergen, eds. (New York, 1958).

Water Resources and the Law, Contributions to the Conference on Water Resources and the Law, September 4–6, 1957, at the University of Michigan Law School (Ann Arbor, Mich., 1958).

E. BOOKS AND ARTICLES

Durward L. Allen, *Our Wildlife Legacy,* 2nd ed. (New York, 1962).

Joseph Kinnicut Angell, *A Treatise on the Common Law, in Relation to Watercourses,* 2nd ed. (Boston, 1833).

Harold J. Barnett and Chandler Morse, *Scarcity and Growth: The Economics of Natural Resource Availability* (Baltimore, 1965), originally published in 1963 for Resources for the Future, Inc.

Wendell Berry, "Strip Mine Morality: The Landscaping of Hell," *The Nation,* CCII, No. 4 (January 24, 1966), 96.

J. I. Bregman and Sergei Lenormand, *The Pollution Paradox* (New York, 1966).

Harrison Brown, *The Challenge of Man's Future: An Inquiry Concerning the Condition of Man During the Years That Lie Ahead* (New York, 1954).

Harrison Brown, James Bonner, and John Weir, *The Next Hundred Years: Man's Natural and Technological Resources* (New York, 1957). Compass ed., 1963. Preface by Lee A. Dubridge.

Ian Burton and Robert W. Kates, eds., with Lydia Burton, *Readings in Resource Management and Conservation* (Chicago, 1965).

Nigel Calder, ed., *The World in 1984,* 2 vols. (Baltimore, 1965).

Robert Callis, *The Reading of That Famous and Learned Gentleman, Robert Callis, Esq., Sergeant at Law, Upon the Statute of 23 H. 8 Cap. 5 of Sewers: As It Was Delivered by Him at Grays Inn in August, 1622* (London, 1647).

Arthur H. Carhart, *Water—Or Your Life,* revised ed. with introduction by Jay N. Darling (Philadelphia, 1959).

Donald E. Carr, *The Breath of Life* (New York, 1965), and *Death of the Sweet Waters* (New York, 1966).

Harry M. Caudill, *Night Comes to the Cumberlands; A Biography of a Depressed Area,* with Foreword by Stewart L. Udall (Boston, 1963).

Stuart Chase, *Rich Land, Poor Land: A Study of Waste in the National Resources of America* (New York, 1936).

S. V. (Sigmund von) Ciriacy-Wantrup, *Resource Conservation: Economics and Politics,* 2nd ed. (Berkeley, 1963).

Fred A. Clarenbach, "Water Pollution Policies and Politics," Seminar on Pollution Control and Abatement, Iowa State University, Ames, November 9, 1965.
———, "Western Regional Planning of Water Resources," Water Resources Center, University of California at Los Angeles, August 1, 1964.

R. H. Coase, "The Problem of Social Cost," *Journal of Law and Economics,* III (1960), 1–44.

Richard A. Cooley, *Politics and Conservation: The Decline of the Alaska Salmon* (New York, 1963).

Thomas D. Crocker, "Air Pollution Control in Polk and Hillsborough Counties, Florida," *Bulletin of the Atomic Scientists,* XXII, No. 4 (June 1965), 17.
———, "The Structuring of Atmospheric Pollution Control Systems," Seminar on the Economics of Air Pollution, United States Public Health Service and American University, Washington, D.C., April 21, 1965.

Raymond F. Dasmann, *The Destruction of California* (New York, 1965).
———, *Environmental Conservation* (New York, 1959).

Betty Eakle Dobkins, *The Spanish Element in Texas Water Law* (Austin, 1959).

René Dubos, *Man Adapting,* XXXIX in the Silliman Foundation Lectures (New Haven, 1965).
———, *Mirage of Health: Utopias, Progress, and Biological Change,* XXII, World Perspectives Series (1959), ed., Ruth Nansha Anshen (Garden City, 1961).

Harold H. Ellis, "Water Rights and Legislation in the Eastern States," in *Water Resources and Economic Development in the South,* Agricultural Policy Institute, North Carolina State University, Series 16, August 1965, p. 109.

Philip O. Foss, *Politics and Grass: The Administration of Grazing on the Public Domain* (Seattle, 1960).

Bernard Frank and Anthony Netboy, *Water, Land and People* (New York, 1950).

M. Mason Gaffney, "Applying Economic Controls to Air Pollution," *Bulletin of the Atomic Scientists,* XXII, No. 4 (June 1965), 20.
————, "Soil Depletion and Land Rent," *Natural Resources Journal,* IV (1965), 537.

Karl Gertel, *Water: Uses, Supplies, Projections,* Resource Development Economics Division, Economic Research Service, United States Department of Agriculture, June 1962.

H. R. Hamilton, *et al., Bibliography on Socioeconomic Aspects of Water Resources* (Washington, D.C., 1966).

Larry K. Harvey, "A Mandatory Permit System for the Acquisition of Water Rights in Idaho," *Idaho Law Review,* II (1965), 42.

Lawrence J. Henderson, *The Fitness of the Environment* (1913), with Introduction by George Wald (Boston, 1958).

Orris C. Herfindahl and Allen V. Kneese, *Quality of the Environment* (Baltimore, 1965).

Edward Higbee, *Farms and Farmers in an Urban Age* (New York, 1963). Foreword by August Heckscher.

Gladwin Hill, "Are We Running Out of Water?" *Look,* December 14, 1965, p. 31.

James Willard Hurst, *Law and the Conditions of Freedom in the Nineteenth Century United States* (Madison, 1956).
————, *Law and Economic Growth: The Legal History of the Lumber Industry in Wisconsin, 1836-1915* (Cambridge, Mass., 1964).
————, *Law and Social Process in United States History* (Ann Arbor, 1960).

Edward Hyams, *Soil and Civilization,* The Past in the Present Series, Jacquetta Hawkes, ed. (London and New York, 1952).

J. Myron Jacobstein and Roy M. Mersky, *Water Law Bibliography* (Silver Spring, Md., 1966).

Peter d'Alroy Jones, *The Consumer Society: A History of American Capitalism* (Baltimore, 1965).

Allen V. Kneese, *Water Pollution: Economic Aspects and Research Needs* (Washington, D.C., 1962).

John Lear, *et al.,* "The Water Crisis: What Brought It On?" *Saturday Review,* October 23, 1965, pp. 24 ff.

Thomas LeDuc, "The Historiography of Conservation," *Forest History,* IX, No. 3 (October 1965), 23–28.

Aldo Leopold, *Round River,* Luna Leopold, ed. (New York, 1953).
————, *A Sand County Almanac* (New York, 1949).

Willard F. Libby, "Man's Place in the Physical Universe," *Bulletin of the Atomic Scientists,* XXII, No. 7 (September 1965), 12.

Arthur Maass, *Muddy Waters: The Army Engineers and the Nation's Rivers,* Foreword by Harold L. Ickes (Cambridge, Mass., 1951).

Arthur Maass, Maynard Hufschmidt, Robert Dorfman, H. A. Thomas, Jr., S. A. Marglin, and Gordon M. Fair, *Design of Water-Resource Systems: New Techniques for Economic Objectives, Engineering Analysis, and Governmental Planning* (Cambridge, Mass., 1962).

Carey McWilliams, *Ill Fares the Land: Migrants and Migratory Labor in the United States* (Boston, 1942).

Roscoe C. Martin, *Water for New York: A Study in State Administration of Water Resources* (Syracuse, 1960).

Roscoe C. Martin, Guthrie S. Birkhead, Jesse Burkhead, and Frank J. Munger, *River Basin Administration and the Delaware* (Syracuse, 1960).

Wesley Marx, "Can Thousand Palms Survive the Sand?" *National Observer,* November 8, 1965, p. 11.

A. R. Meetham, *Atmospheric Pollution,* 3rd ed., D. W. Bottom and S. Cayton, eds. (New York, 1964).

Maurice H. Merrill, *The Public's Concern with the Fuel Minerals* (St. Louis, 1960).

Hermann J. Muller, "Genetic Effects of Chemicals," *FDA Interbureau By-Lines,* No. 3, November 1964.

Lewis Mumford, *The City in History: Its Origins, Its Transformations, and Its Prospects* (New York, 1961).

Earl Finbar Murphy, *Water Purity: A Study in Legal Control of Natural Resources* (Madison, 1961).

Ronald G. Ridker, *Economic Costs of Air Pollution* (New York, 1966).

Michael Roberts, *The Estate of Man,* ed. Janet Roberts (London, 1951).

Robert L. Rudd, *Pesticides and the Living Landscape* (Madison, 1964).

John R. Sheppard, "Total Sediment Transport in the Lower Colorado River," paper presented at the American Society of Civil Engineers, Phoenix, April 10–14, 1961.

Erling D. Solberg, *New Laws for New Forests: Wisconsin's Forest-Fire, Tax, Zoning, and County Forest Laws in Operation* (Madison, 1961).

Ted Trueblood, "Let's Kill Off More Ladies," *True Magazine,* November 1964, p. 39.

Stewart L. Udall, *The Quiet Crisis,* Introduction by John F. Kennedy (New York, 1963).

Charles Richard Van Hise, *The Conservation of Natural Resources in the United States* (New York, 1926).

Samuel Charles Wiel, *Water Rights in the Western States,* 2 vols. (San Francisco, 1911).

Karl A. Wittfogel, *Oriental Despotism: A Comparative Study of Total Power* (New Haven, 1963).

Abel Wolman, "The Metabolism of Cities," *Scientific American,* CCXIII, No. 3 (September 1965), 179.

James C. Wright, *The Coming Water Famine* (New York, 1966).

Erich W. Zimmermann, *World Resources and Industries: A Functional Appraisal of the Availability of Agricultural and Industrial Materials* (New York, rev. ed., 1951).

Index

A note on the author

Earl Finbar Murphy was born in Indianapolis, studied at Butler and Indiana universities, and received LL.M. and J.S.D. degrees from Yale. Mr. Murphy has taught at the State University of New York, Binghamton, and at the Indiana University School of Law, and has practiced law in Indianapolis. He is now Professor of Law at Temple University and an assistant editor of the *American Journal of Legal History*.